Secret Life

Also by Kevin Donovan

The Dead Times (fiction)

ORNGE: The Star Investigation that Broke the Story

Crime Story: The Hunt for the "Body Parts" Killer (with Nick Pron)

SECRET LIFE

The JIAN GHOMESHI
Investigation

Kevin Donovan

Edited by Jill Ainsley.
Cover and page design by Julie Scriver.
Cover illustration inspired by a photo by Peter Bregg / Stringer (Getty Images).
Printed in Canada.
10 9 8 7 6 5 4 3 2 1

Library and Archives Canada Cataloguing in Publication

Donovan, Kevin, author
    Secret life : the Jian Ghomeshi investigation / Kevin Donovan.

Issued in print and electronic formats.
ISBN 978-0-86492-964-8 (paperback).--ISBN 978-0-86492-958-7 (epub).--
ISBN 978-0-86492-959-4 (mobi)

1. Ghomeshi, Jian--Trials, litigation, etc. 2. Ghomeshi, Jian--Relations with women.
3. Sex scandals--Canada--Ontario--Toronto. 4. Trials (Sex crimes)--Canada.
5. Fame--Social aspects--Canada. 6. Radio broadcasters--Canada. I. Title.

HV6593.C3D66 2016   364.15'30971   C2016-904305-3
                                             C2016-904306-1

We acknowledge the generous support of the Government of Canada, the Canada Council for the Arts, and the Government of New Brunswick.

Goose Lane Editions
500 Beaverbrook Court, Suite 330
Fredericton, New Brunswick
CANADA E3B 5X4
www.gooselane.com

PREFACE

In May 2014 the *Toronto Star* assigned me to work with Jesse Brown to investigate allegations that a "well-known Canadian public figure" was assaulting women. The assignment came just over a year after reporter Robyn Doolittle and I saw the mayor of Toronto smoking crack in a video recorded by an alleged gun and drug dealer. When Doolittle and I watched the video on an iPhone on an April evening in a dodgy parking lot, we were not at all surprised. Of course Rob Ford was smoking crack. That explained his behaviour. But when I learned that this new investigation involved the prominent CBC radio host Jian Ghomeshi, I was floored. Shocked. I was a fan, an admirer of Ghomeshi's interviewing prowess who enjoyed his program. It's not that I thought a skilled interviewer was incapable of hurting other human beings; it is just that it did not make sense to me. I listened to his show when my schedule allowed and found him to be very progressive on many levels. I was vaguely aware that Ghomeshi was a former musician, and I had wondered how a musician becomes the CBC's premier interviewer. Now I asked myself how someone who seemed so likeable and progressive could do the things he was accused of doing. Was he never concerned that he was putting his reputation at risk? And why were we only hearing about this now?

This book explores the specifics of the many allegations against Jian Ghomeshi over a twenty-year period, the efforts of women to bring this story to light, and the intense, behind-the-scenes attempts to protect Ghomeshi's secret life. I also examine the emergence of a national conversation about sexual harassment and abuse, and why, in so many cases, people bury these allegations of mistreatment and do not come forward.

Telling these stories, encouraging the national conversation on this issue, is very important. As a former justice of the US Supreme Court said more than one hundred years ago, "Publicity is justly commended as a remedy for social and industrial diseases. Sunlight is said to be the best of disinfectants."

Most of the allegations raised in this book were never heard in court. At time of writing, I have interviewed, and in some cases have written statements from, seventeen women and two men who have alleged that they experienced either sudden violence or sexually inappropriate behaviour at Ghomeshi's hands. The allegations of only four complainants were dealt with in court, resulting in an acquittal in three cases and an apology from Ghomeshi in the fourth. In the remainder of the allegations, most of them far more serious, the women chose to talk to the media and not the police. I am also aware of four other sets of allegations from women who approached me anonymously and whose identity I do not know to this day.

Looking at the totality of the allegations, I can tell you that each person's response was different when faced with Ghomeshi's behaviour. Some stayed. Some left. One pushed him back roughly and warned Ghomeshi that she had three brothers. Another visited him from out of town many times. She said she endured the violence because she liked him and thought he would change, until she had finally had enough. From the first time I contacted Ghomeshi in the summer of 2014, and with the exception of his apology to one of the women, the former radio star has insisted that everything he has done is consensual. In the two years since I confronted him in person with these allegations, neither he nor his lawyers have ever responded to my written requests for his side of the story, requests I sent as each new allegation surfaced and as this book was being finalized. In court, he pleaded not guilty to the criminal charges against him. In his now infamous Facebook posting after he was fired, Ghomeshi wrote he only partakes in sexual activities that are "mutually agreed upon, consensual, and exciting for both partners." The stories of the women in this book are generally described as they were told to me. They remain allegations and have not been proven in court.

I have previously done research into bondage and sadomasochistic practices. I know that some people enjoy experiencing or inflicting physical pain. Some stay in the privacy of their homes, while others go to dungeons with full knowledge that they might be put in a cage, tied up, whipped or spanked. They are willing participants who establish their boundaries in advance. Explicit consent and safe words are paramount. The women interviewed for this book say none of these things occurred when they were with Jian Ghomeshi.

The Ghomeshi story was polarizing and remains so today.

"The evidence to dismiss the bogus charges against Jian was overwhelming. As for broads in general they are manipulative, dishonest, ruthless liars," one reader told me. "Many men are in jail because women lied. We finally get a judge that doesn't wear a dress and you're quick off the mark to brand him. Women are inherently evil. Perhaps you should expose women."

Where do we go from there? Ghomeshi's story made many people ponder two connected issues: sexual assault, and how allegations of this nature are treated by the criminal courts. How do you move forward in a system where the post-incident contact of the complainant is probed, not that of the accused? There is no clear road. I cannot imagine the Criminal Code of Canada will be rewritten to allow for a different approach on sexual assault. Surely, better police and Crown investigations are the way to go. Police and prosecutors need to do more than take a statement from a complainant. They need to look into the story of the complainant and examine post-incident contact — not because an ongoing relationship means the person is lying, but to ensure that when they go to court, they have the full story. Crown attorneys should also consider using expert witnesses to explain a complainant's conduct to the court, something that was not done in the Ghomeshi cases.

As a male journalist investigating these issues, I have found myself walking a tightrope. When we first learned of the allegations, they seemed unpublishable. Complainants were confidential to us, and they asked to remain anonymous to the public. Some said they had deleted their texts and emails. When I questioned elements of each complainant's story, some became angry, wondering why I, a man, did not simply believe them. For those women, I expect the resulting court case shed light on why these questions have to be asked. In our newsroom, some reporters and editors thought it was a valid story to pursue. Others wondered if we were doing what former Prime Minister Pierre Trudeau warned against, getting involved in the bedrooms of the nation. At an event I attended following publication of the first stories, a Toronto businessman, a well-off man in his late fifties, scoffed at the pieces, telling me that "choking is just the beginning" in sex play, and I should grow up and write about something more important.

Out of all the comments I heard regarding the Ghomeshi case this last one worries me the most. My wife and I have two children, a son and daughter, and I coach a competitive female soccer team when I am not out reporting. I worry that the trial failed to explore a very important part of this issue — consent — that teens, and indeed people of all ages, need to be aware of. Consent was never an issue at the Jian Ghomeshi trial. That very important concept has been lost in the vigorous discussion that followed the criminal trial.

We live in a new media world, and stories like the Ghomeshi scandal, as the judge called it in his ruling, show how quickly information travels today, and how technology has transformed journalism. When I spent three months in the desert of Saudi Arabia, Iraq, and Kuwait covering the Gulf War in 1991, at exactly the time Jean Ghomeshi, as he was then known, was running student government at York University and allegedly menacing co-eds, I wrote my dispatches in longhand and drove to a town where a local store with a fax machine allowed me to transmit the stories home to the *Star*.

During the Ghomeshi trial in 2016, I, along with dozens of reporters, "live tweeted" the interplay between witnesses and Ghomeshi's criminal lawyer Marie Henein, sending unfiltered information to a waiting public. The Sunday in 2014 when we broke the story detailing why Ghomeshi was fired from CBC, I watched social media explode on both sides, creating a pool of information that is spreading to this day. I saw tweets that were smart and many that were offensive, wrong, and libelous. Social media is a tool. But like the tools of any trade, it must be used carefully.

When Jesse Brown and I were working on the investigation, I encouraged the women in the Ghomeshi case to come forward publicly, or at least provide specifics that could be verified, since handing out anonymity freely and without proper deliberation invites a host of potential problems. It is important to note that Brown, as he put it, "never urged our [original] sources to use their names." Some of those women have since identified themselves publicly. In the following pages, only people who have willingly identified themselves are fully named. I have used first-name pseudonyms for the women who said they were victims of assault and wish to remain confidential sources, and contrary to concerns that Brown raised in an article he published in 2015, none of the women are identified in this book. In fact, I have taken great care to not to reveal their identities. I have altered or left out all identifying details of these women, from physical characteristics to exact dates to geographic locations. I have left only the essence of their allegations: what they say Jian Ghomeshi did to them.

Some of the women whose stories appear in this book — without any identification — did not want them included, though many of their experiences were originally detailed in the *Toronto Star*. The women argued that retelling their stories would re-abuse them. One woman said, "I am appalled by your appropriation of women's voices to fabricate your own storyline." Another alleged that I was perpetrating a "revictimization of me for your purely commercial reasons." My suggestion that exploring all aspects of this important issue was necessary and overdue was answered with threats of lawsuits and a public denunciation of me. I have consulted other women whose stories appear in this book, and they did not understand the concerns. "I am not worried about any information that might be in the book," said one, adding that such a serious social issue can only be explored "by all of us finally talking." Another said, "I know our voices will lead to change. I only hope these shifts come sooner than later." Ultimately, I decided to publish because history cannot be unwritten. As upsetting as this will be to some people, I want to state this clearly: journalists must do their best to be objective; we cannot be in partnership with sources.

In an ideal world, all people who provide information for a piece of journalism would agree to be identified. In reality, many people, on all kinds of stories, will only speak to a reporter on condition that they will not be identified. To the public, the identity of the person is kept secret. This does not mean he or she is anonymous to the reporter. The reporter knows the person and should do his or her best to determine if that person is credible. In addition to the women who did not want to be identified, I have kept the identities of certain other people involved in the Ghomeshi story, including CBC staff and Ghomeshi advisers, confidential because the information they provided was fundamental to understanding what had happened, and it would not have been related to me without that promise. These promises of confidentiality were not given lightly. In all cases, these sources provided critical information on Ghomeshi's life between 1989 and the present. Finally, conversations in this book are based on recordings made at the time or, in the case of discussions with newsroom colleagues, reconstructed from participant recollections.

1

The Interview

"We are here to explore some information about Jian Ghomeshi," I began, lifting my eyes from the red light of the Sony recorder. "We want to ask you some questions about your experience."

It was Monday, May 12, 2014. Opposite me was Carly. To my right was *Canadaland* podcaster Jesse Brown. His resumé included hosting two CBC radio shows, *Search Engine* and *The Contrarians*, as well as work as a technology writer for *Macleans.ca* and *Toronto Life*. On May 5 he had sent an email with the subject line "URGENT: revelations about a well-known public figure" to *Toronto Star* editor-in-chief Michael Cooke and people at other Toronto newspapers.

Brown's email explained that six weeks prior "a young woman" contacted him "with shocking allegations about a well-known Canadian public figure with whom she'd had an intimate relationship." Brown stated that he was not one for celebrity gossip and that this story was different. He had talked to the woman several times and "verified many aspects of her story." Now he was at a dead end. "I have taken this story as far as I can as an independent journalist. I am seeking a partner publication to work with me on bringing this to light. If you'd like to know more about this, the next step is for me to meet you or your representative in person, where I will present documentation and notes on the story so far."

When Michael Cooke first received that email, he sent a copy to me and to Bert Bruser, the *Star*'s lawyer, telling us he was going to meet Brown even though "this guy may well be a nutter." Cooke meant nothing disparaging. The *Toronto Star* receives hundreds of news tips every week.

Some go to the general assignment reporters on the city desk, some to other departments, and those that are more investigative — long-term or sticky, messy situations like the Rob Ford story — end up in the investigations unit, a group of eight reporters and an analyst that I manage. We get all sorts of tips and ideas: the building department is corrupt, my lawyer stole my money, doctors are sexually assaulting patients and getting away with it, a retirement home is mistreating its residents, standardized school testing is rigged. Most of the story tips go nowhere, and some of them come from, well, nutters. But when I was a cub reporter, Jim Emmerson, an old rewrite man legendary for his pithy quotes, told me that we are like the fire department — when the alarm goes off, we have to answer the call. Most times there will be no fire, but what if there was, and we didn't check it out?

"I can't leave you with any materials," Brown said in his note to Cooke. "The nature of Canadian defamation law, as I understand, is such that I must demand that only two people are present at this initial meeting — either you and I, or your representative and I. I am sending similar emails to contacts of mine at the *Globe and Mail*, *Vice* and *Gawker*. I will meet with whoever is interested this week in the hopes of finding the right publishing partner."

Brown was deeply concerned that, by telling more than one person this tale, he could be found liable for defamation. The reality is that with a story so potentially damaging, more than a few people in the newsroom would have to be involved. We have all sorts of checks and balances that kick in when we are reviewing a story and working on an investigation. In the end, Cooke and Bruser met with Brown. They learned that Carly had contacted him on March 28. She had done some of her own detective work, and she provided him with information about her experiences and those of two others. Brown had then done a preliminary interview of Carly, and he shared the gist of it with Cooke and Bruser. Upon their return, they briefed me and then-managing editor Jane Davenport.

After some more discussions in-house, Cooke told Brown we were interested. The *Star* put Brown on a freelance contract and assigned me to work with him. Brown had some concerns, including his hope that he would have a shared byline. The *Star* assured him he would.

This meeting with Carly was our first time working together. Brown, a tall and imposing man who always seemed to be breaking a sweat, had, of course, spoken to her before. But for the *Toronto Star* to be part of such a legally sensitive story, a staff journalist had to be involved.

Carly pulled in her chair, checked for messages on her phone, and smiled. She was slender and well spoken with a nervous assurance about her. She had made up her mind to be involved, but only to a certain extent and on certain conditions. Her name, the city she was from, and a number of distinguishing details could never be revealed.

The small conference room was bare and windowless. Outside the door was the still-startlingly empty fourth floor, former advertising offices the *Toronto Star* didn't need now that much of that function had been contracted out. Carly was concerned about being recognized, and the barren corner of the fourth floor, one down from the bustling newsroom, seemed a good idea. Upstairs, Bert Bruser, Michael Cooke, and Jane Davenport were awaiting a full report.

"I listened to his radio show, I didn't know anything about him personally. Back in 2012 he was doing a book tour around Canada and I went to his show with a friend." Carly straightened in the soft-backed chair as she began her story. I watched her closely: her eyes, her mannerisms. My job was to determine whether this was a story worth investigating. Was there a fire?

Carly picked up her phone again, checked it, and moved it away. She set the scene. The book reading took place in an old brown-brick building. Ghomeshi read excerpts from *1982*, an autobiographical book describing his year as a David Bowie–worshipping fourteen-year-old in Thornhill, north of Toronto.

"Afterward, during the book signing, I got in line to meet him. I was really nervous when I met him, and he just asked me a lot of questions, including my age and my name, what I did for a living." Carly was in her early twenties, but Ghomeshi thought she was younger and asked if she was eighteen.

"I told him no, and I felt a bit of flirtation going on, so on my way out I said, 'and I have Facebook.' A couple of hours later he contacted me on Facebook and gave me his number and told me to text him."

In my notebook I drew an asterisk. The allegations that Jesse Brown brought to the *Star* suggested that Canada's number-one radio personality was abusive to young women. Many people young and old, male and female, were at the signing. The suggestion here was that Ghomeshi, alone in a strange town, selected one young woman. Were there more? Was this a pattern?

Via text message, Ghomeshi asked Carly to dinner later in the week. By this time he was in the next city on his book tour, and he asked if she was feeling adventurous. If so, she could meet him later that night. In a text message Carly said she no longer had, Ghomeshi wrote: "I thought you were the prettiest one there."

I made another asterisk and wrote on my pad, "text messages deleted."

In 2012, Ghomeshi was forty-five. Carly was roughly half his age, born around the time when he was attending university. She was single; he was single. She was excited that the host of *Q* had asked her out. A fan of his show, Carly knew his easy and bright manner and hoped for stimulating conversation. After all, this was a man who was at ease with rock stars and politicians. She did not know what to expect, but there was no doubt in her mind that this was a date, and Carly looked forward to a very interesting dinner. "I figured that if I didn't go and have a date with him I would probably regret it," she said.

Carly agreed to Ghomeshi's plan, grabbed her car keys, and got on the road. Halfway through the drive she received a text from Ghomeshi: "I am just relaxing and taking a bath. Are you almost here?"

Carly arrived at Ghomeshi's hotel at ten p.m. She followed his instructions and knocked on his door. "He gave me a hug, immediately came on to me," she remembered. "He was super handsy right from the start. He really caught me off guard. I immediately felt sorry for him. I felt he had no game."

They walked a few blocks to an Italian restaurant. They chatted a bit at dinner. Carly was aware that patrons at tables around them were looking over and whispering, recognizing the CBC star. At the table he touched her hands and body a lot, to the point that Carly told him to stop, reminding him they were in public.

Ghomeshi picked up the bill for dinner, and they meandered back to the hotel room. Carly mentioned it was her time of the month and that they would not be having sex. Ghomeshi told her that was fine but said that given the long drive and the time — midnight — she should consider staying the night. Inside his room, Carly said, Ghomeshi instantly became aggressive. It was like a switch was turned on.

"He put his hands around my throat. I could not swallow. He started making growling noises."

"Can you describe them?"

Carly blushed and after a few tries made a guttural sound. "They were animalistic. The sound a dog makes when it is starting to get angry. A very low rumbling."

"Has he hit you yet?"

"No. But it was very strange."

I looked at Jesse Brown, who had been silent to this point, then back at Carly. "I'm married; I have kids," I said. "I had dates with other women before I was married. I don't growl. I don't put my hands around women's throats. Is there something going on out there on the dating scene I don't know about these days?"

Carly chuckled at my question. "No, it is not normal. Normal men do not do this." Carly said she initially had the same question. Maybe this was something that men out there were doing?

I flipped to a fresh page of my notebook and was silent for a minute. The question I was about to ask was an obvious one, and a question that many others involved in the Ghomeshi case would ask over the next many months. Asking the question and other, more probing queries would anger some young women I later spoke to, but Carly faced them all calmly. Over the years I've found that there's usually a moment when it is clear to me that the subject is telling the truth. I've sometimes been wrong, but not often. This was the point — Carly's honesty was apparent. She was not dodging questions; she was answering them even if they were uncomfortable.

"When that happened, when he put his hands on your throat? Having not experienced that before, what did you do?"

Carly sat back in her chair. "This is the thing with me. If you really catch me off guard I will just process it in my head. I won't react to it."

She recalled the unusual growling continued. At one point, Ghomeshi stopped and spoke to her. "Is this scaring you? Let me know if this is scaring you," she remembers him asking.

"No, it's fine," Carly replied, though she was uncomfortable. Ghomeshi led her to his bed, and they began kissing and "making out," clothes on. Ghomeshi told her she was being "rigid" and stopped. They chatted, still on the bed. She told Ghomeshi that she did not know him at all and that things were moving too fast. To slow things down, Carly tried a distraction and asked Ghomeshi questions about himself. Rather than moving to safer ground, she found she had angered him.

Ghomeshi was insulted when it became clear that Carly was unaware of details about his life. He seemed to assume that since he was a celebrity on the CBC, she should know everything about his past. Carly decided to turn interviewer.

"What do your parents think about your career?" she asked.

"Didn't you read my book?" Ghomeshi shot back. "You would know if you read my book."

"Do you know what? I read your book. But I am asking you on a personal level. I am trying to get to know you."

Ghomeshi did not respond. Carly decided it was time to leave. Ghomeshi was immediately concerned and said he was worried she was not attracted to him. Carly said she did not know yet. Ghomeshi offered her the bed for the night — he said nothing would happen, and he would probably snore — but she said goodbye and drove the two hours home.

"I was being really careful with him not to insult him. I really did feel sorry for him," Carly repeated an earlier comment that he seemed not to know how to relate to women. "I felt he had no game."

In the morning, back in her home city, she texted Ghomeshi and apologized for leaving so abruptly. He told her to look him up if she came to Toronto. She told him she was there quite often.

"He had some kind of effect on me. Despite how much he came on to me I was still interested in him. I don't know if it was the intrigue of me having been a fan of his. I am thinking it probably was. I also found him quite nice on that date and interesting. He has a really funny sense of humour, and to this day he is hilarious."

Carly smiled from across the table. It looked as though she was remembering some good parts of the relationship. It was hardly what I expected from a young woman who at some point in this story was apparently going to allege some much more serious and long-term abuse. As I understood from Jesse Brown, her relationship with Ghomeshi became much more intimate in the following days.

Having listened to Ghomeshi for years myself, I would never have pegged him as having a violent nature. I suddenly realized that I had no sense of Ghomeshi's physical presence. I had never seen him in person, never watched the televised QTV podcasts. Carly was tiny. How big was Ghomeshi?

"Five foot eleven," she estimated.

"Is he muscular?"

"Mmmm. He works out probably three times a week. He has a trainer. He is well built, except for his stomach. He thinks he's fat. He stands in front of the mirror and says he is fat. He sounds like a teenage girl talking about his weight, and I have never heard a man talk like that. He would project his body image issues on to me as well. 'I want your ass to get bigger, but I don't want your thighs to get bigger. I want you having abs, you have nice abs, but make sure they are not too toned because I don't want them to be too toned.'"

Within two days of the book reading in the fall of 2012, Carly said, she and Ghomeshi began texting on a regular basis. She was at work in her hometown; Ghomeshi was still doing book events. Calgary, Montreal, and other cities were on his route, and she knew he would meet other young women along the way. Despite that, Carly said she enjoyed the texting and felt there was a mild flirtation going on. At this point in the interview, she paused. "This is where it makes me look, you know, whatever."

She explained that she had purchased a new bikini, mail order, and she tried it on, took a photo, and texted it to Ghomeshi, who responded, she recalled, "I fucking love that you just sent this to me." He asked for more photos, and videos, and she complied. Some were with the bikini on; some were taken in lingerie. At that point, they all included some form of clothing.

"It completely spiralled from that point. He requested that I send him a new video every day. I had to keep him interested because if I didn't he would move onto another woman." Carly raised her eyes to look directly at me. "Please don't judge my frame of mind here because I was so out of my mind here."

In my notebook I made an observation. Carly rarely referred to Ghomeshi by his name, only as "him." This might mean she had him on a pedestal and never thought of him as an equal partner in the relationship, or she might simply be so angry and betrayed that she could only refer to him that way.

Plans were made for Carly to visit Ghomeshi in Toronto. She dragged her feet. Christmas was coming, and she was concerned about the cost and what she was getting into. Eventually, just before the end of the year, she booked her ticket. By that point, Carly was sending a video of herself to Ghomeshi every day at the radio star's request, more graphic as time went by.

Brown leaned forward in his chair, eager to get to the point. "Do you remember the first time he mentioned anything outside of . . . any threat of violence?" he asked.

"Yes," Carly answered quickly. "Shortly after I sent him videos. It was something about beating me up. I almost wasn't surprised after I got it for some reason." Carly explained that she had been watching Ghomeshi on Twitter and had noticed a real anger and aggression in his tweets. When people challenged him on the smallest point, Ghomeshi would become upset and angry and fire back. Carly did not remember what her answer was to his introduction of the rough sex idea, and she had already deleted all of his texts. "This was a while ago so I don't remember, but it certainly wasn't 'please beat me up.'"

I wanted to see if there was any chance that, at this point in their relationship history, Carly had any previous connection with any of Ghomeshi's friends, colleagues or former colleagues, or former dates. She said she had not and that beyond what she had heard on *Q*, Ghomeshi was a closed book to her. I went back to Brown's question about the threat of violence, and Carly said she must have provided a cold response because Ghomeshi texted urgently, asking when would be a good time to phone her. They arranged a time when she was working late, and Ghomeshi called.

According to Carly, Ghomeshi told her, "I can see that you are getting a little standoffish about my violent texting, and I just want to assure you that it is purely fantasy, and we will come up with a safe word. I want you to know that I would never hurt you."

Carly responded that Ghomeshi should not worry; she was still coming for the visit but, she told him, she hoped he wasn't planning to "have his way with her" and "toss her aside."

Ghomeshi has had three houses in Toronto over the last decade. In late 2012, he was living in Cabbagetown, a gentrified area of east Toronto dotted with stately Victorian houses and old buildings. Ghomeshi's home was in a renovated industrial space, once a peanut factory. A 2010 *Toronto Star* story by arts reporter Rita Zekas described the interior as uncluttered yet homey, with a spread of shoes just inside on the tiled floor. In the foyer, the ceiling stretched up almost fifty feet to the top floor of the townhouse, which was lined with well-worn Persian carpets, a nod to Ghomeshi's Iranian heritage, and musical touches on the walls — photos from his days with nineties Toronto folk-pop band Moxy Früvous and a drawing by singer Lights, whom Ghomeshi managed. On the top floor he had a rooftop deck fitted out with lounge chairs and a table.

Carly flew in late in the afternoon on a Friday, a plan she said she made clear to Ghomeshi, hoping he would pick her up. Ghomeshi was at work that day. His morning radio show wrapped up just before noon, and he then typically spent a few hours working on future shows. She texted him that she had arrived, and the timing was not to Ghomeshi's liking.

"I have to leave work right now!" Ghomeshi replied. "If you're standing outside my house waiting for me there's nothing I can do about that because I don't know if I will get back in time. Try to stall. Take a cab."

I was puzzled. "Was he trying to protect his neighbours from seeing a young girl there?"

"No, I think he was just annoyed."

Carly took a taxi. She arrived around dinnertime. It was dark. She waited outside and saw him drive up in his Mini Cooper.

Opening a folder, I took out a picture of Ghomeshi's current house, in the Beaches, another area in Toronto's east end. Carly looked at it and said no, the house she went to was the Cabbagetown house on Sackville Street. She knew Ghomeshi had moved since then, and she had been to the house in the Beaches, too. Carly resumed her story.

The driveway of the Sackville Street house was long by city standards. She waved when he got out of his car, but Ghomeshi went inside without saying anything. Carly walked up to the front door and knocked. No answer. The door opened and she went inside.

"He did not speak to me. He put my luggage down and threw me against the wall and started making out with me." She said it was like a scene from a movie.

"Like the scene from that Glenn Close movie?" I asked, referencing the steamy, aggressive sex scenes in the 1987 movie *Fatal Attraction*, which co-starred Michael Douglas.

Carly said it was exactly like that, very intense, no dialogue. Ghomeshi led her upstairs, where she noted mirrors everywhere, particularly on the closets in front of the bathroom, just outside the master bedroom. She said Ghomeshi ordered her to perform fellatio.

"Just like that?" I asked.

"Just like that. So I obliged."

"Why?"

"I was there already. It was assumed we were going to have sex anyways, so I just thought this is what we are doing. I didn't want him to think I was a cold fish."

I must have looked puzzled. Carly explained further.

"Also, too, I froze. I am the type of person who is really bad in an emergency. If something major happens I just freeze. I was just going through the motions with him and not knowing what else to do, and that's when he hit me across the head."

"While you were giving him oral sex?"

"Yes."

"Once?"

"Repeatedly."

"One side?"

"He would vary. I would say he mostly did it with his right hand."

"Did you stop doing what you were doing?"

"I think, for a minute. I could not believe what was happening. I was in so much shock. I thought, you know, he was going to be a little rough but not physically hurting me."

"Then what?"

"He led me to the bathroom."

"Did he ejaculate?"

"No. He goes a long time. Especially for his age."

"Then what?"

"He kind of shoved me against his vanity so there's a mirror in front of me and behind me."

"Who's wearing what?"

"I had my top on and underwear and nothing else. He had his pants off. My memory is a little bit fuzzy. He would face me in front of the mirror and grab my throat. Him wanting me to give him oral sex; him hitting me across the head. I remember him pushing me really hard against his counter and it had a sharp edge and it was hurting my back."

I looked straight at Carly. "'Stop.' Are you saying that?"

"No. And that's where it's my fault. I didn't tell him to stop. And I remember him taking his belt and leading me around his bedroom like a dog on a leash."

Brown broke in. "Is he talking at all throughout this?"

"Yes, like 'you're a dirty whore' kind of conversation."

We took a brief pause. After three decades of reporting on all sorts of stories I was well aware that people are not always the same in the bedroom as outside of it and that lots of people engage in sexual role play. One story I investigated a few years back, involving allegations against a man who by day worked for a public service agency in Ontario and by night was known as Lord Morpheus and a self-styled kink expert in BDSM — the art of bondage-discipline-dominance-submission-sadism-masochism — took me briefly into the world of dungeons and rough-sex role play. That world, as I recalled, involved a lot of gadgets, collars, ropes, leather gags, and other paraphernalia. I wondered if this was what was going on with Ghomeshi, some kind of consensual role play. I asked Carly, and she said there was no agreement, no safe word, no discussion of consent.

I was clenching my teeth. I found Carly's story deeply troubling. The scene she was describing was baffling. A major celebrity, one of Canada's biggest stars, risking it all with this terrible behaviour did not make any sense.

"Okay, so he's put one hand around your neck, now he's put his belt around you and now he's leading you, and you still say nothing. Which is an issue with this story, and you obviously understand that?"

Carly nodded. "Yes, I do, yes."

I wasn't blaming Carly, but I wanted her to understand that some readers would question whether she was consenting to certain parts of Ghomeshi's alleged behaviour.

"Then what happened?"

"We went to his bed."

"Still on your neck? The belt?"

"He would have taken it off and started whipping me with it."

"Did he? Or would he?"

"Oh, yes, absolutely. I just don't remember the exact order of when it happened, but it happened for sure."

"Whereabouts on your body?"

"My back and shoulders. Never on the head or face area."

"Hard?" I asked.

"Yup. It hurt."

"Did you have marks from that?" Brown asked.

"Probably. I had a lot of bruises and marks and stuff when I got back."

Carly described the next hour. She said Ghomeshi pinned her down, straddled her, and hit her hard enough to blur her vision. "He would do that a lot, lay me on my back, straddling my face, and shoving it down my throat. He would have his whole weight of his body on me, and he was pinning my arms with his legs so I couldn't say anything, and I couldn't get him off me. I would be choking and crying, and I couldn't breathe, and that made me panicky. When I was pretty much at the breaking point, that's when he would get off."

She said this was her first introduction to Ghomeshi's stuffed animal, a blue teddy bear he called Big Ears Teddy. It was always in the room when they had sex. She said Ghomeshi would turn it around, saying, "This is too inappropriate for Big Ears to see."

Carly said they had intercourse after that, which included more hitting by Ghomeshi. Then he asked her to massage his back, and he fell asleep.

I was curious about something. "I listen to his show a lot. He's a very good interviewer. You're not getting any of these questions where he is asking about you as a human being?"

"Nope. He didn't even give me a tour of his house."

Carly stayed the weekend with Ghomeshi. She said he was violent every time they had sex. One particular incident stood out. The morning after her arrival, a Saturday, she was getting dressed in a spare room where her luggage was, and he walked in and went at her again.

"He made me face the mirror and pushed me up against the mirror and was choking me, and I started to black out. He would cover my nose and mouth and choke my neck. This is where I was trying to tell him to stop, and he wouldn't stop. I would try and pry his hands off and make a noise, and he would still wait a few seconds longer. When you think you are going to black out, a few seconds is a long time. I would panic. I would say to him, 'You almost made me black out, I couldn't breathe.' And he said, 'That is so hot, I wish you had passed out, it would have been hotter if you had passed out.'"

I put my pen down on my notebook. Journalists have a duty to seek the truth, just like lawyers in a courtroom, and that often involves asking tough questions. The next question was one that might seem insensitive, but it was one that had to be asked.

"That's frightening stuff," I said. "I think a lot of people would ask this: why didn't you get your bags and get the hell out of there?"

2

Rape Culture

"Well, hi there. Happy Monday. And what better way to begin the week than with a surprise pop quiz." Jian Ghomeshi's voice was sunny, building up speed like a rolling freight train, punctuation and grammar sometimes be damned. Just another day at the *Q* office, and he had a good though controversial show in store for his listeners across Canada and around the world on Monday, March 24, 2014, two months before Jesse Brown and I began our investigation.

Downstairs in the bustling CBC lobby, a two-storey-high poster of Ghomeshi made it clear that he was one of the national broadcaster's top talents. In the control room of Studio 203 at the Front Street headquarters of the CBC, a group of loyal producers and production assistants watched their star perform in the dimly lit studio that was both stage and cave for the forty-six-year-old. First, his trademark opening, a daily monologue, always under three minutes, that he called his "essay." Though the listening public generally believed the *Q* host was the author of these essays, they were the work of two *Q* writers, Sean Foley, who was also a producer, and Matt Tunnacliff.

"Ready? Here we go. What superhero are you? Okay, what *Buffy* character are you? What, what kind of dog are you? What *Breakfast Club* character are you? Who should play you in the movie of your life? What minor *Friends* character are you?" he said, with the slightest pause and forced seriousness that would bring a smile to listeners in offices, cars and homes.

"What cheese are you? Seriously, dear audience, what cheese are you? It is an important question that needs asking and answering, or so it seems by millions of people on the Internet in 2014. If there is one trend that defines our web culture in the first few months of this year, it is the amazing popularity of the online quiz where you pick a subject to answer a few random questions and the quiz spits out an answer—Hey, I got gouda!—which you can then instantly share with your friends or followers over social media. That's all it is, a few minutes of your time, a few clicks and you could instantly know which Muppet you are, because everyone needs to know which Muppet they are. Stat. And sure, it's a lot of fun, kind of, and a well-worn distraction from real issues and life, right? It's certainly shameless click-bait for Buzzfeed, the site that first popularized the quizzes, although they have now spread across the Internet at large. Nearly twenty million people took the 'What city should I actually live in?' quiz, the one that might have truly clicked off the trend a few months ago. But the wild popularity of these Internet quizzes does reveal a couple of things…"

As he spoke, Ghomeshi's voice sped up and slowed down; the pitch rose and fell. "Smooth as silk baritone" was how one reviewer had described it. "Comforting yet inquisitive baritone," said another. A friend of mine, a woman who was in her late forties when she first heard Ghomeshi, remarked, "His voice is like a spider, it draws you in." Speaking quickly was part of the charm, and when he occasionally stumbled on air, he corrected effortlessly and moved on. Ghomeshi continued his morning essay.

"First, it turns out the Internet is not just about awesome communications or creativity or education or even surveillance or promotion or a nefarious plan to take over the world, no, it may be all of that but it's also about self-involvement, yes, real genuine old-school narcissism. But it's more than that too, particularly in the popularity of quizzes like 'What career should I actually have' or 'What city should I actually live in.' There's that melancholy undertone, that feeling that we should really be somewhere else doing something else. When it comes down to it, one might say this taps into our belief, nay hope, that we could be somebody else. Because deep down inside, apparently, we all want to be Ironman or Wonder Woman or Kermit or Piggy or Buffy or Spike or Ross or Rachel or Captain Kirk or… Sulu.

"I'm Jian Ghomeshi. This . . . is *Q*."

That was the cue for the trademark opening music, recorded by Toronto artists Luke Doucet and Chris Murphy. When the last guitar chords and drumbeats were still in the air, Ghomeshi breezily announced, "Okay, on your program today, do we really live in a rape culture? Is the term accurate or just plain alarmist? We convene a *Q* debate."

Across the country, ears perked up. *Q* had tackled some big issues, but this one promised to be contentious. This was not another interview with an indie rock artist or a legendary comedian. This was a serious, timely, and significant issue. And in pockets of the country, here and there, an unknown number of women who had been on dates with the CBC host listened even more intently.

Ghomeshi listed off two more segments on the morning show, including one about captivity in Iran, and then with that perfect mix of fun and gravity — plus a rhyme as always — he announced he would end the program with a look at the rise of online eating shows in South Korea. "Here's looking at chew . . . This is *Q*."

In his seven years as *Q* host, Ghomeshi talked to a lot of big stars. He had the ability to be serious with just the right hint of fun. This balance was a large part of his enormous success.

Ghomeshi began his career with the national broadcaster at the start of the decade, working mainly in television on a series of shows including *>play* and *The Hour*. When *Q* began in April 2007, it had an afternoon timeslot, something that changed inside of a year. Jennifer McGuire, the executive director of programming for CBC Radio, told the *Toronto Star*'s Bruce DeMara before the launch of the new show that the broadcaster had made a detailed study of the network's audience and their music tastes. Putting Ghomeshi on the as-yet-unnamed afternoon program was done as an attempt to attract a younger audience to its core. At the time, half the CBC audience was older than sixty-five.

"We went into people's homes and looked at their record collections. It was a fairly in-depth and exhaustive piece of research," McGuire told DeMara. McGuire said they discovered that of approximately thirty thousand songs produced annually by Canadian artists, only about 0.8 per cent received decent airplay. "So there is a huge amount of Canadian creativity that has no … opportunity for exposure to other Canadians. We felt as a public broadcaster, we should be reflecting the diversity and range of creativity happening out there," McGuire said in the interview, one of many she did that year as the CBC fought an ongoing battle for a younger audience.

In a talk Joe Mahoney, the CBC engineer when Ghomeshi's show started, gave to Ryerson radio students, he noted: "*Q* is a show not afraid to have a little bit of fun, and … at its core it's a show about creativity. And the sky's the limit."

According to Mahoney, one of the biggest dilemmas in creating *Q* was coming up with a name. The CBC brass wanted a catchy name that would draw listeners to the arts and culture show. *Radar* was one option put forward. *Awesometown* was another. Mahoney and others were put into a SkyBox at the SkyDome (now the Rogers Centre) and told to come up with a name and a concept. *Skybox 3* was another name bandied about, followed by *Studio Q* and, finally, *Q*. That name was taken to Ghomeshi, who went for it.

Seven years later, the name had stuck and *Q* was a success. Before that first launch in 2007, during those SkyBox brainstorming sessions, the production team spent a lot of time figuring out just what the show would be. Would it be confined to arts and culture? What are the parameters of arts and culture? Mahoney recalled an intense time period that gave birth to a very good radio show. He said the production crew took courses to help them prepare, including courses on ethics and interviewing. Over time, the show would tackle some serious issues in addition to its arts coverage. Depression, suicide, concussions in the NFL, Russia's treatment of gays and whether or not a celebrity's bad behaviour should stop fans from listening to the celebrity's body of work were just some of the many serious topics over the years. More than three million listeners tuned in to hear *Q*, coast to coast on CBC in Canada, on Public Radio International in one hundred and eighty cities in the United States and by podcast in far-flung countries. *QTV*, a weekly highlight show of filmed interviews in the studio, was also turning in record numbers.

Despite the show's clear external success, however, things were not as tranquil behind the scenes at *Q* as the celebrity host portrayed. For some of the young staff, both women and men, Ghomeshi's outward stance as a progressive, supportive host was at odds with his behaviour toward them, which was often demeaning and belittling when the microphones were off and the *Q* cameras were not rolling. It was not unusual for Ghomeshi to fly into a rage at some perceived slight, then an hour later be seen giving a back or shoulder massage to a young female staffer. Young interns from journalism schools coveted jobs on *Q*, but as the years went on, some of the schools decided to skip *Q* because of fears of Ghomeshi's inappropriate behaviour — flirting, asking young female interns on dates, touching their bodies with his hands, grinding his pelvis against them, giving long embraces in full view of staffers. When guests were not in the studio, Ghomeshi enjoyed discussing his sexual escapades, frequently remarking on his love for anal sex. Producers were not sure if his stories were true, but they had given up trying to get him to stop. He was a popular host, and they all knew their futures were tied to his. The show was a massive success, and no one was willing to risk hurting *Q*.

It was also very clear to the predominantly young staff who worked at *Q* that Ghomeshi was the boss. That was apparent during meetings, when show plans were hatched over email late at night, and when, from time to time, Ghomeshi had his staff run out the side door of the CBC building to meet him and park his car, so that the perpetually late host made it to his chair on time. On paper, control might seem to belong to the executive producer, Arif Noorani, but Noorani, like Ghomeshi, was in the CBC union and held little sway over his star host. The managers above them were Chris Boyce and Kim Orchard, executives who had a great deal of their own success vested in Ghomeshi's. On a day-to-day basis, Ghomeshi called the shots, and he was very good at catching the ear of higher-ups at the CBC. Orchard, who oversaw the arts and entertainment portfolio, was very close with Ghomeshi, calling him "my poor baby" and "poor darling" when the host complained of problems he perceived on the show.

Over the years, staffers had whispered complaints about Ghomeshi's rude behaviour on the set: disrespect bordering on harassment. He was a demanding host and would sometimes fly into tirades if he didn't get his way. Producers who worked on Q discussed the possibility that Ghomeshi was a psychopath, a clinical term that describes someone who is uncaring, insincere, but often charming; someone who lacks a conscience, has no sense of right and wrong, and, in the extreme, can be prone to violence. One day, several producers discovered an online test for psychopathy and filled it in, answering questions as if they were the Q host. Their test scored twenty-six out of a possible twenty-seven, although that likely owed a debt to the bias of the producers who completed it.

In 2012 many Q staff sent management a highly critical document they called "Red Sky," an ominous play on Blue Sky, the name of the yearly think-tank meeting Q producers held to see how the show could be improved. Though watered down from its original form before it was sent to CBC brass, the one-page letter complained that Q producers and other staff worked in a highly stressful environment, and though it did not name him, it laid the blame at Ghomeshi's feet. The letter writers noted their fear that if they did not do as the host requested, they would be punished in some way.

But as a CBC-commissioned report by lawyer Janice Rubin would find in the spring of 2015, the bosses at the CBC were not paying attention to complaints about their golden boy. The show was simply too important. The other reality is that many of the young producers stayed silent because they wanted to keep their jobs; complaining against the boss would put them in a vulnerable position.

Successful producers learned to script shows the way Ghomeshi spoke. On a script, from which Ghomeshi rarely deviated, they would write "pause here" or "sigh here" or even suggest a place to stammer a word if it would make him seem endearing. In the control room during a live show or taping they had two options for prompting Ghomeshi: his earpiece, which the host hated to use, or a teleprompter in the desk. "Our relationship with Jian was like the story of Cyrano de Bergerac," one producer said. Ghomeshi had the face and the voice — they provided the words. Joe Mahoney recalls how important it was for these young producers to curry favour. Sometimes, one would get to do a small segment on the air. Mahoney recalled one female producer in that situation. "If she wanted to get back on the air, she would have to play ball." That meant treating Ghomeshi as a star, not questioning his decisions and generally making the host feel that he was the most important person at the CBC.

Like many *Q* topics — Toronto's controversial, crack-smoking mayor, Rob Ford, was another example — the debate about rape culture that took place on Monday, March 24, 2014, sprang from the headlines. In the month immediately preceding the debate, two incidents of sexual assault related to universities hit the news. Ghomeshi's introduction to the segment went like this, his voice taking on a more serious tone than when he had rattled off the pop quiz segment in his opening essay:

"In recent weeks several Canadian universities have been at the centre of a heated public conversation about sexual assault. At the University of Ottawa, for example, two recent incidents have made headlines. First, a sexual assault investigation involving members of the school's hockey team and second, revelations about a group of male students making so-called jokes online about raping a female student leader. These incidents and earlier ones have prompted discussions about what role online comments and general cultural attitudes have in creating an environment where sexual assault is tolerated or even encouraged. And the term most often used to describe that complex of attitudes and behaviour is 'rape culture.' The term has become common in feminist discourse and popular media, but not everyone agrees it is helpful or accurate. The notion of rape culture has been criticized in the pages of national newspapers and even by some advocates for victims of sexual assault. So, we've decided to convene a *Q* debate. Do we really live in a so-called rape culture? Is that term accurate, or is it alarmist?"

Ghomeshi introduced the panelists to his listeners. One was linked by phone, the other in a New York studio where the CBC rents space. According to CBC's explanation of the debate on its website, *Q* had invited Lise Gotell, chair of the Department of Women's and Gender Studies at the University of Alberta, "to make the case that the term 'rape culture' is valid and useful." Gotell was one of the people behind the public education drive "Don't Be That Guy," a behavioural marketing campaign to raise awareness surrounding alcohol-facilitated sexual assault and promote understanding that sex without consent is sexual assault.

To make a counter-argument, *Q* invited Heather Mac Donald of the Manhattan Institute. According to the CBC, Mac Donald "has carried out research that questions whether the incidence of rape is as high as claimed on college campuses."

The segment began with opening statements from each guest that set the table for a talk that *The Atlantic*, in an understatement, later referred to as "tense." Gotell in her first comments said the term "rape culture" was a good one, though she admitted it can be too sweeping and general. "I think it is a meaningful term, it really helps draw attention to the prevalence of sexual violence which is well documented. It is really drawing attention to the ideas that normalize and trivialize sexual violence," Gotell said.

Mac Donald shot back by condemning the "one in four, one in five" statistic often used to describe how many women are victims of sexual assault while on a post-secondary campus. She said that statistic, which she challenged, is trotted out to prove the existence of rape culture.

"That is simply a fantastical claim, that is a level of criminality that is unprecedented in human history," Mac Donald argued. "If colleges were this tsunami of sexual violence and predation that is claimed, we would have seen a stampede to create and demand alternatives, whether sending girls to single-sex schools or private tutors. Instead, every year the onslaught to get females as well as males into colleges increases."

The segment ran just over twenty minutes. Among the comments Mac Donald made that incensed listeners was her suggestion to "tell all girls: do not drink yourself blotto at parties and get in bed with a guy and take your clothes off. That could wipe out campus, what is being called campus sexual assault, overnight."

Before the segment was finished, calls and emails began pouring in. The enormous response continued while the two other segments aired — and for the rest of the day. James Hamblin noted in *The Atlantic* that "the segment swelled out of the amiable host's control." By lunch hour, the CBC, Ghomeshi, and the *Q* staff were in a firestorm. While some writers insisted the CBC had the right to air such spirited dissent, most were downright angry about the program and particularly the decision to let Heather Mac Donald come on the program in the first place.

One listener, a St. Catharines woman, criticized Mac Donald for being thirty years behind the times in her view of women and sexual assault. "If we follow her submission that women should be taught to avoid situations of danger and blaming men for being sexually assaulted, then would we not teach everyone to avoid being hit by drunk drivers?" she asked. "We don't blame the victims who are injured or killed by a drunk driver—why then do we blame the victims for injury or death by sexual assault?" Shortly after that day's show concluded, a wise decision was made to, as is said in the media business, "get out ahead of the story." They would do it by devoting the start of next day's show to the thoughts of the listeners, beginning with a reading of the letter from the woman from St. Catharines—the first time a show began with listener reaction. The hope was to clear the air before they had to pack up and head to Winnipeg for the much-hyped *Q* live show organized around the coming weekend's Juno Awards, a celebration of the Canadian music industry.

In the turmoil that afternoon, as the CBC and its host tried to figure out if anything more needed to be done to respond to these criticisms, a different kind of message popped into Ghomeshi's personal email in-box. This note was from Paula, one of the numerous women Ghomeshi had recently been dating. The email was direct and to the point. It alleged that Ghomeshi had been violent with her and others and accused him of being "sadistic." No reference was made to the Gotell/Mac Donald rape culture debate, from earlier that day but Paula did question how Ghomeshi could speak passionately about human rights and the need to abolish violence against women and still carry on the way she alleged he did. Paula wrote that she had become a sort of lightning rod for complaints about Ghomeshi. Other women had contacted her, women who, in complaining about Ghomeshi, provided photos and videos of "significant bruising on their bodies." Including herself, she said, the number of complainants she knew of numbered six.

Ghomeshi was in the middle of the *Q* debate turmoil as well as preparing for the Winnipeg show. Now he had to deal with a personal crisis.

An hour later, Ghomeshi emailed Paula back. "I'm shaking as I read this. Can we please talk?"

3

Big Ears Teddy

Jian Ghomeshi paced. He had a hard time sitting still. The email from Paula had heightened his anxiety to an uncomfortable level. When he finally did sit down at the table in his lawyer's boardroom, his left leg fidgeted, and he tapped his hand on his knee rapidly. In what people present perceived as a calming device, Ghomeshi repeatedly took the palms of both hands and rubbed them on his inner thighs.

The boardroom of Dentons LLP in downtown Toronto's financial district was filling up with his advisers: people from his publicity firm, his management firm, his newly hired crisis communication firm, and several lawyers, including Tiffany Soucy, a senior associate in the firm's litigation and alternative dispute resolution group, who was managing the file. One of the people present remarked later that so much expensive talent was on hand that if you added up the preparation and meeting hours, this was a "$20,000 meeting."

The meeting had been called to discuss the ongoing issue of allegations — still secret from the public — that Ghomeshi had been abusive to Carly. A new concern, Paula's email to Ghomeshi the day of the rape culture debate, listed allegations of similar violent sexual behaviour, but only a select number of people had seen it. The main reason for the meeting was to bring everyone on the Ghomeshi team up to speed and discuss both the Paula development and some of the allegations contained in an obscure Twitter account. Nobody from the CBC was present. Ghomeshi informed his advisers that just after the rape culture debate he alerted his employer to a potential problem, but only at a junior level. In late March 2014, during a quiet moment off set at the *Q* live show connected to the

Juno Awards in Winnipeg, he told two *Q* producers — Sean Foley and Brian Coulton — that an ex-girlfriend, by whom he meant Carly, was threatening to tell the world about his interest in rough sex. Ghomeshi's fear that Carly would make these allegations public began back in late February, shortly after he returned from hosting CBC programs at the Winter Olympics in Russia and they stopped seeing each other.

The two producers later told CBC's *fifth estate* in its program "The Unmaking of Jian Ghomeshi" that Ghomeshi broke down in front of them. "He basically said, 'I like rough sex. I have an ex-girlfriend who is angry at me, and she is threatening to tell everybody that I am into this,'" Sean Foley said in his *fifth estate* interview. Foley recalled Ghomeshi saying that he wasn't worried that he'd done anything that could be considered "illegal." Rather, he was concerned about being "tried in the court of public opinion" and worried that the CBC might not back him if he was "outed," according to Foley. Ghomeshi swore Foley and Coulton to secrecy, and they abided by that for months, although Coulton later recalled that the secret he was carrying induced "mild panic attacks" in the months that followed. "I carried this with great emotional weight," he said.

Ghomeshi pulled Coulton aside a second time and told him of an anonymous Twitter account that was making allegations against him, allegations that Ghomeshi told the producer were unfounded. Coulton looked up the Twitter account out of curiosity and shared it with Foley, who found the anonymous allegations shocking. Coulton didn't know what to do with the information, and for the time being, he did nothing. If it was true that a jilted ex-lover was making unfounded allegations, he said, he did not want to "tarnish anyone's reputation who does not deserve to have it unduly tarnished."

In the boardroom, Ghomeshi and his advisers discussed his recollection of his talks with Foley and Coulton. Ghomeshi had made it clear to the producers that he was not making a confession of any sort. That Ghomeshi liked his sex rough was not a complete revelation to people who worked at *Q*, in light of his habit of talking about his sexual habits to the production staff. But the concern that Carly and now Paula were about to go public moved Ghomeshi's anxiety into overdrive.

Despite the issue at hand, the mood in the boardroom was upbeat. They were trained professionals, smarter than the media, and they could handle this. Ghomeshi's legendary agent, Jack Ross, who had plucked Ghomeshi from busking obscurity a quarter of a century before, made his position quite clear to anyone who asked, including those in the meeting. "I don't believe it," Ross told the people involved in dealing with the crisis. "It's not in his nature." The goal of this meeting, and others to come, was to find out the extent of the problem and to stop these allegations from becoming public. Also firmly in Ghomeshi's camp was Chris Taylor, a musician turned lawyer whom *Billboard* has called one of Canada's most influential entertainment lawyers and whose clients have included Drake and Nelly Furtado.

The stakes in the late winter and early spring of 2014 were enormous. Should a story hit the news, even if it was eventually proven untrue, the public fallout would be devastating both to Ghomeshi's brand and to his employer, a national broadcaster fighting a perpetual cutback battle with the ruling Conservative government of Stephen Harper. Jian Ghomeshi was popular with veteran listeners and — just as the CBC hoped — a new thirty-something audience. A statement his lawyers eventually prepared for a lawsuit against the CBC would describe Ghomeshi as "one of the best, if not the best, in the business." The host, in discussions with his advisers, also noted that *Q* was the most popular show CBC had ever aired in the key ten a.m. weekday timeslot. It had long surpassed the ratings of beloved host Peter Gzowski, whose *Morningside* show earned him the nickname "Captain Canada."

For his work on *Q*, the CBC paid Ghomeshi $320,000 annually, one of the highest salaries at the publicly owned corporation. Ghomeshi was also very much in demand on the speaking circuit and earned at least another $100,000 a year from hosting and speaking duties across the country. Paid and unpaid, Ghomeshi's engagements included such luminous events as the annual Scotiabank Giller Prize, which celebrates the best in Canadian fiction every fall. Ghomeshi had hosted the Gillers the previous year and was tapped again for this coming November. As he told some of his friends, Ghomeshi had designs on something beyond his current job, perhaps a run for politics. He had also spoken about the dream of one day becoming Canada's governor general, following in the footsteps of former CBC host Adrienne Clarkson.

Of particular concern to everyone in the boardroom that spring was the sudden appearance on social media of an allegation that linked Jian Ghomeshi's name with violence. On April 9, two weeks after the rape-culture debate, a tweet was posted from a person using the Twitter name Sidnie Georgina and the Twitter handle @bigearsteddy. The Twitter account was new, and almost all its activity related to Ghomeshi.

The first tweet appeared late in the evening on April 9, at 9:29 p.m. "Hi there @jianghomeshi. Remember louring me to ur house under false pretences? Bruises don't lie. Signed, every female Carleton U media grad." Since the tweet used Ghomeshi's own Twitter handle, Ghomeshi received a notification on his Twitter account that he had been mentioned. That spring, Ghomeshi had 246,000 followers and was very active on Twitter, happily engaging with fans about issues on his show. Inevitably, this tweet caught his interest, and the eye of others in his camp. Strangely, though — and this is perhaps a product of how much garbage surfaces on social media — the tweet had been missed by the public and the media — so far.

Between April 9 and April 11, nine more tweets followed. Among them:

"BREAKING NEWS: @jianghomeshi keeps an impressive anthology of videos and photos of the young girls he chokes out…#howromantic #rapeculture." Another: "Yes, a friendly FYI @jianghomeshi to cement your great depression. Snuck a viddy of you punching me — OOOPS this is my confession #staytuned." And another: "@jianghomeshi you think you know me but you have no idea. I'll make you second guess me like North Korea. #happyhitting #rapeculture." And: "Ever wake up wishing you could live a day in @jianghomeshi shoes? All you gotta do is Eat. Sleep. Degrade women. Repeat. Yes. It's THAT easy."

Other tweets from the account alleged that Ghomeshi was the "real life monster" behind American pop star Britney Spears's smash hit "Hit Me Baby One More Time." The Twitter account retweeted only once, a message from an anti-CBC account suggesting that the cuts to the national broadcaster might force Ghomeshi to "have to find a job in the real world." Most used the hashtag #rapeculture, allowing others who followed topics connected to that debate to easily find these Ghomeshi tweets. It was clear to the Ghomeshi advisers who reviewed the account that whoever was behind it wanted the world to find their message.

The account went silent on April 11, 2014. There was only one mention of anything specific and that was Carleton University in Ottawa, a school with a journalism program that had, according to one tweet, sent dozens of interns to work at the CBC and *Q*, where they had been abused. When I later tried to run down the Carleton allegation, it appeared, as far as I could tell, to have been invented by the author of the tweet to provoke Ghomeshi. Carleton embarked on an investigation for naught, as the university found no evidence of any issues involving Carleton students who worked on *Q*. The *Star* later reported that another journalism school, the University of Western Ontario (now known as Western) declined to send students to fill *Q* internships, partly because of concerns dating back to 2008 that students were assigned to run mundane errands not connected to journalism, but also because of concerns about Ghomeshi's alleged "inappropriate" behaviour to female students, according to a former student and one of the journalism professors. In an interview, the dean of the Faculty of Information and Media Studies said the school dropped *Q* because it insists that students acquire real journalism experience on internships. The dean did not respond to follow-up questions regarding allegations of inappropriate behaviour by Ghomeshi.

In the weeks since the Twitter messages had surfaced, Ghomeshi continued to assure his advisers that he had done nothing wrong.

"He told us at these meetings, and there were a lot of meetings, that he had long had an interest in consensual, rough sex. But it was all consensual," said one insider.

One substantial question that came up at the twenty-thousand-dollar meeting was about the @bigearsteddy handle. Ghomeshi explained, somewhat to the surprise of his advisers, that his therapist had suggested he get a teddy bear to help with his anxiety. He named the teddy for his boyhood family dog; an earlier iteration of the bear had had the same name. Ghomeshi explained that he had generalized anxiety disorder, and the bear provided a sort of safety net that helped him get through the day. It was clear to Ghomeshi that only someone who knew him well would have come up with that Twitter handle.

"It's her for sure," Ghomeshi told those in the meeting, naming Carly as the suspected Twitter culprit. The CBC host's eyes were lidded, and he did not look up at his advisers. "I just know it. She knows how to push my buttons. She knows how much that teddy bear means to me." Later, in his *fifth estate* interview, *Q* producer Brian Coulton said that when the tweets first surfaced, Ghomeshi took him aside a second time and told him he was sure they were authored by his ex-girlfriend, because the tweet referenced, Coulton said, "a Teddy Bear [Ghomeshi] used for anxiety" and only people who had access to his "personal areas" would know of its existence.

Someone at the meeting asked a question: who was Sidnie Georgina? Ghomeshi didn't recognize the name, and Google searches failed to yield any results. Ghomeshi's advisers determined it was a made-up name. But by whom? Despite Ghomeshi's assurances, they weren't yet convinced that Carly was behind the account.

The person who had been handling many related concerns for the better part of six months was Debra Goldblatt-Sadowski of rock-it pro-motions. Named public relations professional of the year at a Toronto event in 2012, Goldblatt-Sadowski was a force to be reckoned with in the industry, one who had started her company out of her parents' basement in early 2000, about the time Ghomeshi was beginning a stint on CBC television. Ghomeshi was one of her marquee clients. At the meeting to discuss the tweets, Goldblatt-Sadowski showed unwavering support for her client. She put her hand up when a discussion was held as to who was best suited to deal with Carly or any other woman who was making allegations.

"Deb was put in charge of woman management," said one person who was present at meetings where these matters were discussed. "She had shown her success in that field."

Goldblatt-Sadowski had been putting out fires for her celebrity client for some time, most notably two incidents prior to the current issue that had brought so much talent to the Dentons boardroom. Through her skilled work — "I did my job," she later told me — a lid was kept on stories about Ghomeshi's love life. That experience gave her the credibility at the meeting to take the assignment of dealing with Carly — and any others making complaints.

On June 10, 2013, ten months before the anonymous Twitter account popped up, a young Toronto woman wrote an account of a bad date with "Keith," a man people in Toronto's arts and culture scene widely believed was Jian Ghomeshi. The post was published on *xoJane*, an online US publication that bills itself as the place "where women go to be their unabashed selves, and where their unabashed selves are applauded — regardless of age, size, ability, location, occupation, race, ethnicity, sexual orientation, economic status, relationship status, sexual preferences or lifestyle choices."

The *xoJane* story was called "IT HAPPENED TO ME: I Accidentally Went on a Date With A Presumed-Gay Canadian C-List Celebrity Who Creepily Proved He Isn't Gay." In the story, Carla Ciccone wrote that she attended an outdoor concert in 2012 and had a horrible encounter with Keith, a successful radio host. She had thought Keith was gay and trying to pick up a male movie star at the event, actor Jake Gyllenhaal. She described Keith's lecherous advances on her over the course of the evening — "I felt a sweaty hand travel across the back of my dress and grab my ass" — right up until he drove her home and tried to kiss her. Ciccone wrote that she tolerated his advances because she did not want to damage her "fledgling career in Canadian media." She recounted Keith's frequent attempts to grope her and proclaimed that "Keith had gone from harmless dork to repulsive sexual predator."

Just as Ghomeshi's publicist, Goldblatt-Sadowski, was dealing with that story, *Toronto Life* magazine decided to do a light piece on Ghomeshi's penchant for serial dating, a frequent topic of gossip in entertainment circles. Editors at the magazine had noted that Ghomeshi seemed to be out with a different woman every night, at restaurants, arts events, and on red carpets at award shows. The concept was "Fifteen women Jian Ghomeshi has dated," and in August 2013 a young reporter named Ryan Kohls — who had worked briefly at *Q* — was assigned the task. When

Goldblatt-Sadowski heard from women Kohls was contacting that a story was in the works, she became very angry.

"We feel this is a really unfair and absurd piece," she wrote in an email to Kohls. "Surely we could work with *Toronto Life* on a more interesting story in the future (with our cooperation) vs. going behind an incredibly established and well-respected public broadcaster's back looking for anonymous sources for women he has taken out."

Goldblatt-Sadowski earned her pay on the *Toronto Life* story. She pushed hard at *Toronto Life* editor Sarah Fulford. "Jian is upset by the idea of this type of a story," she wrote in an email. "Not only would it not be an inappropriate [*sic*] representation of his personal life, but would also be unfair to those included in the story."

Toronto Life killed the story and assigned in its place, a deep profile of Ghomeshi. The profile, published a few months before the @bigearsteddy tweets surfaced, was mostly flattering, though it did include the Carla Ciccone allegations in *xoJane*. Fulford later told me no deal was made to drop one story for better access to Ghomeshi. She said the research presented by her freelance reporter was "thin" and would not have amounted to a story for her magazine.

Back at the boardroom table, Goldblatt-Sadowski was sitting near the person who, second to Ghomeshi, was the most important man in the room: Jaime Watt, chairman of Navigator, the top crisis intervention firm in the country. Navigator's website describes how it aims to do both "crisis response and reputation recovery":

> Corporations and individuals sometimes find themselves on the wrong side of public opinion. We quickly pull together the right team to manage issues before they escalate into major crises. But when disaster strikes, our clients depend on our custom-built communications plans to minimize reputational damage. We formulate crisp messaging, handle media inquiries and provide media training. Once the crisis has passed, we develop strategies to quickly rebuild and recover.

Watt, a political communications whiz whose strategy and branding helped bring the Ontario Conservatives to power during Mike Harris's Common Sense Revolution, has said that he takes on clients who are "good people who have done a bad thing." When former Ontario attorney general Michael Bryant was charged with criminal negligence causing death, he turned to Navigator and Jaime Watt. Bryant and his wife had been out for dinner and ended up in an altercation with a bike courier who was inebriated and aggressive. Thanks to Watt and the Navigator team and the efforts of defence lawyer Marie Henein, who would play a prominent role in the Ghomeshi case, all charges were dropped. Bryant went on to write a book about the collision and its aftermath.

Watt brings a personal depth of experience to his work, particularly when it comes to resuscitating careers after embarrassing incidents. As a young man in 1984, Watt pleaded guilty to five counts of fraud and one count of forgery relating to a clothing business he was running in Oakville. According to a *Toronto Star* story detailing the events, Watt used false documents suggesting he had lost $25,000 in a credit card transaction to convince a group of men at the Oakville Rotary Club to loan him money. Watt served twenty days, only at night, in jail. He recreated himself as a communications consultant and then a political strategist. He would have become a member of the bureaucracy in the Mike Harris government if news of his old conviction hadn't surfaced. That event from his past was the type of incident that would prompt him to tell clients that the only sure way to ensure something embarrassing does not enter the public realm is not to do it in the first place. As Watt once said to a confidant, "I tell people, the only way to stop photos of your genitals leaking out is not to take photos of your genitals."

Jian Ghomeshi engaged Navigator, through lawyer Tiffany Soucy, within days of the Twitter account surfacing. According to an account of the call provided by a source, Soucy did not name Ghomeshi at first.

"I act for a Canadian celebrity," Soucy said. "I can't tell you who it is, but I want to know if you will act for him." Soucy provided some bare details of the allegations. The consultants at Navigator, based on rumours they had heard, quickly figured out that it was the host of *Q*. They agreed to take the assignment.

Navigator had several consultants present at this meeting. Their job was to dampen the crisis and prevent news of the allegations from getting out. The hope was that there would never be a need to develop recovery strategies. Ghomeshi said that the whole issue was manufactured by Carly, an ex-girlfriend who, he told them, did not like that he was seeing other women. With two women now making allegations, the question was how to best deal with them. Someone would need to reach out to the second woman and determine if there was some way to stop her from repeating these allegations. The team also needed to determine whether Carly and Paula were connected and if either was behind the anonymous Twitter account.

"Ghomeshi, at these meetings, provided a complicated explanation for how these two women had met and were conspiring against him," said a source with knowledge of the events. The assignment did not sit well with some of the Navigator staff. Not everyone believed that Ghomeshi was telling the truth. Though the team was cohesive, one junior member would later contact me to say that some of the Navigator consultants, primarily the female members of the team, were suggesting during the summer that Watt should fire his high-profile client.

Watt had two requests and a question. First, he wanted to conduct a lengthy interview with Ghomeshi to learn everything he could about the man and the situation he was facing. The lawyers told him that would be arranged. Second, given that Ghomeshi had been relatively open about his pursuit of rough sex, Watt asked members of his team to do some sleuthing to find out how common and acceptable BDSM activities were these days. Was there published material that would help? Court cases? Should the story come out, proving that Ghomeshi's tastes in the bedroom were mainstream would be extraordinarily helpful. Finally, there was a persistent rumour reaching the Navigator team that these women were talking to someone in the media. The name that had surfaced was freelance journalist and podcaster Jesse Brown, a relatively unknown commodity in early 2014 and certainly not someone who would be able to investigate and make such damning allegations stick against a celebrity with deep pockets.

"Let's find out who else is involved," Watt told the Navigator team.

4

The Newsroom

Bert Bruser cupped his hand to shield the wind off Lake Ontario and lit his cigarette. It would not be long until Pier 27, the massive condominium complex south of the *Toronto Star* headquarters, would all but obscure the view. Sailors enjoying the light spring gusts tripped back and forth across the harbour, masts leaning, canvas full. For now, it still meant something to have an address at the foot of Yonge Street.

"Do you believe her?" he asked me.

Carly was gone, headed back home, and I was having a pre-meeting with the company lawyer before we went up to the fifth floor to speak to the editors. I had known Bruser for almost three decades, and there hasn't been a story of substance in that time that he has not been involved in.

I was silent. Keeping silent instead of jumping in with a comment is one thing I had learned in almost three decades of knowing Bruser. When enough time had passed, I ventured, "Sure, I believe these things happened. Whether they can be proved, well, that's another story."

"So, you will have a story for tomorrow's paper?" Bruser chuckled.

"There's others to talk to."

"With this guy Jesse Brown?"

"I don't see that I have a choice. He brought us the tip. The woman contacted him. He's a smart guy, but he has no experience with anything like this," I said.

"Let's go upstairs and find Cooke and Jane," Bruser said.

But when Bruser and I arrived at editor-in-chief Cooke's office, there was no Cooke. That was not surprising. He was out somewhere in the newsroom stirring things up. Managing editor Jane Davenport was over in the "hub," the central area of the newsroom where all the department heads sit. Davenport was the person who kept the *Star* newsroom running smoothly. She's cool and sharp and was young for the job. Cooke was the splash; Davenport was the details. We approached Davenport.

"Are we supposed to have a meeting?" Bruser asked, hovering.

"I'll text Michael," Davenport said. A few minutes later, Cooke, who had been down hassling some of my investigative team reporters, walked up.

"Do we have a story?" Cooke asked me.

"We are a long way from that," I answered. We moved to Davenport's office.

Jane Davenport's office looked across at the condominium tower that faces the *Star* building. A window washer was slowly making his way down the building. Three of us settled into the couches. Cooke took a hard-backed chair.

In our newsroom, you are either a *Star* person or you are not. The majority of reporters at the *Star* began in the newsroom as interns. We grew up there, covered fires, murders, wars, and published exposés together. It takes about ten years to become a *Star* man or a *Star* woman. Jesse Brown had spent less than a day in the building. We spent some time going over our new relationship with an outside journalist before dedicating our conversation to Carly. I had my notes from the interview in front of me.

"Do you believe her?" Bruser asked again.

"Yes. The problem is, there is no proof. She has deleted all her texts, all her emails."

Cooke hunched forward in his chair. The questions that would be asked of me were similar to the ones I had asked Carly and were an important part of the process of determining if the information was credible and if we had a story worth pursuing.

"Were they dating?" Cooke asked. "For how long?"

"I told her that would be an issue, and she agreed. The relationship started in the latter part of 2012, ended a year and a couple of months later. She came into Toronto to visit him from time to time."

Everyone in the managing editor's office understood the difficulty of breaking the cycle of abuse in a domestic relationship where the couple lived together. In the mid-1990s, I had been the project editor on "Hitting Home," a groundbreaking series on spousal abuse. Three *Star* reporters — Rita Daly, Jane Armstrong, and Caroline Mallan — probed the difficulty of getting convictions against men who attacked their partners. With Carly, who did not live with Ghomeshi but repeatedly travelled to visit him, we had to wrap our minds around the nature of their relationship.

"How many times did she say she was beaten?" Bruser asked.

"Every time she visited." I watched as the three of them took that in. "The choking allegations are even stronger. Carly says that choking was often a prelude to sex. He would choke her until she almost blacked out and then tell her how hot that was. She complained a bit but rarely said no outright. Though he once promised they would have a safe word, they never did."

"Why did she stay?" Jane Davenport, the only woman in the room, asked.

I pursed my lips and exhaled. These discussions are one of the best parts of my job. When a story is published, particularly a sensitive story, twenty discussions like this might be behind the piece. It was the job of the editors to ask questions that readers might ask or that might one day be asked in a courtroom. Davenport's question was a good one. From our 1990s domestic violence series to many other cases of abused and murdered women, I had dealt with the issue a great deal. People stay for all sorts of reasons — love, economic need, a sense of loyalty, or a desire to be the one who fixes a person. What was different about Carly's relationship was that she and Ghomeshi did not live together and only saw each other occasionally, though over a long period of time. She did not have to visit him, but she chose to. There is a lot of talk these days about victim blaming — heaping scorn on the person who stays instead of focusing on the alleged abuser's actions. In the newsroom that day, and throughout the Ghomeshi investigation, we were not blaming women who stayed. But as journalists we were asking questions about the nature of those relationships so that we could better understand them. As anyone who paid attention to the criminal trial two years later would realize, many questions come into play inside a court, particularly about what is known as "post-incident contact." I looked at Davenport and did my best to answer.

"She liked him. She thought he was funny and charming. He told her they might have a future together. She's in therapy now to deal with all of this, and thank goodness for that. No matter how it started or continued, she has been through a lot. She's twenty years younger, and she lives in small-town Canada. All of a sudden she meets one of the most famous Canadians of the day, and it is very exciting. She thinks if she stays with him she can change him. It is as if she was trying to tough it out in hope that they would have a future."

Davenport took that information in. For some readers, staying in a relationship would indicate consent, at least on the surface. That was not something we could ignore. It is not that we did not believe Carly or were blaming her for this situation — the issue was the lack of proof that this was abuse, not a consensual dominant-submissive relationship.

"I guess it speaks to the harmful power dynamic that can develop between a high-profile, charismatic man and a woman." For Davenport, the probability that we would land this story was low. She noted that we might have just paid a fair bit of money to a freelance reporter that would not result in a story, and this would also occupy my time and perhaps others' as well. We needed more than the words of a confidential source to publish this story. A he said/she said story is extraordinarily difficult to prove. And if we published and were wrong — if Carly was lying — then Ghomeshi would be destroyed, or at least forever dogged by the allegations. Plus, as we say around the newsroom in legally sensitive situations, if we were wrong, then Ghomeshi would own the *Toronto Star*.

"On the other hand," Davenport said, "we need to look into this because of the real and awful possibility that this is true and his pattern of behaviour is continuing with others." She looked out the window for a moment. The window washer was on the move again.

"What changed?" she asked. "She was with him for quite some time. What happened to make her want to get this story out?"

I shifted on the couch, which was a little too soft for my liking. "I think it had been building for a while. She noticed he was texting other women. She was jealous. She memorized the names of women he was in communication with. She and Ghomeshi were fighting a lot, and she did not think the relationship was going anywhere."

"How recently were they in touch?" Cooke asked.

"Sochi, the Olympics in Russia in February," I replied. "She told us he was texting her while doing *Q* on location. They had broken up in Christmas but then were in touch again after. It didn't last long, and she thought about it and decided she'd had enough. She said she complained" — I looked in my notebook for the reference — "and told Ghomeshi, 'I don't want all this violence.'"

Nobody spoke, so I continued. "When she complained about the violence, he would then have bland sex, and she found it boring. One time she pushed him back. I found this interesting: she said he complained to her and asked, 'Why are you being so aggressive?'"

Cooke checked his BlackBerry. "Jane, we have the news meeting. I think we should postpone it for an hour." He turned to me while Davenport alerted the other editors on her iPhone. "Did she ever contact the police?"

This was an important question, and it would remain so throughout the investigation. I told them she did not. Cooke asked why. I flipped through my notes and read quotes from Carly explaining why she did not contact the authorities.

"'I'm nobody. No concrete proof. It would be hearsay. He's a very powerful man I am nobody from a small city.'" I dropped the notebook on the table. "She thought about going to the cops but not seriously. Look, it took her therapist telling her she was assaulted and abused before she realized what had happened to her over all those months. Ultimately, she said nobody would believe her. It would be her word against this big CBC star."

Bruser had a question. "What about other women? Jesse Brown said there were others."

"Yes. Carly has a list. The most promising is named Paula. Jesse tried to talk to her but had no luck. Carly is going to try and help. She is very interesting because . . ." I hesitated. I had a sense I might be losing the room. My job right now was to give Cooke and Davenport the "top of the waves" information. Brevity was key. Bruser and I could discuss the details.

"It looks to me like Paula and Carly overlapped. Carly found out about Paula from text messages on Ghomeshi's phone and looked her up on Facebook. All this was very recent. Carly told Paula that Ghomeshi beat her up in the bedroom and told Paula that she suspected she had had the same treatment. Carly said Ghomeshi bragged that other women — maybe Paula, too — enjoyed the abuse. That pissed off Paula, and she sent a blistering email to Ghomeshi just six weeks ago. Around the same time, somebody created a fake Twitter account to taunt Ghomeshi about his violent, his allegedly violent, ways."

Bruser nodded his head. I could almost see his brain dissecting the information, following the twists and turns. "So Carly and Paula are in cahoots, and they are out to get Ghomeshi. And maybe one of them created this account."

"Yup. And I am pretty sure there must be more women out there. I think we need to find others who have similar allegations but did not stay with him. Carly knows of one who says she was assaulted once and then got out of Dodge. My hunch is these women are in small-town Canada, places he visits to emcee events or maybe as part of his book tour. Problem is, I can't exactly wear a sandwich board saying, 'Looking for victims of Jian Ghomeshi.'"

Cooke stretched out his legs. He was wearing a pair of colourful socks, something that had become a bit of a signature for him; he frequently teased me about my boring socks.

"What about the CBC? Is there any hint that he does this to women who work there?"

"No. These women seem to be people who have careers outside the CBC. There is one woman, a former producer, who says he was rude and demeaning to her and once made a comment in a meeting about wondering if he should 'hate fuck' her to wake her up. She says he touched her inappropriately at work as well, came up behind her and 'cupped her buttocks.' That woman is a long-time friend of Jesse Brown's. Apparently, Ghomeshi's bad behaviour at work has been the talk of dinner parties for years."

The "hate fuck" allegation was made by a woman we referred to in conversations at the time as "K," but who has since revealed herself to the public as former *Q* producer Kathryn Borel. She had been a victim of Ghomeshi's harassing behaviour on the job in 2007, though it was not until years later — even after her experience was described in a *Star* story — that police told her that what she had experienced was actually a sexual assault. Borel was deeply angry with Ghomeshi, but in 2014 she was not willing to go on the record to the *Star*, and even if she had been, this was not an allegation that on its own would support a major investigative story that had as its focus a central allegation that Ghomeshi choked and beat women he dated. Borel, in 2009, while still at *Q*, was featured on the program as a guest, discussing with Ghomeshi her recently released book, *Corked*. I heard this interview when it first aired and reacquainted myself with it as part of the investigation. It was a friendly interview, and while Borel seemed a bit cool to Ghomeshi, I detected no hint of any animosity between them.

Davenport tapped her pen on the notepad in front of her. "How did Jesse get involved?"

"Carly had contacted Paula, and they began sharing Ghomeshi stories. They wanted to stop him. They had no interest in getting involved publicly so they hatched a plan to get the story out. Paula knew somebody in public relations who suggested she reach out to a male journalist. I would have figured a female journalist would be better, but that was the PR person's advice. Carly did the reaching out. Jesse thinks he was contacted because he covers media and the CBC. Now Jesse and I are hoping to interview Paula and hopefully find other women. The problem is these women do not want to come forward publicly."

That was an issue we were very familiar with. Most journalists strive to give the names of all sources of information in a story because when a person puts a name to a comment or allegation, it is seen as trustworthy. The *Toronto Star* and other major media organizations have policies in line with this. We try to get people on the record if possible. There are, however, very good reasons that a person would want to remain confidential. Personal safety and fear of retribution (losing a job, for example) are chief among them. During the Rob Ford investigation, which involved many confidential sources that Ford's supporters liked to ridicule as "anonymous sources," the *Star* took a lot of heat for not identifying the witnesses to his bad behaviour. I had a sense the Ghomeshi story would have very few named sources, if any, and that was understandable, given the women said they were victims of sexual violence. There was another concern: public shaming. After Carla Ciccone published in 2013 her veiled account of a date with Ghomeshi, an online video calling her the "scumbag of the Internet" was viewed more than three hundred and fifty thousand times.

"Just how famous is this Ghomeshi?" Bruser asked, moving to a new area of questioning. "I've never listened to him." You either are a CBC fan or you are not, and Bruser was not. As far as I knew, he only listened to 1960s rock on satellite radio in his car.

"In certain circles, Jian Ghomeshi is pretty big. He's relatively young, personable and I have to tell you, he's a very good interviewer. Gets great guests. Do you know how he got his big break? The Billy Bob Thornton interview?" Nobody spoke so I plunged ahead with the story, speaking quickly so as not to lose the room again.

In 2009, the *Q* guest list included Hollywood actor and director Billy Bob Thornton. He'd won an Oscar for adapted screenplay for *Sling Blade*, which he'd also directed and starred in. Billy Bob was in a band, a rockabilly group called the Boxmasters. At the time of the *Q* program the Boxmasters had been around for just two years. Ghomeshi frequently had musical guests, and as a musician himself he had a pretty good understanding of the craft and how difficult it is for most acts to achieve sufficient fame to be booked on national radio programs. Billy Bob was here because he was already well known. For the *Q* staff that day, it was not entirely a surprise that the interview went off the rails. Billy Bob arrived at the studio at eight a.m. asking if anyone had some Bud Light beer for him to drink. When the show got underway, Ghomeshi naturally asked his guest some questions about his movie career. He also asked how long the Boxmasters had been around. Billy Bob grew surly and uncommunicative and said that the deal with *Q* was that the host would not talk about his movie career. As Billy Bob grew more ornery, he commented on how Canadians are boring at rock concerts and just sit in their chairs. He accused Canadians of being "mashed potatoes with no gravy." In what became an online sensation, Ghomeshi paused perfectly and responded in defence of Canadians: "Oh, we've got some gravy up here."

Bruser's eyes were almost closed. They opened. "That's it?"

I laughed. "Look, I heard the interview, and it was excruciating. I thought Ghomeshi handled it really well. On live radio."

"So he's got moxy," Bruser said. "Michael, make a note: reporter likes the person he is investigating." He chuckled then grew serious. "Let's assume this other woman talks and tells a similar story of abuse that seems to hold up, but you have no proof, and even if you and Jesse get other women to talk, none of them will come forward as sources. What do you do next?"

"Try to get Ghomeshi to help," I replied. "Get him to plead guilty with an explanation." The term describes the journalistic goal to get subjects of an investigation to say that what they did was wrong—and help themselves by explaining why they did it. These sorts of stories are much easier to defend, because the subject has made an admission.

Cooke looked at Bruser. "Counsellor? What are your thoughts?"

Bruser had a cigarette in his hand. He'd have to get to the smoking patio immediately after the meeting. He had brought in one of the legal briefs he uses to teach classes on libel law at two Toronto universities. He knew the law by heart, but having spent his entire career dealing with documents, I think he took comfort in bringing them along. The heading was "Public Interest Responsible Communication," and it was the result of a hard-fought legal battle by the *Star* that went to the top court in the land, a case called *Grant v. Torstar*, in which a businessman named Peter Grant sued former *Star* reporter Bill Schiller, the finest interviewer I have ever had the pleasure to sit beside, for libel. Schiller's story suggested, based in part on interviews with local residents, that Grant used political influence to bypass the normal approval process for a new golf course on a lakefront estate in northern Ontario. The *Star* lost at trial, and a jury fixed the paper's penalty as $1.475 million in damages. Through a series of appeals and cross-appeals, in conjunction with another case involving the *Ottawa Citizen*, the case made it to the Supreme Court of Canada. The *Star* won, and the court noted in its decision how the "reporter, an experienced journalist, attempted to verify the allegations in the article, including asking [Peter Grant] for comment, which [Grant] chose not to provide." That was a very happy day in our newsroom — rivalling the day years later when Toronto Police Chief Bill Blair announced that the missing crack video of Mayor Rob Ford had been located.

"Do we have a story? Not now." Bruser paused. "Before this," he said, tapping the binder, "we would not have a hope in hell of publishing this type of allegation from confidential sources. We would have had to prove the truth of the allegations, and since we don't think this woman will, as Kevin would say, 'come to the party,' there would be no story."

Bruser put his cigarette back in its pack. Nobody spoke. The "party" is a newsroom way of describing a libel trial. At the *Star*, we are not afraid of trials, but they are extremely costly, and we want to know going into a story how strong our defence will be if that's the way things go. We all waited patiently for Bruser to continue. "Things, as you all know, have changed. Now, the Supreme Court says that we can use confidential sources and maybe, *maybe*, do a story like this if it is of compelling public interest and if we diligently try and verify the information. That includes what Kevin is proposing: talking to Ghomeshi sooner rather than later. This law that the *Star* won is the most important freedom-of-expression case in the country. If we do everything right, we are now able to publish stories that we wouldn't have dreamed of publishing prior to the Grant case."

"Can I sum up?" Cooke was great for the short meeting and getting us out the door with a plan. "We have talked in detail to one woman, who won't go on the record but who is telling a story of abuse. Others, one or two, may do the same thing in the next week or so. You and Jesse are going to run down these leads but as of now we don't have a story and we may not. I suggest you both keep going and keep us posted, but there might well be nothing we can print at the end of it."

5

Road Trip

"I didn't buy this big house to throw parties, but to raise a family. I bought this house for kids and a wife. I want to have them with you."

"Ghomeshi said that?" I asked Paula. "When you were just getting to know him? Seems pretty forward."

"Yes," she said. This interaction happened at the tail end of 2013, just five months before, in Ghomeshi's new home in the Beaches. A massive ice storm had left three hundred thousand Torontonians without electricity, including Ghomeshi, who lit candles to brighten his home.

"I can't stop thinking about you," Ghomeshi told Paula.

Over the next six months I would come to learn that those these lines — "I bought this house for kids and a wife and I want to have them with you," and "I can't stop thinking about you" — were part of a well-worn repertoire. I think this repertoire is what Carly was referring to when she told us that Ghomeshi had "no game." Just as he did on *Q*, Jian Ghomeshi followed a script in his private life.

At Carly's urging, Paula had agreed to an interview. I was keen to ask her if, as I suspected, Paula had a clandestine role in trying to get the story out on social media earlier in the year. Jesse Brown and I were about to do our second interview together.

The drive out of Toronto to meet Paula was like almost every other late-afternoon drive out of Toronto: slow. The highway seemed perpetually jammed. Construction cranes and dump trucks were everywhere as condominiums continued to rise over the congested waterfront and preparations for the 2015 Pan Am Games persisted.

Jesse Brown and I did our best to get to know one another. He has young children — mine are teens close to being adults — and he was reminding me of those early days of parenthood when little kids seem to be moving off in all directions, all the time. Workwise, Brown's main focus since 2013 had been his media-critic podcast, *Canadaland*. I was paired with someone who, at his core, thrived on criticizing big media. I work for big media, the largest-circulation newspaper in the country. Our parent company, Torstar, owns a variety of other papers. So, with vastly different backgrounds, Brown and I tried to find some common ground on which to build our working relationship.

The word "journalist" covers a wide gamut, but as far as I could tell Brown did not yet have experience covering complex investigations and then publishing and defending them. It's part of what brought him to the *Toronto Star*, but it also made it difficult for us to relate and discuss the project at hand. When I talk to young journalists I often explain how our craft is a series of building blocks. You begin covering flower shows, accidents, court cases, murders — the lower-stakes cases that eventually allow you one day to take on the big cases. It's like a uniformed constable rising through the ranks to make detective: it takes time. I have been blessed with some terrific work partners over the years, including Nick Pron and Moira Welsh, to name the best. We fought a lot in the course of doing investigations, but we had one important factor in common: we came up through the trenches of daily journalism at the *Toronto Star*, learning the ropes from the people who had gone before us, defending our stories to tough editors and tougher lawyers. Brown did not share this experience, but the *Star* wouldn't be chasing this story without him.

During our drive we talked a great deal about the Ghomeshi allegations. Brown seemed desperate to get the story out and wanted to know when that would be. I did my best to explain that, at the *Star*, we work on many stories at once and due diligence takes time. I also reiterated that we did not yet know if we even had a story. Brown referred to the information he had as "credible," but at this stage these were all allegations, a case of "she said." I told Brown that we needed the "he said" as well as some sort of proof of the allegations to have a story, and getting complainants on the record would be very helpful.

As my car ground its way through the gridlock, Brown told me that allegations of abusive behaviour relating to Ghomeshi were not news to him. As far back as 2007, at a dinner party, he had heard people talk openly of Ghomeshi's penchant for rough sex, though it was always described at the time as consensual. He was very good friends with former Q producer Kathryn Borel, who was at the dinner, and who alleged she was a victim of on-the-job sexual harassment by Ghomeshi; at that point Borel was still a confidential source. Brown regretted that he had not done more over the years to support Borel, having heard her complain of sexual harassment on the job at Q. He had suggested she keep a journal of all sexual harassment offences, and when Carly contacted him with new Ghomeshi allegations, he sought help from Borel. This was very important information for me to know. Brown was just being a good friend to Borel, but I was becoming concerned that he was not an objective investigator on this case.

Traffic was improving. Paula had asked to meet at her office late in the day, presumably so we would have time to talk over the sensitive matter at hand. Brown had questions about libel law, and I did my best to fill him in.

Over the course of my career, I have been involved in dozens of lawsuits and a couple of trials. In early days, our only real defence was the truth. Now, thanks to Schiller and the able legal counsel provided by *Star* lawyer Paul Schabas in *Grant v. Torstar*, we had a new defence, and it applied to cases like the Ghomeshi story. The Supreme Court established a new defence in libel matters, and it has two essential elements. First, the matter being written about has to be of public interest. Second, the journalist must show "that he or she was diligent in trying to verify the allegations."

The responsible communication defence makes it easier for journalists to probe sensitive stories. However, with the defence comes guidelines. In Ghomeshi's case, I was focused on the "public interest" issue. The court said the matter being written about must not be a subject inspiring "mere curiosity or prurient interest." Rather, the journalist has to show that the public has "a genuine stake in knowing about the matter published." In the fledgling Ghomeshi probe, we were looking at a well-known host of a popular Canadian show allegedly abusing women. Did that meet the test? Pierre Trudeau had once said, "There's no place for the state in the bedrooms of the nation." Did we have the right to question bedroom activities? Then again, domestic violence and sexual violence against a partner in a casual relationship were important social issues. Two decades earlier, the *Star*'s groundbreaking project on domestic violence led to the creation of special domestic violence courts and protocols. There was certainly a true public interest in this topic, which twenty years later still affects many women in Canada.

The second issue was due diligence. In Carly's case, we were told there were no texts, no emails, no witnesses to substantiate her claim. What if she was lying? And Paula? What about her? Part of the defence is the need to make the other side well aware of what you are investigating and give them ample time to respond. That was something that I would be doing with Ghomeshi sooner rather than later.

We arrived at Paula's place of business in the early evening. Her office was utilitarian: a desk, a computer, and a guest chair. We found a third chair in another office, wheeled it in, and sat down. Everyone else at her office had gone home. Brown began with some small talk. I took that opportunity to size up Paula. Carly had told us during her interview that the two women were very different in looks, suggesting that Ghomeshi did not have a "type." I agreed that they looked quite different, but they were both petite, tiny even, which in itself may be a type. I had begun to read up on dominant-submissive relationships, and now I was wondering if the *Q* host sought women physically a great deal smaller than he.

Our interview with Paula was preceded by a discussion of how to treat her information in any eventual story. Paula stipulated that nobody could know she was talking to us. I asked to record the interview so we would have an accurate record and she was firm — no recording. I wanted to take notes. At first Paula said no, but she relented. I was already upsetting her with basic requests; I found that concerning. Having been on a witness stand in a libel trial, I am well acquainted with lawyers from the other side. I could imagine Jian Ghomeshi's lawyer raking me over the coals: "Mr. Donovan, you did not record the interview and, am I correct, you did not even take notes?" Notes are essential to document an interview, so I was relieved when Paula gave permission. I began a fresh page in the notebook, the page after the Carly interview ended.

Paula first met Ghomeshi a few years earlier at a cultural event. They had very little interaction. More recently, in the summer of 2013, they reconnected. She said Ghomeshi began texting her "incessantly." She was dating someone at the time, and she let Ghomeshi know this. Still, Ghomeshi would text her out of the blue, and she said she had a vivid recollection of their communications, though she had deleted most of them: "You are the most beautiful girl I have ever seen," he texted at one point.

Paula said she was not interested. "I told him I did not want to be a locker-room joke."

Ghomeshi texted back that he was "happy to just be your friend."

This time period, according to information we had from Carly, overlapped with Carly's relationship with Ghomeshi. As I would come to learn over the next few months, there was in fact a great deal of overlap — other women, other relationships. In the late fall of 2013, Paula said she and Ghomeshi were "hanging out." On one occasion he kissed her suddenly, so hard that his teeth banged against her mouth, giving her a bloody lip. "You are an animal," Paula said to Ghomeshi.

"Fuck, you are so sexy when you are angry," she recalls his retort.

Around this time — I had flipped my notebook back to check — Carly had told Ghomeshi they were finished, though they would see each other again following his Sochi, Russia trip. Carly said Ghomeshi had called her, screaming, in December and warned there was no turning back. Timelines are crucial to investigative journalism, and I was already building one.

The ice storm hit Toronto while last-minute Christmas shoppers were frantically finishing playing Santa. Power outages were recorded across Ontario and Quebec. Throughout the investigation, I checked to see whom Ghomeshi had interviewed on days that were flagged as important on my timeline; CBC has a public archival system that allows fans to search old shows. Later I looked up who had been Ghomeshi's guest on Q that icy day. In a curious twist of fate, just as Ghomeshi was himself heading into a maelstrom of complaints from women he had dated, he had done a live interview about sexual abuse complaints involving a well-known American musician, R. Kelly. The interview took place December 23 with eminent Chicago music journalist Jim DeRogatis, who for fifteen years had been investigating sexual predation allegations involving the singer. *Q* billed the R. Kelly interview thus: "Is it okay to like songs by alleged offenders?" The core question of the interview — whether or not it's ethical to enjoy the work of someone who is alleged to have hurt people — was about to take on new meaning.

After that day's program, many parts of Toronto still dark after the ice storm and the streets a magical, glistening mess, Ghomeshi was off on Christmas vacation. He made it very clear to Paula that he wanted to see her.

At some point in this time period, he called and invited her over, saying she was in his thoughts and that she was the one he wanted to marry and settle down with. When Paula arrived at Ghomeshi's house, he had candles burning and wine on offer. Ghomeshi did not drink that night. Paula had a glass of wine. They began kissing and within thirty seconds, she said, he suddenly grabbed her hair, jerked her head back and hit her, first with an open hand, and then with a closed fist. She said he choked and struck her, and accused her of "liking it." At one point, he told her to kneel on the floor in a room and put her hands under her knees. He took his erect penis out of his pants and circled her while masturbating.

The sudden violence took her by surprise, she told us. "Had you ever experienced anything like this?" I asked.

"I had never been hit before," she answered. I asked her what Ghomeshi was saying, to the best of her recollection, and made notes of her responses.

"If we are going to give this an honest go, you have to give in to me sexually," he said at one point. Ghomeshi told her he had to know if the two of them were "sexually compatible."

"You have to let me enjoy this the way I want," she also quoted Ghomeshi as saying. By this time, she told us, he was naked.

When Ghomeshi called Paula a degrading name, she exploded. "Don't you ever fucking say that again," she told him.

Ghomeshi's transformation was instantaneous. He shied away from her. "Now you are making me feel like a creep. You're making me feel like a weirdo. You are not being a good girl," he told her. "Get the fuck away and leave. You need to go." With that, Ghomeshi picked up his phone and made his way to his leather couch, where he sat down, still naked, and started either texting people or checking Twitter, according to Paula.

Had I not heard the earlier story from Carly, I would have been shocked. But I was more prepared for it this time, less surprised to hear of the same bizarre and abusive behaviour. In fact, it was almost a carbon copy.

"Was there any warning before this happened?" I asked. "Any request from him?"

Paula shook her head. "There was no consent. No safe words," she said. Shortly after Ghomeshi sat on the couch, Paula left in a taxi. Two weeks later, she still had bruises from the night. Her throat was very sore from the choking.

"Did you call the police or consider calling them?"

"It never crossed my mind to call the cops," Paula said. She did not feel she had been raped, though she was beaten.

I had the same reaction to Paula's decision not to call police as I did to Carly's. Many important factors went into her decision, of course — fears about not being believed, reluctance to get involved in pressing charges, and perhaps embarrassment at being caught up in such an odd situation. Still, as a father of a daughter, I could not help hoping that, in the same situation, my kid would make the call.

Late-day sun spread a pool of light on the desk in the office. Paula continued telling her story. Two weeks after the incident, Paula emailed Ghomeshi, wondering why he had not contacted her. She let him know she was upset. My initial understanding of the situation was that Paula was hoping for an apology, though she was unclear on her motive for contacting him when I pressed her.

In the weeks after her visit to his home, Ghomeshi had his wisdom teeth removed, a long-delayed procedure for a man in his late forties. Instead of apologizing, Ghomeshi was angry that she had not asked about his wisdom teeth operation. He also appeared concerned that Paula might say something about what had happened, that she would impugn his character. "I can't sleep and eat," he told her, saying that was due partly to his anxiety and partly to the wisdom teeth operation. Ghomeshi told Paula, and others I would interview, that he had no friends to pick him up and drive him home after the operation. Like many other celebrities, Ghomeshi led what seemed to be a very lonely life. In the end, he relied on Ashley Poitevin, the trusted assistant he personally paid $50,000 a year, to drive him and care for him.

Working himself into a near fit after his operation, Ghomeshi showed up outside Paula's house in January, his face swollen, tears in his eyes.

"I am not that kind of guy. I will make it up to you to the end of days," he said.

Ghomeshi's anxiety was running high in the month of January. First there was the on-again, off-again relationship with Carly that had recently collapsed after a bitter phone call in which Carly told him it was over for good. Now there was the Paula episode. Ghomeshi routinely took the drug Atavan to control his anxiety and a powerful sleeping pill to get to rest at night. He told people close to him he was having frequent panic attacks, and during this time, he showed signs of stress to others. Paula did not know it, but Ghomeshi was snapping at people at the CBC and behaving poorly at public events. Women were letting Ghomeshi know that they were angry with him, and he was obviously rattled.

The sun was going down when Paula finished talking about her time with Ghomeshi. They had been intimate on just the one occasion. Though they kept in touch after, she had never gone to his house again. At my urging, she showed us the few electronic conversations with Ghomeshi she said she had kept. These related to the time period before and after the incident at his home. None of them could be classified as evidence of abuse or consent. However, the timing of one of their exchanges, which seemed very amicable, didn't make sense when I flipped back in my notebook and compared it to the timeline. Paula had sent Ghomeshi a video of herself, accompanied by a pleasant message telling him she was near the CBC offices and thinking about him. She told us she sent the video prior to the attack at his home. But in one of the few text messages from Ghomeshi that she had kept, he referenced the video, and the date of his text suggested to me that she had sent the video after the alleged attack. I asked her why she would make and send a friendly video to a man who hurt her.

Paula did not like me asking questions in this vein, and I could tell Jesse Brown did not like it, either. It seemed to me that he did not want to irritate and risk losing a key source. But the job of a journalist is to ask all the questions, even the tough ones. Two years later, at Ghomeshi's trial, answers to questions like that about what the justice system calls post-incident contact would undo criminal cases against Ghomeshi. I persisted, and Paula answered. She explained that she continued to be friends with Ghomeshi. They eventually attended more events together, though they were never intimate again.

The friendship between Paula and Ghomeshi finally ended in March 2014. Shortly after that, Carly, who had earlier spotted Paula's name and telephone number in a text message on Ghomeshi's phone when the CBC host was showering, phoned her. Carly shared a lot of information with Paula, some of which was particularly offensive to her. Carly had once asked Ghomeshi if other women had a problem with the choking and punching, and Ghomeshi apparently said no, they all liked it. He included Paula in that group. When Carly shared this with Paula, she saw red. Her anger boiled over, and she immediately sent off an angry email to Ghomeshi — the email that the host received the day of the rape culture debate.

I now had a sense of how angry Paula was at Ghomeshi, though the anger seemed to have developed a month or two after the alleged assault. Hearing her words and thinking about the mysterious Twitter account, it became clear to me that Paula was Sidnie Georgina, the author of those mysterious tweets from @bigearsteddy, although I suspected that Carly had a hand in helping devise the tweets. During the course of interviews for this book, both women at different times suggested the other was the driving force in the Twitter assault. I pressed the issue in the office that day and Paula, reluctantly, confirmed that she was involved in the

@bigearsteddy campaign. Later, however, in a conversation regarding this book, Paula angrily denied she was the author of the tweets.

Less mysterious was the signed email to Ghomeshi from Paula the day of the rape-culture debate. It was sent just over two weeks before the Twitter jabs started.

Ghomeshi responded to the angry email by asking Paula if they could talk. He also used a line we would become quite familiar with.

"I swear everything I have done is consensual."

6

The Women Out There

How hard could it be? Lucy DeCoutere's summer was all about getting in shape for the annual Shubie Dooby Triathlon in Dartmouth, Nova Scotia, set for September 2014. As often as her busy work schedule allowed, DeCoutere rode her bike along the trails lining the Saint John River Valley in Fredericton, New Brunswick, ran the trails in Odell Park, and swam in Killarney Lake. The swimming was the toughest part. "I had to learn how to swim properly to do a tri," DeCoutere told friends. "I could always swim, but this was a different kind of stroke." From time to time that summer she listened to CBC, including *Q*. Reruns in the summer—billed as the best of *Q*—included boxer Mike Tyson, who had just published a book about his tumultuous life, and an interview with comedian Rob Delaney discussing how he had survived depression and overcome "dark days." DeCoutere enjoyed the guests. She did not like listening to the host. His opening line—"Well, hi there"—summoned the ghost of an unpleasant flashback. As she had done for more than a decade, she pushed it back down. "If you don't have somewhere to put it, then it has nowhere to go," she told me months later.

DeCoutere, a star of the TV show *Trailer Park Boys* and now a captain in the Royal Canadian Air Force, first met Ghomeshi at a barbecue in 2003. She was two seasons into playing the on-again, off-again girlfriend of Ricky on the hit show, and Ghomeshi had just begun hosting the CBC's late-night interview show *>play*. There was chemistry between the two, and they began to exchange some flirty, racy emails. Later that year, when DeCoutere visited Toronto, she and Ghomeshi had a dinner date.

"You don't know how lucky you are to be with me," DeCoutere recalls the CBC host telling her. "Lucy, I am famous, and I am going to be even more famous."

Arguably, at the time, DeCoutere was more famous than Ghomeshi. She was not a fan of that sort of boasting, but she laughed it off and went back to his house. He gave her a tour. DeCoutere noticed how perfect everything was: the temperature was exactly right, the cushions on couches almost geometrically placed. In his large closet, she observed a long row of perfectly pressed shirts, moving from lightest to darkest, left to right.

They began kissing. She recalls a sudden change in Ghomeshi, an aggression she was not familiar with. The memory she would almost immediately suppress was this: she said Ghomeshi used his hands to push her against the wall of his house, hard. She felt his hands go around her neck and choke her until she could not breathe. She said he slapped her — three times, she recalls — with an open hand.

What happened after that incident was a series of post-incident contacts that would be analyzed and cross-examined at Jian Ghomeshi's criminal trial two years later. DeCoutere sat on Ghomeshi's couch with him and talked and kissed. She wrote him in an email the next day "you kicked my ass last night and that makes me want to fuck your brains out. Tonight." They did not have sex, but they did see each other again, attending a barbecue at singer Murray Foster's house. Foster was an old friend of Ghomeshi's from Moxy Früvous days. On the Sunday of that weekend, DeCoutere cuddled in the park with Ghomeshi and one of them took a selfie photo of the two of them. A few days later she sent him a handwritten letter and flowers. She closed the letter: "I love your hands."

In the summer of 2014, across Canada and in at least one city in the United States, a group of women had stories eerily similar to DeCoutere's to tell and no idea that anyone was interested in listening. In some cases, those stories came with the baggage of a relationship, however brief, and with post-incident contact both minor and major.

Linda Redgrave was another of the women out there. Back in 2002, Redgrave was a struggling actor who worked as a host at media events in Toronto. She was in her late thirties at the time. Ghomeshi, a couple of years younger, was in his first season of >*play*. The show was taped in front of a live audience at eleven p.m. in downtown Toronto in the bar at the old Mövenpick restaurant near CBC headquarters. Ghomeshi approached Redgrave at a CBC Christmas party she was working one night, and they chatted.

"You should come to a taping of my show," Ghomeshi suggested. "It's fun."

The following Thursday night found Redgrave at the taping. Ghomeshi spotted her and they spoke. Afterward, they had a drink at the bar. The spot was a popular watering hole for thirsty journalists, and other CBC people wandered in. Ghomeshi was fun, and Redgrave, a single mother, was enjoying the night out. He offered to drive her a drive to her car. She accepted, and they chatted on the short trip along snowy streets. She would later testify at Ghomeshi's trial that he was driving a yellow Love Bug, a Disneyesque car that made her feel safe, a recollection that, among others, came under attack in court. During the drive Ghomeshi, who was in his mid-thirties, insisted that he was twenty-six years old. Ghomeshi stopped his car near hers and turned to face her. What follows is the account told to me, the CBC, and police.

Ghomeshi did not kiss her. Instead, she felt his right hand wrap tightly around her long hair, and her head was pulled back, hard.

"Do you like it rough?" Ghomeshi asked. Surprised and tongue-tied, Redgrave pulled back. She got out of his car and left. He kept in touch, however, and two weeks later she returned at his invitation to watch another taping of >*play*. She found the television host charming and wondered if the incident in the car was an aberration. They went on a real date to see a concert by singer-songwriter Kathleen Edwards, who was just releasing her first full album, *Failer*. After the concert, Redgrave agreed to join Ghomeshi for a drink at his Riverdale home. They were only in the house for a short time when, with no warning, she said, Ghomeshi grabbed her hair, pulled her to the ground, and hit her in the head at least three times with a closed fist. Redgrave began to cry. She was on the floor, sobbing. Ghomeshi was standing over her. They were both clothed.

"You should leave," he said. Redgrave dialled a taxi company, watched out the window, and left when the cab arrived. Ghomeshi, she recalls, said nothing else to her. The taxi took her to a girlfriend's house. She did not consider reporting what had happened. "What, I am going to tell the authorities that Jian Ghomeshi hit me? What are they going to say? Who do you think they are going to believe?" she asked me when I interviewed her. "It just seemed to me it would be so easy for me to be made out to be the bad guy."

Reva Seth was busy in the summer of 2014. The last thing, the very last thing, on her mind was Jian Ghomeshi. She was best known at the time for *The MomShift*, a groundbreaking book that profiled women who achieved career success after having children. Seth and her husband, businessman Rana Sarkar, have three boys. Though it was a struggle at times to fit in all the moving parts, she had managed to find a balance. After completing two law degrees, Seth practised for a time at the firm that would eventually become Dentons.

In the summer of 2014, having published two books and with a successful coaching and public-speaking career, Reva Seth was proof that a woman did not have to choose between family and career. She was developing a new communications agency and working on her third book. She and her husband were also making sure their three young boys were raised in a home with love and quality family activities — and that they got to their lessons, sporting events, and school on time.

Seth had built the life she wanted, but from time to time events would trigger memories of experiences with Jian Ghomeshi she would have preferred to forget. What follows is from an account of her interactions with Ghomeshi as described in an article she published in the *Huffington Post* in the fall of 2014.

Seth and Ghomeshi first met in the water aisle of a Loblaws in Toronto in 2002, when she was twenty-six and single, and started chatting. Seth found him "funny and charming," and he invited her to a taping of *>play* at the Mövenpick restaurant. Seth's world was law and politics. His was music and the arts scene. She never bothered to go to the taping, but she agreed to meet him for dinner during the week on the Danforth, a bustling area of Toronto known for good restaurants, most of them Greek. The dinner was fun. Seth wrote that Ghomeshi thought she was Persian — she is South Asian. They discussed their immigrant parents, books, "sex and shame." Ghomeshi was just a decade older, and they seemed to have a lot in common.

Over the summer they "hung out very occasionally." A couple of parties, a movie night at his house, all what she would describe as "low key." There was a bit of kissing, but not much. He was very proud of his Riverdale house and enjoyed having her over. He showed her a large glass jar with matchbooks he collected during his years of touring with Moxy Früvous. One Sunday night, Seth went over to his house where they had a drink, "smoked some pot," and chatted. They began kissing.

Without any warning, she felt Ghomeshi's hands around her throat. It was jarring. She remembers thinking, "What the fuck is going on here?" She wondered what was wrong with Ghomeshi. As she wrote in the *Huffington Post*, "it was like he became a different person. He was super angry, almost frenzied and disassociated."

He pulled her pants down and "aggressively and violently" penetrated her with his fingers. In her account, Seth does not say how long the attack lasted. When it was over, it was clear she was very angry. She felt violated. There had been no discussion of consent.

"I remember he gave me some weird lines about how he couldn't tell if I was actually attracted to him or not, and somehow this was meant to explain his behaviour," Seth wrote. She called a cab and left quickly. She was stunned. A lawyer, she ran through her options.

"I hadn't been raped. I had no interest in seeing him again or engaging the police in my life. I just wanted to continue on with my life as it was. And even if I had wanted to do something, as a lawyer, I'm well aware that the scenario was just a 'he said, she said' situation. I was aware that I, as a woman who had had a drink or two, shared a joint, had gone to his house willingly and had a sexual past, would be eviscerated."

Seth saw him again soon after the attack, in a situation that made her very uncomfortable. Ghomeshi telephoned her six weeks after the incident at his home. She was being called to the bar the next day, and her mother was in town. Seth told Ghomeshi she could not talk because she and her mother were on their way to the liquor store to purchase a bottle of wine. As the women browsed at the Danforth liquor store, Ghomeshi showed up. Seth was annoyed — "creeped out," as she put it — and they left the store quickly.

The next time she saw him was in early 2014. Just as Ghomeshi was caught up in separate dramas with Paula and Carly, the CBC star was preparing to host a very important event. The man who was the star of *Q*, front and centre at CBC's Canada Reads, the Giller Prize, and many other galas, was the darling of the Iranian-Canadian community. He was tapped to host, alongside Iranian comedian Maz Jobrani, the annual Parya Trillium Gala at Le Parc conference and banquet centre. The foundation behind the gala is a charity that seeks to improve Persian-language activities and services available to Iranian Canadians. Ghomeshi's father and mother attended, and he introduced them proudly to some of the dignitaries, including former federal politician and Ontario premier Bob Rae. What follows is an account according to people who were present at the event.

Seth and Ghomeshi spotted each other, and he jostled her from behind then appeared to stare at her from his adjacent head table with a "simmering anger." When Ghomeshi's name was announced, his face softened, a smile took over, and he bounded to the stage to begin his hosting duties.

Toronto political candidate Lily Pourzand, also an Iranian Canadian, was at the event as well, and just before Ghomeshi took to the stage, she made her way to his table. Pourzand was pregnant, due in a few weeks, and she was seeking the federal Liberal nomination for the riding of Willowdale in anticipation of a coming election. Pourzand knew Ghomeshi from events over the years, and she had previously sought him out. Given their shared heritage, she was hoping that he would at least give advice, if not public support. Ghomeshi had not responded to her email. When she approached him at his table, she asked him why he had not responded to her request for help. Pourzand does not remember Ghomeshi's reply, but it was instantly "harsh and aggressive," she said. "It was not the same Jian he always was; he did not like me asking why he was not offering help."

"Why are you talking to me like this? Why are you asking me these things?" Ghomeshi demanded, standing up.

Pourzand was taken aback. This was not the "gentle and respectful Jian I had always known," she said. She knew his book had come out and he was busy with *Q*. Perhaps stress was making him angry. Still, she wondered if something else was at play. Earlier, Pourzand had seen Ghomeshi standing near Seth. Something aggressive about Ghomeshi's attitude toward the lawyer stuck in her mind. It flashed back months later when the Ghomeshi story broke and Reva Seth revealed publicly that she had been a victim. "It made no sense that he was acting like he was," Pourzand said in a later interview. "I wondered what sort of pressure he was under that night."

Around the time Ghomeshi's CBC career was taking off, the host of *>play* had developed a habit of inviting women to tapings. Many of these women — it's impossible to get to an exact tally — ended up feeling abused in one manner or another. None of the women I interviewed about their negative interactions with Ghomeshi felt comfortable doing anything about it at the time, publicly or privately. None of them stayed with him very long, but they were able to make some observations. Ghomeshi emanated insecurity. He would frequently tell his dates how important he was to the CBC and to the cultural scene in Canada. If the date was not aware of this, or perhaps did not know he had been the front man for a well-known Canadian satirical band after his time at York University, Ghomeshi would turn angry or petulant. Or both.

Ghomeshi talked about his father a great deal on dinner dates. His father, he said, wanted him to be a doctor or an engineer. Not a musician, certainly. Back when Ghomeshi was starting out he was a busker, playing music on Bloor Street for money. His father thought that was "begging," Ghomeshi told his dates. A lot of how he felt about himself seemed wrapped up in what his father thought of him. Ghomeshi seemed to seek comfort and security but not to know how to find it. When he convinced one date to cuddle on the couch, Ghomeshi seemed at peace. In years to come, after one alleged violent incident with a woman, he curled up on a hotel-room bed in London, England, and began to read, in a child's voice, chunks of copy from the manuscript of his autobiographical book *1982*—the story of his grade-nine year at Thornlea Secondary School—describing the moment he kissed Wendy, the object of his dreams, on the dance floor to the sounds of Phil Collins's "In The Air Tonight." He told women he dated during his early years on *>play* that they made him feel like he was in eighth grade again.

With his newfound role on CBC came more public appearances and more opportunities to meet women. During *>play*'s years, Ghomeshi created a start-up company called Wonderboy Entertainment—he was Wonderboy. He eventually discovered and managed a young talent from Timmins, Ontario, named Valerie Anne Poxleitner, who was renamed Lights and would go on to have a successful career as a singer.

Long before Lights, however, Ghomeshi let it be known that he was available to manage new musical talent. Jessica, a new independent artist, sent him a CD in 2003 with some of her songs and a letter inquiring about potential management. Ghomeshi called her, and they set up a meeting, her very first in the music business. Before the meeting he sent her a short email telling her to watch *>play* and his interview with Split Enz and Crowded House singer Neil Finn. Ghomeshi and Jessica got together for an afternoon chat at the Joy Bistro in Leslieville, not far from Ghomeshi's Riverdale home. Jessica found the meeting unusual, having expected the talk to focus on her career aspirations. Instead, Ghomeshi talked about himself. He then asked her to come to his office to listen to some music. When she learned his office was in his home, she balked. He became quite aggressive, she recalls, and pressured her to go to a movie with him. He said he needed to watch the movie as part of his job. In several encounters in the space of a few days, Jessica said, Ghomeshi aggressively tried to kiss her, groped her, and reached his hands over to touch her inner thighs, crotch, and rear end, both outside and inside her pants. He told her he called her after receiving her CD because she was "so hot." Jessica did not report Ghomeshi's behaviour to anyone.

"I was a small-town girl who had very limited experience with men, period," she explained. The incident, she said, traumatized her greatly. She did her best to forget what had happened.

. . .

Ghomeshi was also pursuing a solo music career at this time, and in late August 2002 he was at the Summerfolk music festival in Owen Sound on the shores of Georgian Bay. Simone, who was the same age as Ghomeshi, said she was "selected" from the crowd that afternoon. She was not there by accident. Simone, who lives in the US, was what was called, when Moxy Früvous was together, a "frühead." She had been a big fan of the band since the mid-1990s and listened to "King of Spain" and other Früvous songs on her drive to work. Moxy Früvous had an almost cult following in parts of the northern US, in spite of a Ghomeshi video selfie he made in which he fumed, lyrically, that "all my fans make me sick . . . I'd like to beat them with a fucking big stick."

Ghomeshi and Simone had already met years before at a music festival in the US. Although he did not recognize her at Summerfolk, Ghomeshi zeroed in on her from the stage and afterward invited her out for a drink, suggesting she pick him up at his hotel. Simone arrived at the appointed time, and he greeted her at his hotel room door, drinking a can of Sprite and eating a tuna fish sandwich.

"We can't go out," Ghomeshi told her, explaining that he would be swarmed by fans, and they would never have any time alone. Simone agreed to stay. Ghomeshi began kissing her, which was fine. She liked him and thought she might want to date him, but she had no intention of sleeping with him that night. The kissing intensified and then Ghomeshi, she said, wrapped his hands around her neck and began squeezing. They were both clothed.

"I want to fly you to Toronto and fuck you in every orifice of your body," Ghomeshi said. Simone was upset, and she told Ghomeshi she was going to leave. Ghomeshi begged her not to go and he lay on the hotel bed, writhing, grabbing his crotch and making it clear that he was in pain because she would not have sex with him. Simone walked to the door. Ghomeshi jumped off the bed and tried to convince her to stay.

"I am tired, so I should go," she told him. He slapped her across the face, hard. Simone was shocked. She slapped him back. Ghomeshi grabbed her, forced her mouth open with his fingers and started looking at the back of her mouth, her teeth and gums, "like a dentist." Simone pushed him off and left.

According to Simone, that should have been the end. It was not. Over the next few months, they exchanged emails and calls, which Simone freely shared with me when I asked.

"You should go to New York City sometime. I hear there's great humans to hang with," Ghomeshi emailed, two months after the summer concert incident.

Simone emailed back, thinking that what had happened, the aggression and odd behaviour, was an aberration, and she would give him another chance.

"I was just thinking of you and wanted to be in touch. How fortuitous to hear from you," read another email, signed, "Yours, as ever, jian." He invited her to see him do his solo act at Hugh's Room in Toronto when she was next in town.

Simone agreed to come but said she would stay in a hotel, and Ghomeshi suggested a few spots that were nice and inexpensive. "Of course I'd invite you to crash at my place but we may want to hang a bit again before we jump into such deep waters!" he wrote.

Simone watched the show, and Ghomeshi drove her back to her hotel. He kissed her goodnight, and she went upstairs alone. They kept up an email relationship for a bit until she told him she was engaged. She never heard from him again.

All of these interactions with Ghomeshi were in the early 2000s. The women involved were relatively close in age to him at the time, most a bit younger, one a couple of years older, but the age gap was not as pronounced as it would become as he aged. None of the women had heard the others' accounts. It was only when the story broke that they realized they were not alone. As upsetting as their experiences were, the women who encountered Ghomeshi in later years — Carly and Paula and other similarly young women — would reveal even more distressing accounts of abuse. The level of violence alleged would increase, and in some cases, the women continued to date Ghomeshi for weeks, months, and in at least one case, more than a year. Over the course of research for the *Star* stories and this book, I spoke to seventeen women and two men who alleged that they experienced either sudden violence or sexually inappropriate behaviour. I also received communications by email or written letter from five anonymous individuals who made strong allegations but would not agree to be interviewed. In three cases, the anonymous email accounts were disabled immediately after the strongly worded and very detailed letters of allegations were sent. Not one of the individuals I spoke to — some of whose experiences dated back to the earliest known incidents at York University — felt comfortable bringing their allegations forward at the time they occurred.

7

Responsible Communication

Jesse Brown and I were not the only ones investigating the issue of sexual assault in the summer of 2014. Two reporters on the team I manage at the *Star*, Jayme Poisson and Emily Mathieu, were looking into a story idea with a similar theme. The reporters wanted to tackle the issue of sexual assault on university campuses. Was it being reported and dealt with properly? Did young female students know to whom they should report allegations? If they did report, did each college and university have a protocol in place to deal with their allegations? My role at the *Star* — I describe it as a player-coach for lack of a better descriptor — involves serving as a listening board for reporters with an idea and then, if the idea is sound, guiding their investigation and helping them get it into the paper. The most difficult part is choosing what to investigate. Stories come to us in all kinds of different ways.

There are the tips, similar to how the Ghomeshi story came to Jesse Brown and then to us. Someone in the know, or claiming to be in the know, contacts a journalist. A good example of that was my ORNGE air ambulance investigation, the probe of a $150 million government-funded enterprise plagued with financial impropriety and safety woes. Tips from people involved — in that case pilots and paramedics at the agency — have the most chance of becoming a story, provided the tipster has not invented or oversold the story. The other way ideas grow is from a hunch. It could be the supposition of a reporter, an editor, or a member of the public. My favourite example of this occurred in 1989. My mother, Norma Donovan, a bit of a news junkie, had been noticing small stories about Catholic priests across Canada who had been charged with sexually assaulting altar boys. But the charges, she pointed out to me, all related to events twenty years ago. "Why did it take so long?" she wondered. "Where was the church in all of this? Where did those priests go in those twenty years?" This is a common theme now, but in the 1980s it wasn't. I took my mother's advice and spent several months travelling across Canada, schmoozing with cops, Crown attorneys, defence lawyers, and parishioners in more than thirty jurisdictions where charges had been laid. I also spoke to victims who told stories the *Star* published in a series called "Silent Sins," when lawyer Bert Bruser and I were just starting to work together. It laid out the Catholic Church's practice of moving priests to a new parish after an allegation was made rather than addressing the allegations.

What Poisson and Mathieu were embarking on with post-secondary sexual assault protocols grew out of an informed hunch based on the news of the day. "Definitely worth poking around," I wrote in response to their original pitch early that summer. Given the new Ghomeshi allegations, I was keen to have the issue explored further, using a wider lens than complaints against just one person. The reporters made a list of all universities in Canada and all provincial colleges in Ontario and set out on the phone and in person to determine the state of sexual assault investigation on each campus. These "cold calls" are the staple of journalists. A young intern once sat beside me and watched as I looked for a relative of a man killed overseas. The man's name was a common one, and I had to go down a long list in a phonebook and call literally a hundred numbers. "That's not reporting," the intern observed. He did not make the cut that summer.

Poisson and Mathieu also began looking for personal stories that would highlight this sensitive issue. I told them that although it might prove impossible, they should try to get people to come forward and tell their stories as named sources. The investigation would carry more weight as a result, but the sources would need to agree to be named, which rarely happens in the case of sexual violence. If a case has gone to criminal court, there is usually a ban on publicizing the name of the victim. The *Star* also has a policy against identifying victims of sexual assault unless the person agrees. The victim can waive the ban, and the *Star* can waive its policy, but we would only do that if identifying the victim is clearly in the public interest.

Star policy also requires journalists to make their best efforts to get people to speak on the record. We would prefer not to have a story filled with confidential sources who are anonymous to the public. If everyone is allowed to spread information anonymously, well, that's an invitation to people to lie with impunity.

Jayme Poisson and Emily Mathieu were just starting their probe. My experience told me that, assuming there was a story, it would publish in the fall. An editor can make that assumption on a story that has a strong policy side. But a publication date for a story like Ghomeshi's? That was impossible to estimate. I knew Jesse Brown believed we had the story. I did not.

It was time to spread out my notebooks and determine what we had and what we needed to move the story along. Over the years, I have published investigations that have caused dozens of high-profile people a lot of problems. Some of those people have been investigated by police as a result of the stories and have gone to jail. Many have lost their jobs — businessmen, lawyers, doctors, government officials, politicians, and others. One prominent lawyer attempted suicide after a story I did with Nick Pron about how the lawyer had abandoned a woman dying of a drug overdose in a cheap hotel room hit the front page. The dangers of printing misinformation are many, and stories like the one about the lawyer and the one we were now working on have to be researched thoroughly. Journalists have a very important role in society and do not serve the public by rushing to judgment. I am of the belief that it is more important to be right than to be first. Better to take your time than to publish and be wrong.

This story was very different than most I had dealt with. There were no court records to support the allegations that Ghomeshi beat women during intimate encounters. I spent some time over the summer looking, both civilly and criminally, and came up empty-handed. Using my contacts, I spoke to three veteran CBC hosts, all women, to see if they knew anything. One of these was Anna Maria Tremonti, the host of CBC

Radio's *The Current*. I ran into her in early June, after the interviews with Carly and Paula, at a Canadian Journalism Foundation event. Taking Tremonti aside, I told her about the abuse allegations and asked if she had ever heard anything about Ghomeshi, anything at all "untoward" or abusive relating to women. Knowing so little at the time about how CBC Radio worked, I assumed that since *Q* came on the radio right after *The Current*, perhaps there was some overlap. The two shows are completely separate — produced in the same building but in different areas. Tremonti, whom I have always greatly respected as a journalist, was shocked to hear the allegations but said she knew nothing. I asked Tremonti what I should do, given the difficulty we were having in proving the story. She urged me to keep investigating to see if the story was valid. "I think you have to," she said.

The absence of any sort of documentary evidence posed a real problem. Had Paula or Carly made a report to the police, we could have used that. But they had not. Neither woman was willing to come forward publicly, and although sources in previous stories have committed to help in the event of a libel suit, Paula was adamant she would not assist us if Ghomeshi filed suit; Carly was on the fence. Since Carly was not willing to be a named source, and since people in her world knew she and Jian Ghomeshi had dated, I wanted to make sure that she would not suddenly rise to his defence if we published a story. My fear, based on my own experiences and those of my colleagues, was that we would extend her the protection of confidentiality, and she would then turn around and pronounce Jian Ghomeshi a gentle, caring lover. I cautioned Carly that if she had lied to me or went on to publicly defend Ghomeshi after telling us he had abused her, I would consider that a violation of the source-reporter contract. This is something that I have said to many sources over the years as a way to get the source to focus on the serious nature of what they are doing — making a strong allegation against a person and doing so on the condition of anonymity, with the newspaper taking the public and legal risk. Carly said she would honour the agreement and did not seem at all troubled that I had raised my concern.

If ever there was to be a cautionary tale warning journalists of the dangers of failing to conduct due diligence, it would come later in the fall of

2014, after *Rolling Stone* published "A Rape on Campus: A Brutal Assault and Struggle for Justice at UVA." The article's account of seven men at a fraternity party at the University of Virginia alleged to have brutally raped a female freshman was retracted after online commenters and a *Washington Post* investigation raised serious doubts about the tale's veracity. A subsequent police investigation found no truth to the allegations, and a Columbia Journalism School probe found a series of "systematic" failures of *Rolling Stone* reporters and editors that led to publication of a story that ultimately could not be verified. Subjects related to the story were not questioned properly — and sometimes not interviewed at all. The targets of the story, the alleged rapists and a student who facilitated the alleged attack by taking the young woman to a room, were not tracked down and interviewed. The fraternity was never given a full account of the allegations so that its members could respond. One simple piece of information that was not checked: there was no party at the fraternity the night the rape was said to have taken place. The Columbia investigation found that *Rolling Stone* failed to exercise "basic, even routine journalistic practice" in researching and editing the story.

With nothing to go on other than the word of Carly and Paula, we were left trying to attack the story from other angles. I had asked Carly if she had told her mother and father about the alleged abuse. She said she had. I contacted her father by telephone right away: I wanted to find out what Carly had told her parents at the time.

Carly and her parents were close. I was impressed with how much she shared with them. I liked her father, Thomas, immediately. It's best to describe him as "salt of the earth," a man who clearly cares very deeply about his daughter but who also knew she had gotten herself into a very sticky situation. Both fathers of daughters, we found ourselves on common ground, and during the interview I could see him struggling with what had happened. His daughter, not long out of the house, had dated a man two decades older, and she told her parents she had been mistreated.

Thomas had been a fan of *Q* and of Ghomeshi. Not much older than Ghomeshi himself, he was struck by the age difference when his daughter mentioned she had run into the radio host at a book signing and not long after was going to visit him in Toronto.

"I guess I warned her a bit. I suspected something was not right quite quickly," Thomas told me. "She told me he was putting her down all the time, demeaning her, mistreating her. I told her, be careful, a lot of men don't have a lot of respect for women." Thomas said that as the months went on, Carly began telling her parents more and increasingly frightening stories.

"At one point she told me that Ghomeshi locked her out of a room. Another story she said was how he choked her to the point of passing out and punched her," Thomas recalled. In addition to the violence, Thomas said his daughter reported that Ghomeshi was controlling. "He told her get a boob job, gain weight, get a bigger butt and hey, I can see myself being with you if that happens." Thomas and his wife counselled Carly to "move on."

I asked Thomas if he had any knowledge that this was part of a pattern.

"No. But when I heard all of this from her I figured, this guy has done this before. He knows what kinds of girls are vulnerable; he uses his charm and social status to get girls. He gets off on this. You listen to him on the radio, and he has the charm, not a bad-looking guy. Intelligent. I am sure he knows the type of girl he can manipulate."

I tried to put myself in Thomas's situation. As a parent, you learn to let your children fight most battles, but in the case of something like this, stories of disrespect and mistreatment at the hands of a man almost twice her age, I would be inclined to pay Ghomeshi a visit and tell him to stay away from my daughter. I wondered if Thomas had ever considered taking matters into his own hands.

"Well," Thomas said and paused, choosing his words carefully, "It's a good thing we don't live in the same city. I'd end up with charges."

We finished by talking about lawsuits. Both Carly and Paula were nervous about coming forward because they feared that Ghomeshi, whom they saw as wealthy and powerful, would sue them. Thomas said the same thing. He was concerned about an "escalating" legal battle that would drain the family finances. I explained that should a story ever be published and Ghomeshi were to sue, his target would unquestionably be the *Toronto Star*.

. . .

At my desk in the *Star* newsroom, I was continuing to go through my notes on the investigation when Bert Bruser ambled over. Bruser makes his rounds of the newsroom several times each day, and as much as I wanted to get his advice, I asked if he could come back after I had completed my review. Bruser shrugged and went over to see how Jayme Poisson and Emily Mathieu were coming along with the campus sexual assault investigation.

One reason Jesse Brown was so confident in the truth of the story we were investigating is that he had worked at CBC and heard accounts over the years of Ghomeshi's caustic and harassing behaviour. *Q* seemed to have a revolving door of producers, as far as I could tell from broadcasting sources. Brown's friend Kathryn Borel was one of them. On its own, without Borel coming forward as a corroborating witness, the *Star* would not print a story saying that Jian Ghomeshi had made a vulgar comment and sexually harassed her in the workplace. Still, it was another piece of the puzzle.

Dale Brazao hustled into the newsroom.

"I got your boy," Brazao said, and plunked down a couple of eight-by-ten photos. They were taken that morning outside Jian Ghomeshi's house in the Beach, not too far from where Brazao lived. Brazao — Braz — seems to have been involved in some way in just about every important story the *Star* has done in my memory. Braz is a sleuth, a stakeout genius, and a very good reporter.

I had asked Braz, based on Carly's remark to me that Ghomeshi leaves for work each day at 8:45, to see if he could get a shot. We had lots of photos of Ghomeshi, given the public nature of his work, but I wanted to see if what Carly said was correct and to see if Braz noticed anything unusual. Carly was bang on about the timing, a minor detail that helped improve her credibility in my eyes as it showed they had had a relationship. Braz photographed Ghomeshi at 8:32 that morning pulling out in his black and red Mini, a colour scheme that, he pointed out to girlfriends, was the same as the *Q* show palette.

"Thanks, Braz," I said.

"I always get them. Your source had good information."

I did not doubt that Carly and Ghomeshi had been involved romantically. The central question, as I saw it, was whether these were outright assaults or there was consensual behaviour as part of some sort of sex practice. I was leaning toward the former because when we questioned Carly and Paula, neither used the acronym BDSM.

I asked Carly and Paula if Ghomeshi used the term, had any sex toys indicative of BDSM, or if he instructed them on the use of a "safe word." They both answered no to all of these questions, though Carly did say that at one point he purchased a dog leash and a collar, and she was "pretty sure" he used it on her. "Pretty sure" was not good enough for me. At times in the Ghomeshi investigation it felt like I was grabbing smoke — a piece of information initially looked substantial, but when I dug into it the story changed or was not as strong as it had appeared. Carly's recollections were, in most cases, strong. Why would she be hazy on that detail?

I decided it was time to find out whether the law allowed people to consent to be hurt during sex. I used CanLII, a searchable online database of Canadian court decisions. This area of jurisprudence seemed pretty thin. I found a few cases with the keyword "BDSM," but they did not deal with the issue of consent. Other cases in the database showed up in a search with the keywords "consent" and "sexual assault" but did not reference BDSM.

The case that seemed most on-point was the Ontario criminal appeal decision *Regina v. Welch*, from 1995. In this case a man was charged with sexual assault causing bodily harm and forcible confinement. The allegations were severe: the female complainant said she went to the man's home, and he tied her arms and legs to his bed, beat her up with a belt on her breasts and buttocks, and then had intercourse with her. Following this he put his finger in her vagina and a wooden spatula in her rectum. The man admitted much of the conduct but said it had all been done with the woman's consent. The trial judge and the appeal court disagreed, and his thirty-four-month sentence for sexual assault causing bodily harm and forcible confinement stood.

What was most interesting about the case was the conflicting testimony of the two people involved. The man accused of the crime told the court that they had frequently dated and had sex. On the evening of the attack that became the focus of the trial, he said, they were kissing and "fooling around," and she consented to be tied up. He said she asked to be spanked, which he did with his hand and belt, and that during the sex play they were both "laughing and giggling." The complainant's story was very different. She said she tried to leave the man's apartment after a date, and he told her she was not going anywhere. She said he poured baby oil on her, struck her with his belt, and at one point, when she protested, said, "You know what happens to bad girls when they scream." The court papers state the man placed a pillow on her face and pushed down until she stopped screaming. "The complainant testified that she felt like she was going to die," the court judgment stated.

The provincial appeal court, likely in a reference to injuries that can be caused in sport or other approved social purposes, found there was no social purpose in this type of sexual conduct, which they said was "inherently degrading and dehumanizing." The court found that "a victim cannot consent to the infliction of bodily harm upon himself or herself unless the accused is acting in the course of a generally approved social purpose when inflicting the harm."

Several more recent legal writings were critical of the court's decision. The Internet is filled with information about dominant-submissive behaviour and activities that have grown more mainstream since the publication of the *Fifty Shades* trilogy. Legal decisions regarding BDSM are clearly in a state of flux, and based on what Paula and Carly said, it was not entirely clear whether their complaints against Ghomeshi would stand in a court of law, should they ever get there.

We had found another woman with a story to tell. Molly had come forward to Carly and spoken to Jesse Brown before he approached the *Star*, but she was reluctant to go any further. At one point she agreed to an interview but changed her mind on the advice of a friend. We had been able to review documents and emails Molly still had that described her allegations against Ghomeshi, and we did our best to substantiate her story. Molly has since told me that parts of the account published in the *Star* were incorrect, but she has not said which parts are at issue, and she expressed anger to me that her story would be retold in this book. What follows is her account as published in the *Star* in 2014. Her account alleged a sudden act of violence on Ghomeshi's part—she said she was slammed against a cement wall in a Toronto building, choked, and hit five times—after the two had been flirtatious over text and email.

Molly met Ghomeshi at a book signing in 2012. She stood in line to get her copy of *1982* signed, and Ghomeshi was overwhelmingly friendly, asking her name and many questions about herself. The next day, she received a private Facebook message with Ghomeshi's telephone number and an invitation to call him. The two chatted online and Ghomeshi introduced violent sexualized language into their conversation, but he stressed that it was fantasy. On a visit to Toronto, Ghomeshi walked her back to a friend's University of Toronto dorm room, where she was staying. Molly described a sudden attack on her in the building's stairwell that left her stunned. As we later reported in the *Star*, "he demanded that she kneel, then hit her repeatedly about the head while she stared up in shock. She asked him about bruising, and he laughed and replied that he knew how to hit her so there wouldn't be any."

In a follow-up email conversation between them, Ghomeshi responded to accusations from Molly that he had abused her. "It IS about sex," wrote Ghomeshi to Molly, asserting that she had consented. "it WAS...that you've decided to turn this ugly is disappointing. i wish for good karma into 2013."

The timeline I was building indicated that Molly's relationship with Ghomeshi overlapped with both Paula's and Carly's. It was clear that we needed to talk to more women who knew Ghomeshi. It would also help if they had not had contact with each other. The problem was how to find them. Carly had been trying to help behind the scenes. She gave me the names of five women who, for various reasons, she thought Ghomeshi had dated and harmed. I interviewed or attempted to interview all five women.

I approached them with caution and circumspection. It would not be fair to call up people, immediately provide them with specific, detailed allegations of abuse, and then ask, "Did Jian Ghomeshi hit you, too?" Instead, I said the *Star* was "looking into reports that a media personality has in some fashion been abusive to young women." The women typical-ly entered into a conversation with me; some raised Ghomeshi's name on their own. Some of them were prepared when I reached out. Before I became involved in the investigation, Carly had created an anonymous Facebook account identifying herself as a woman hurt by Ghomeshi to look for women with similar experiences.

One woman told me she had only a "platonic relationship" of "an en-tirely friendly nature" with Ghomeshi, although she encouraged me to seek out information that would help me assess whether the allegations were true. Several of the women I spoke to expressed, in eerily simi-lar language, their outrage that I was asking such provocative questions about someone they considered a good friend. One woman, Sheila, was progressively angrier each time I tried to talk to her.

"Hi Kevin. The more I think about this, the more it bothers me. Please don't use my name in anything you publish, but I did date Jian and I know for certain that he wouldn't do anything non-consensual. I feel that this is a terrible smear campaign and I hope that comes to light."

Carly had contacted Sheila through the Facebook account, and she shared Sheila's emails and Facebook messages with me. Sitting at the desk I went through them. Sheila was horrified at Carly's account of abuse. She asked Carly in their email exchange, "Why did you not go to police?" Carly responded by email, using a pseudonym: "He's powerful and I didn't think the police would be able to do anything because I didn't reach out to them at the time it happened."

Over the course of the period when we were trying to reach out to more women, it became clear to me that some were telling Ghomeshi about the *Star* investigation as soon as they hung up the telephone with us. After the story broke, one of the women who told me there could be nothing to the allegations contacted me and apologized for so quickly "running to Jian's defence." The woman said she knew Ghomeshi had a "history of strange behaviour" that, at the time, she assumed was "be-nign." She never shared the details with me, but said she regrets that she "contributed to that resistance by believing Jian." Why did she believe him? "I was seduced by his charm."

. . .

While we were trying to contact other women, Carly emailed me with an idea. She was toying with the notion of putting her name to her allegations solely for any attempts we would make to contact Ghomeshi for comment. That did not mean her name would ever be in a story. Rather, it would be in a letter to him saying "Carly alleges..." It would be better to give Ghomeshi names, dates, and times—as much detail as possible. Carly, however, did not want to be the only person doing this. "Unless other girls come forward," Carly wrote in an email to me, "I just don't want to be the only one named."

"My thought would be that we would only tell him names if we had a critical mass of women coming forward," I replied. "For now, we are still in the gathering stage. I think it is important for women to know that some are willing to have their name used. Whether we do that is something to be decided down the line."

My intent was to help Carly understand the process and her crucial role in securing further cooperation. Nobody wants to be the only person involved in ruining somebody's reputation. And it is true there is strength in numbers. I was also hoping the bravery of one or two women would make others feel more comfortable.

Throughout the first month of my contact with Paula and Carly, I found the lack of retrievable messages on their phones particularly troubling. Other women I interviewed later readily provided their electronic messages, but both Paula and Carly said they deleted all of their significant conversations with Ghomeshi. In Paula's case she had a few text messages and emails but nothing that supported either her allegations or his statement to her that he only took part in consensual sexual relations. Carly said that there had been very strong text messages from Ghomeshi that would be proof of violence—but they were gone. She said it was a "girl thing," that she deleted them because she wanted to rid herself of those memories once she had moved on. With her cooperation, we made a minor and unsuccessful attempt to retrieve them. Molly, who had some emails still, had also deleted her text conversations with Ghomeshi. Those, she said, had captured some steamy discussions that she fanned with curious, flirtatious texts.

I was suspicious about the content of these text messages. I believed, overall, that these women were telling the truth. I was, however, convinced from these interviews that though they had experienced some form of abuse, there were text messages that could muddy the waters, and at least some of them had been deleted to make the story more clear-cut. They were also likely highly embarrassing. In one of my later interviews with Carly, she told me that she had sent Ghomeshi "texts that I consented to some level of roughness." To properly assess the quality of the information we were dealing with, I wanted to have it all. You may not be able to consent to sexual violence legally, but if there had been anything resembling consent, we needed to know. I also had a feeling that Ghomeshi never deleted any of his text messages or emails or threw out other correspondence and that one day, at some proceeding, I would see the missing exchanges.

The timeline I was building was something I considered vital to the investigation. An accurate chronology of incidents and communication is key. It can help an investigator determine cause and effect, why something happens or does not happen. Unlike many of us, what Jian Ghomeshi does most days is quite public. I had pulled together some of his book promotion dates, speaking engagements, and public appearances using the *Star*'s archival system and the ever-reliable Google. This helps with the first rule of an investigation: get to know your target. If you're investigating an air ambulance agency, you have to know everything about flying medevacs. If you're digging into the Catholic Church, you need to learn about faith, priests, and hierarchy. And if you're looking into Jian Ghomeshi, you have to listen to his show.

I had made a note during my first interview with Carly to look up his May 2012 interview with E.L. James, the author of the *Fifty Shades* trilogy. Given the accounts we had been collecting, I expected a steamy interview from Ghomeshi on *Q*. No dice. Instead he conducted a tame discussion that focused on her self-publishing success, although at one point he asked James where she got her ideas for the sex play. "I did a lot of research, and I have a vivid imagination, and I have a very willing and cooperative husband," she told Ghomeshi, a comment that seemed to embarrass the host.

If there was one specific time that Ghomeshi was first starting to feel the pressure from his accusers, it was in the days leading up to and the duration of the December 2013 ice storm, when Carly had told Ghomeshi in very strong terms that their relationship was over. She said he was very upset and that he had a sore throat. I checked those shows and noticed nothing remarkable about them, no sign of stress, though his voice sounded a bit more raspy than usual. The only show during that time period that caught my attention as unusual was on December 23, 2013, close to the day Ghomeshi allegedly assaulted Paula — I had not been able to nail the date down during the interview with her, but I had determined it was around this time. The segment featured the DeRogatis conversation about the R. Kelly accusations and the morality of enjoying work produced by alleged sex offenders. Listening to the show, it seemed to me that Ghomeshi went out of his way to note repeatedly that these were allegations that had never been proven in a criminal court. DeRogatis, intriguingly, published his original investigation at the *Chicago Sun-Times* while current *Star* editor Michael Cooke and *Star* publisher John Cruickshank were running that paper. DeRogatis went to great lengths in the interview to point out to Ghomeshi that many of the victims had received settlements in civil court and a great deal of compelling evidence against the singer was laid out in public court files.

It was hard to tell from the interview if Ghomeshi was just being fair and following CBC rules or if he had a soft spot for R. Kelly and was willing to give him the benefit of the doubt. Regardless, I was finding a lot of what my old partner Nick Pron would call "nice to know" information. It was not getting me anywhere. My timeline also included the date when Paula had sent her angry email to Ghomeshi, the day of the rape-culture debate. Amazingly, according to Paula, the timing was a coincidence. More "nice to know" information.

We had not yet approached Ghomeshi, but it would be soon time to do so. I don't like to wait too long to try to interview a target, but we needed to assemble the framework of the allegations before seeking the other side of the story. I stretched in my chair and figured it was time for a coffee.

A Starbucks had recently opened on the ground floor of the *Toronto Star* building, a welcome addition to the landscape. Before I could head down, Bert Bruser came in and settled into "his" chair at my desk.

"Got the story yet?"

I filled Bruser in on what we had. Jesse Brown was eager to publish a story, but I was not.

"How's it going with Brown?" Bruser asked.

"It's not a seamless partnership, but I suppose they never are. He's a sentence finisher, for one thing."

"A what?"

"You know, when you ask someone a question and they are struggling for an answer, and you know that the struggle will bring gold so you keep your mouth shut. Jesse's one of those guys who finishes sentence and cuts off the thought."

Bruser crinkled up his face. "You don't have a story. Yet. Right?"

"The difficulty with Carly's story is she stayed with him for so long. I have a lot of sympathy for people who get trapped in abusive relationships, but that is more common in situations where the couple lives together or there is some sort of dependency, maybe financial or they have kids together. I think she was abused, but we can't prove it. Look, these two were a long way geographically from each other. She was very flirtatious with him right up to the end. When he was in Sochi, Russia, covering the Olympics in February, they were in touch. She also told us when I asked that at a certain point she began to enjoy his violence. There is a whole culture of BDSM out there that indulges in some of the behaviour these two engaged in. I think it would help to find women who were assaulted and who walked away. And we need to try to get them to come forward."

"How are you going to find them?"

"I'm not sure we can use conventional methods." I explained that I had reached out to women who had dated Ghomeshi, and each one had defended him. "I've put out feelers to others and am waiting to hear back. A story like this could take months."

"What about Ghomeshi?"

"Let's assume at least one of the women I spoke to, who defended

Ghomeshi, has given him a heads-up. By now he knows the *Star* is looking at this. I have toyed with the idea of Jesse and me confronting him on the street, at his house, or at CBC, but I think that is the wrong approach."

Bruser agreed. We talked about the Supreme Court decision and how it related to this case.

"To publish a story it needs to be in the public interest and not just because it interests the public," Bruser said.

I looked around the newsroom, watching reporters and editors busy with the job of putting out hundreds of stories a day. Hundreds, likely thousands of decisions, are made before each paper goes to print and on-line. When readers criticize newspapers, they sometimes say we just put out sensational stories to "sell newspapers." If they could see how we laboured over these tough decisions, it would be clear that investigative reporting is not cost-effective.

Bruser continued. It was not unlike being in one of his journalism law classes.

"Do you remember when we first heard about this story from Jesse Brown?" Bruser asked. "All of us understood that Ghomeshi's sex life — however bizarre and even if it involved BDSM — was not a matter of public interest within the meaning of the responsible communication defence." But, as Bruser reminded me, we undertook the investigation because the allegations included sexual assault and violent physical assaults without consent. "That was the compelling public interest," Bruser said. In the context of the growing debate in North America about what constitutes consent to sexual activity, allegations of this kind against a well-known and highly respected CBC personality are of a matter of public interest.

"But we can't publish them, not at this stage." That was a statement from me, not a question.

"Right. But as you were saying the other day, maybe it's time to try and get the other side. The Supreme Court tells us we have to seek Ghomeshi's side of the story diligently and report it accurately. What are your plans?"

"I think I should just call him up."

Ghomeshi, unlike some of the people we investigate, was not going to hide from us. He was an easily accessible public figure. In a libel suit, such as the one that could come from this story, lawyers for the other side usually attempt to paint the journalists as untrained cowboys or gunslingers, firing off metaphorical shotguns and trampling over the rights of their clients. More and more these days it's best for the first contact to be professional. Bruser and I agreed that I would call Ghomeshi but have a letter ready to send him detailing as much about the allegations as we were comfortable with. Using input from Jesse Brown, I spent a couple of hours writing the letter. Bruser, Cooke, and Davenport all weighed in on the final product. Some of my sources had given me Ghomeshi's cellphone number. I dialled the seven digits.

8

Fifteen Hundred

"He's fishing," Jaime Watt sniffed to Ghomeshi and his other advisers. "He doesn't have a story. He's looking for help from us."

It was June 25. The intense, high-level, and expensive meetings that began in April when the @bigearsteddy Twitter account surfaced had become less frequent. Public relations consultant Debra Goldblatt-Sadowsky of rock-it promotions had reached out to Carly, who, according to Ghomeshi, was at the centre of a smear campaign. She told Carly that her goal was to be "in touch with this journalist" working on the Ghomeshi piece. Goldblatt-Sadowski reported back to Ghomeshi that she had a friendly exchange with Carly, but the young woman rebuffed her request to reveal the journalist's identity. Another adviser of Ghomeshi's reached out to Paula, suggesting it would be best if she did not cooperate with any journalist. This adviser told Paula to make a statement to any who inquired that the CBC host was a "gentleman" and nothing untoward had happened. Paula angrily refused. But as the weeks passed and no story appeared, Ghomeshi and his team relaxed. By mid-June, it seemed the story had all but gone away.

And then Ghomeshi received a letter that breathed life into the dangerous possibility that the press would expose his sex life in a spectacularly embarrassing fashion.

June 24, 2014

Dear Mr. Ghomeshi,

The *Toronto Star* is investigating allegations from women who say that you have been physically and verbally abusive to them during sexual encounters.

These are very serious allegations and we want to give you every opportunity to respond and give your side of the story.

We are continuing to investigate. The women we have interviewed to date, from different parts of the country, tell similar stories. In brief, they say that you physically attack them, without consent.

The women allege that you strike them with a closed fist or open hand; choke them with your hands around their neck to the point that they almost pass out; cover their nose and mouth so that they have difficulty breathing; and that you verbally abuse them before, during, and after sex acts.

The women have told us that they did not consent to this behaviour.

No doubt, this is a difficult letter to receive. We feel obliged to pursue this story because you are a highly respected public figure with a great deal of influence.

In undertaking this investigation we have conducted lengthy, detailed interviews with the women alleging this conduct. We have also looked at email and text information related to your involvement with these women.

We are writing today to request an interview with you, in person and at your convenience, to hear your response to these allegations. As stated above, we want to give you every opportunity to provide an explanation for the alleged behaviour.

The letter was signed Kevin Donovan and Jesse Brown.

I emailed the letter on June 24 after making several attempts to reach Ghomeshi by phone. Jesse Brown thought a swift confrontation would be best. Bert Bruser and I disagreed. With a media-savvy person like Ghomeshi, I ruled out what journalists call the "door stop" — going to the person's house and planting a foot inside the door frame. I had certainly done this type of confrontation in the past, but the provocative door stop generally just angered the target. The goal was to get Ghomeshi to talk and give his side of the story.

I purposely telephoned him in the mid-afternoon, after his show was done for the day, because I wanted to get him in person. I have never liked making a "lunch shot" — a phone call made at a time when you are certain the target will not pick up. My hope was to have an actual conversation with Ghomeshi, one that, ideally, would lead to some admissions. With our current sources providing very limited cooperation, we couldn't print anything. If Ghomeshi said yes, he had choked and hit women, but it was consensual, that might be enough to justify publication. Ghomeshi held the key, and I, of course, wanted to see if he would plead guilty with an explanation.

Ghomeshi's cellphone went straight to voicemail every time I called that afternoon. I finally left a detailed message asking to speak to him because we were investigating serious allegations of violence against women he had dated. I also offered to send him a letter detailing the issues I wanted to interview him about and asked him for his email address.

Ghomeshi emailed me at 5:45 p.m. with the subject line "here's my email addy..." The first thing I noticed was something Carly had told me: when Ghomeshi was under pressure, as he surely was now, he never used capital letters. "hi kevin. got your message. sorry i couldn't pick up - was in a recording. please send the letter you were referencing to this email address. jian." Ghomeshi provided his personal email address, jian@jian.ca. In a voicemail he left later in the day, he sounded pleasant and unconcerned. He thanked me for the call and said he wanted to make it clear to me that he was the victim of a smear campaign. He had done nothing wrong.

My letter already prepared, I sent it immediately. He emailed at 8:35 p.m.

Hi Kevin,

Got your letter and wanted to respond right away to you and Jesse Brown. Obviously, it contains very serious allegations and I want you to know that they are completely false.

I'm quite sure that you have been contacted by an ex of mine who has been harassing me for several months and has tried to find allies along the way. Just to be clear again, the allegations you have alluded to about lack of consent are categorically untrue.

She has been shopping this story around and everyone so far has rejected it. In turn, I've had to engage lawyers to try to stop this harassment.

I can't comment on gossip and manufactured stories about my private life, and I never have. I don't intend to comment further but I've asked my lawyers to reach out to you.

Thanks, Jian.

When Ghomeshi contacted his lawyers at Dentons LLP about my letter, they promptly scheduled a meeting of his advisory team. Each person at the meeting read and reread the *Toronto Star* letter. The absence of names of alleged victims and specific allegations was noted. Jaime Watt explained to the team that this was a good thing. The letter's general nature suggested either that the sources had not given permission to mention their names and specific alleged incidents or else the reporters simply did not have that information. The letter was a fishing expedition, Watt concluded. Still, they could not ignore it. "Why don't we go see him, one of us, try and charm Donovan into dropping the story?" one of the advisers suggested.

Watt laughed. "No. He's a pretty serious dude. You can't charm him."

Watt and other consultants at Navigator were familiar with my work and that of other reporters at the *Star*. They had advised other clients I had investigated and knew of other interviews I had conducted and letters I had sent about other stories. They had seen me provide specific information. Not this time. Watt was also familiar with some of the big players at the *Star* — editor-in-chief Michael Cooke, chairman John Honderich and lawyer Bert Bruser. He knew they were all solid newsmen, the kind of journalists who do good work and do not publish celebrity gossip. He was also well aware of the responsible communication defence's rigorous requirement that journalists present specific allegations and offer a chance to make a full response. This was not quite what this letter represented; there was not enough detail. But the letter revealed the *Toronto Star* was very much engaged in the story, and he knew that the most widely read paper in the country had power.

Ghomeshi paced the room. He had a hard time sitting still in these meetings.

"I know Cruickshank." John Cruickshank, who had worked at the *Chicago Sun-Times* with Michael Cooke years before, was the publisher of the *Toronto Star*. He was also a former boss at CBC, the chief of news, though he had never been in charge of Ghomeshi, who came under the arts and culture umbrella. But Cruickshank had for some time appeared on the *Q* media panel as a regular guest. In fact, he had been on the show just the previous week discussing the headlines of the week with two other panelists.

"I know Cruickshank," Ghomeshi repeated. He told those in the meeting that he thought an appeal should be made to the publisher. Cruickshank was a reasonable man. Surely he would put a stop to this investigation. But the Navigator team recognized the risk in that type of approach. Navigator had many clients in various stages of crisis, and a call from its chairperson to a top newspaper official was not a move to make lightly.

Watt decided both to respond to my letter and to go above my head. He suggested that while the lawyers from Dentons dealt directly with me, Ghomeshi should talk to Cruickshank. Ghomeshi agreed.

My letter was not Ghomeshi's only source of concern. Although I didn't know it at the time, at 9:49 p.m. on Monday, June 23, the night before I sent my letter to Ghomeshi, Jesse Brown sent an email to a person who was close enough to Ghomeshi to pass the email to him and his team: *Q* producer Julie Crysler.

Hi Julie, Something I need to ask you about. First, some context.

Some time ago I was approached by a young woman who had been in a sexual relationship with Jian, during which, she alleges, she experienced non-consensual assault. I have since spoken to a series of other women who have told me similar accounts.

I am working in partnership with the Toronto Star on this, specifically with Kevin Donovan. We are seeking as accurate and truthful an account of Jian's behaviour as possible. He has been given an opportunity to tell his side of the story.

I have information indicating that inappropriate behaviour may have crossed over into the workplace. If you know this to be true, or if you know it to be false, or if you know anything else we should know, I'm hoping you might talk to me.

If you choose to do so, the Star can grant you complete anonymity. We are not interested in celebrity gossip and we are not on a fishing expedition: We are investigating serious allegations made by several people.

If you have anything to share, now is the time.

thanks, Jesse.

I learned of Jesse's email when Rabinovitch, fresh from his meeting with Ghomeshi, sent a one-page letter to me and Jesse, copied to John Cruickshank, Michael Cooke, and the *Star*'s corporate counsel, Marie Beyette; I immediately forwarded it to Bert Bruser and Jane Davenport with the subject line "We're into it now."

Dear sirs,

We are counsel to Jian Ghomeshi. We have your letter to him of June 24, 2014, and Mr. Brown's email to Ms. Julie Crysler of the same date [*sic*].

We are familiar with the situation which has led to your inquiries. Mr. Ghomeshi has been harassed by a former girlfriend for several months. She has contacted other women friends and former partners of his in an effort to find support for her allegations. She has also attempted to have a similar set of allegations published with at least one other newspaper, without success.

We have reviewed email and text messages, as well as related material, between Mr. Ghomeshi and women he has had relationships with that will discredit the individuals we believe to be your sources and demonstrate that the allegations that are now being made about our client are false.

Mr. Ghomeshi does not engage in non-consensual role-play or sex and any suggestion of the contrary is defamatory, wrongly suggests criminal conduct by our client and is actionable. As you can appreciate, given the public profile of our client, such a story would cause additional damage to his public and professional reputation. In the event that such a story is published, we will take immediate steps to bring a defamation claim, and seek compensation for all related damages, on behalf of our client.

In addition, Mr. Brown's email to Ms. Crysler is malicious and defamatory. We are requesting that Mr. Brown, or anyone else on behalf of or associated with the *Toronto Star*, immediately cease and desist sending such communications about Mr. Ghomeshi, and failure to do so will leave us no choice but to take legal action.

I trust this responds to your inquiry.

Yours truly,

Neil S. Rabinovitch

Brown's email made me furious. He promised anonymity up front, something that should be agreed to only after careful consideration of the need for confidentiality, and he implied an urgency that did not exist. More concerning, when combined with my letter, his email could seem to allege that Ghomeshi was beating and choking employees at Q. We had no indication that was the case. Should Ghomeshi bring a libel suit, literally everything we said, did, or wrote during the investigation would be part of the case. We would have to disclose everything to the other side under civil discovery rules. And if there was a libel case, Ghomeshi would go after not a crowd-funded podcaster but an established newspaper with deep pockets.

We later learned after publication of the first investigative stories that Jesse Brown's email to Julie Crysler caused a stir at the CBC. The email made its way to Brian Coulton, one of the two Q producers in whom Ghomeshi confided. Coulton and fellow producer Sean Foley went to see Chris Boyce, the head of CBC radio, and gave him a copy, plus the anonymous tweets, at a meeting on Canada Day weekend. In his later interview with the *fifth estate*, Boyce said that most of what the producers shared with him was not too different from what Ghomeshi had earlier shared. Brown's email was different, as it alleged a workplace issue. Boyce called it a "red flag," and it prompted a deep look at Ghomeshi's human resources file. Nothing came up. Ghomeshi was interviewed again, and he stood by his claim: an ex-lover was unfairly tarnishing him.

In their response to the *Star* in late June, Ghomeshi's lawyers delivered an unequivocal message: Jian Ghomeshi does not do *anything* non-consensual in the bedroom. Their letter went further, acknowledging that the allegations I made in my letter were potentially criminal. But the letter also provided us with more information, and it was helpful as we tried to determine whether publishing this story would truly be in the public interest. Both Carly and Paula had told us that, other than a few short messages, they had deleted their text and email correspondence with Ghomeshi. Now his lawyers were saying they had reviewed texts and emails that would "discredit" the women making allegations. I had suspected that Ghomeshi retained all of his electronic correspondence, and it appeared I was right. The man was a pack rat.

I checked in with Bruser and my bosses, Cooke and Davenport. We all agreed that the next step was to ask Ghomeshi's legal team to provide the exculpatory email and text information they had referred to. I emailed a letter back to Rabinovitch.

> Dear Mr. Rabinovitch, I would be pleased to review that information at your office as soon as you are able to set up a meeting. While I cannot reveal sources, and there are a number of them, it would be helpful at this stage of our investigation to review any information you have in your possession.
>
> You also state that your client does not engage in non-consensual roleplay or sex. The information we have gleaned from interviews indicates allegations of lack of consent. Our information comes from more than one person. There is a commonality between the allegations and to the best of my knowledge there is no collusion.
>
> We are continuing to explore this.

I concluded by asking for an appointment to view the materials. In retrospect, I would change one item in my letter. I had written "to the best of my knowledge there is no collusion." Collusion is when people conspire secretly together for a harmful purpose. Looking at the correspondence months later, I would agree that Paula and Carly were certainly communicating secretly in their attempt to get this story out, and the story would be a harmful one to Ghomeshi if published. However, their over all goal was to end harm they believed was being caused to women who knew Ghomeshi. I should have told Rabinovitch that while some of the women may have spoken to each other, I did not think they were colluding to invent a story.

The final letter in this communication string arrived the next day, June 27. It was disappointing. The lawyers were not biting on my suggestion to allow us to review the emails and texts they suggested would clear Ghomeshi. Rabinovitch wrote:

> As you can appreciate, the material we have reviewed is of an incredibly private and sensitive nature. It has been

exchanged between Mr. Ghomeshi and women he has been involved with in a private and intimate relationship. It has only been reviewed by us, as his legal counsel, as it relates to possible allegations against him; but it is not appropriate to make the material available for wider consumption or publication.

As such, we are not prepared to disclose the material in question to you, particularly without identifying the women who you have spoken to in advance; to do so would only sensationalize the baseless allegations you are investigating, and more importantly, it violates the privacy of all involved, including our client, and it risks unnecessarily exposing women who have been involved with Mr. Ghomeshi but are not otherwise involved in your investigation.

You have stated that to the best of your knowledge there is no collusion between the women. Our client has been notified by several women friends and former girlfriends that they were approached by the woman we believe to be your primary source and their accounts have made it clear that she was seeking others to collude with her story. Further, we understand that these women are in semi-regular contact with one another. To believe there has been no collusion of any kind is not reasonable.

Further, your letter refers to information you have "gleaned from interviews [which] indicates allegations of lack of consent." That statement is not as emphatic as the statements made in your earlier letter. Moreover, it is curious, at best, that the women you have met with have elected to raise these serious allegations with the media, rather than the police. In light of that, you can appreciate our heightened concern that these allegations are fabricated in order to damage the reputation of our client, and for no other purpose.

Yours truly,
Neil Rabinovitch

Perhaps Rabinovitch and his fellow counsel had a legitimate concern for the privacy of the women Jian had dated. Another way to look at it — and the one I believed to be the case — was that the texts and emails contained information that would be both helpful and harmful to Ghomeshi. Releasing that information, which we might publish, would open a barn door that could not be closed. At any rate, Jian Ghomeshi was not going to assist us in getting to the bottom of the story.

Rabinovitch also raised an issue that had certainly been discussed by our close group in the newsroom: the police. The women chose to make their allegations to reporters, not to the cops. How seriously should anyone take criminal allegations that were made to a newspaper — not to law enforcement? In fact, many of the big criminal investigations begin with journalists or are aided by journalists doing their own stories. Watergate is a perfect example. In my own recent experience I can point to the cases of Mayor Rob Ford and ORNGE air ambulance. Both criminal probes began with newspaper investigations. Police have a tendency not to take on big, complicated cases if they can avoid them. In Canada, more than in the more aggressive US, it is much easier for police to hand out traffic tickets than to launch into an expensive, often years-long criminal investigation.

Three things in Ghomeshi's reply to me stood out. The first was that, contrary to my expectations, he did not deny choking or beating women. Instead, he wrote that the allegations about "lack of consent are categorically untrue." Second was his allegation that a woman — presumably he referred to Carly — had been harassing him for several months and trying to find allies along the way. I took the mention of "allies" as a reference to Paula. The third item was more puzzling: Ghomeshi's claim that this ex-girlfriend had been "shopping" this story around without success. Jesse Brown had offered the story to other publications — that had been part of his original pitch to the *Star* — including to my former colleague Robyn Doolittle, now at the *Globe and Mail*. Before the *Globe* responded, Michael Cooke of the *Star* indicated interest. Had Carly done some shopping around of her own? Brown immediately contacted Carly, and she said she hadn't talked to anyone else before him. I wondered why Ghomeshi made that allegation.

Not to be ignored in Rabinovitch's letter was the threat of legal action. Defamation is committed when something is said or written that would cause a reasonable person to think worse of the individual who is the subject of the report. Publishing a story alleging that Jian Ghomeshi chokes and beats women would certainly qualify as actionable. Defending lawsuits is expensive for the newspaper and gruelling for the reporter involved. I once spent several years defending a libel suit filed by a convicted conman who did not like what I wrote about him. The *Star* spent hundreds of thousands of dollars in legal fees and at the end, when he finally dropped the suit, it received only $14,000 to cover its costs. Ghomeshi's lawyers had waved a red flag: publish these stories, and we will take you to court. We take threats like this seriously. Ghomeshi's damages, should he be successful, would be enormous as he had an excellent reputation and a solid career, and the damage to his standing would severely restrict his future earnings.

"John, you guys can't possibly believe that I do this."

John Cruickshank said Ghomeshi called him a half-dozen times over the span of the next several months, each time telling him that a "jilted ex-girlfriend" was spreading a campaign of lies. At one point, Ghomeshi tried through Cruickshank to appeal to my ego. "Kevin Donovan is a distinguished journalist. He can't possibly believe this. Does Michael Cooke think I do things like this to women?" Ghomeshi demanded. "John, you have to come to my defence here."

"Jian," Cruickshank said in one telephone call, "Kevin has done this a hundred times. It is part of his job. It is part of a process."

"What the fuck? This is crazy! This is tabloid journalism. I thought you were a serious news organization. You know, another national news organization has thoroughly investigated this and found nothing," Ghomeshi insisted, and then he went after my freelance partner. "I can't believe you guys are involved with Jesse Brown. You are making a big mistake, and my lawyers are going to shut this down. He has been shopping this story around."

Cruickshank later recalled in an interview that because of Ghomeshi's attempts to influence the investigation, he decided to create an ethical wall between him and the newsroom in relation to this case. Though he was not privy to the details of our probe, he had a strong sense that there was a story still worth investigating. In effect, he was stalling for time, telling Ghomeshi not to be too concerned, that the *Star* was going through a process and there was no story yet. "I felt bad about it, but I had no choice," he later said to me. "I had to allow our process to work and to allow you to do your job. I was certainly emotionally supportive [to Ghomeshi] during that time, although it was agonizing for me."

When Ghomeshi and his advisers reconvened in the Dentons boardroom later that summer so the CBC's star host could report on his progress, he was very reassuring. He had spoken to Cruickshank. "It's all good," Ghomeshi told his advisory team. "The *Star* is not going to do a story. It's just my personal sex life. We are fine."

Some of his advisers still worried. As they dug into the case, they had begun to wonder if there was much more to the story than Ghomeshi had initially led them to believe. This was concerning. The advisers, particularly Navigator, would have preferred to shut down the chance of a story completely. As the chair, Jaime Watt's goal was to prevent a story coming out, not to deal with a published exposé. The best way to attain success, according to Navigator principles, is to convince the journalist that the story is wrong. If the story is not wrong, then the goal is to get the client to admit to something—to rip the Band-Aid off quickly. Ghomeshi rejected all suggestions that he needed counselling for aggressive sexual behaviour or should admit to a problem. He insisted everything he did was consensual, and he particularly did not want Lights, the female singer whose career he managed, to learn of his behaviour in the bedroom, although at *Q* and with his team of advisers he was forthcoming about his sex life.

The process with a crisis team is similar to what good defence lawyers do—better to know all of the secrets before trial, or before a story hits the papers. During one of the discussions of his sexual activities, according to a Ghomeshi team member, he paced around the room and moved his arms wildly as he described sexual scenarios he had been involved in with various women. Some women had alleged bruising in various parts of the body, and Ghomeshi explained how it was possible to bruise someone in a consensual relationship. Ghomeshi said women frequently recorded selfie videos of themselves in all sorts of provocative positions and they sent them to him by text and email. He described a very open freewheeling sex life that was, as far as he was concerned, completely normal. Those of his advisers watching Ghomeshi noticed that he seemed to become aroused as he described how rough sex is done: his voice rose, the timbre of his voice changed, and he provided more detail than needed. One witness said he seemed to "get off" on telling these stories. He told his advisers that he had enormous experience with the opposite sex. He provided an estimate of the number of women he had had sexual relations with, per year, since he was in university.

One of the advisers at the table did the math. "That's fifteen hundred women."

9

"I Don't Hurt Women"

Jean Ghomeshi, as he was then known, wheeled his new black Jeep YJ into the student parking building. It was the 1990-91 school year at York University in the north part of Toronto. Gathering some papers into a backpack, Ghomeshi stepped out, locked the Jeep, and walked onto campus and to his office on the main floor of the Ross Building.

"Yo, Mook, wot up?" he called to Jim Hounslow, his friend and the communications director for the recently renamed York Federation of Students. Ghomeshi was the president.

A creature of habit, with mannerisms just beginning to grind on Hounslow and other members of the student government, Ghomeshi was a fan of the popular movie of the day, *Do the Right Thing*, which told the story of a hot day in a predominantly black Brooklyn neighbourhood, where simmering hatred and bigotry flare in a dispute over the celebrity photographs on the wall of a white-owned local pizza joint, resulting in a race riot. Actor-director Spike Lee's character was Mookie, and one of his screen pal's greetings was an oft-repeated hello for Ghomeshi.

"Yo, Mook, wot up?" Ghomeshi said again, laughing.

Ghomeshi aimed to be a public force for change on the York campus. Though student voter turnout was always low, his election the previous school year saw tremendous support and a solid majority for the long-haired, tight-jeaned twenty-one-year old musician from Thornhill. His was a progressive platform: lower tuitions, freedom of speech, women's rights. As tensions in the Persian Gulf built towards a conflict with Iraqi leader Saddam Hussein, Ghomeshi also railed against the war and the gathering coalition in the desert. A child of Iranian immigrants, he attended rallies opposing what he saw as the naked aggression, with oil rights the goal, of US President George Bush.

That morning, as he did most mornings, Ghomeshi stopped into the office of the health administrator in the small student-run complex and played the Tetris video game on a vacant computer for a while. The campus papers, *Excalibur* and *Lexicon*, were filled with stories of discontent with both the university administration and the federal government. Ghomeshi was front and centre on most issues. He had been elected on a platform of change, and he was hell- bent on convincing York students to join the Ontario Federation of Students and the Canadian Federation of Students. It was one of many goals Ghomeshi would achieve, though he was not without his detractors. Ghomeshi ran for the presidency against Kate Collins, who remembers a post-election dispute about Ghomeshi's alleged overspending on his campaign.

"He was outraged by this point," Collins recalled. "He tracked me down on a number of occasions and tried to convince me he was innocent and a feminist and that I should join forces and support his work. I eventually told him I believed him just to get him to stop trying to convince me." Collins also said that female students — called Ghomeshi-ites or Ghomeshi Girls — hung around the polling booths, apparently trying to influence voters.

Other critics called him a "champagne socialist," and his brand new Jeep did not help that image on a campus where most students were middle class at best and struggled to pay rent and tuition. Ghomeshi earned $17,500 for his year as president, but he also, as he frequently reminded his detractors, held down a part-time job at a Queen Street West clothing store.

Ghomeshi's other stated campus plan was to push what he called a "national anti-racism on campus awareness campaign." In the cheekily named *Up York* student handbook he helped publish, Ghomeshi laid down a challenge in a harbinger of the essays he would read on the CBC's Q program years later:

> Greetings fellow York students, Well, well, another tedious obligatory introductory address from the "president"

of the Federation to kick off this year's handbook? I truly hope not. I've always found these ridiculous messages boring and useless. So instead of wasting trees by writing what I should write in this space (i.e. "Hello my name is... York's a big place eh? ... get involved with us... good luck with academics... party!"), I'll discuss the role I think the York Federation of Students should play in the student movement for 1990-91, and the initiatives we are embarking on for the year.

Nestled beside his words in the student handbook was a photo of Ghomeshi, on the phone in his office, his more-than-shoulder-length hair tossed and hanging down as he scribbled a note. This essay ended with a call to arms, particularly in defence of women.

"It is important that we focus upon sexism, homophobia, and heterosexism at York. In the context of a rise in sexist attacks on women at university campuses — the offensive reaction to a Rape Awareness campaign at Queen's University; the murders at the École Polytechnique in Montreal; and last year's (council) refusal to fund the York Women's Centre — it is essential that the York Federation of Students support campus and community women's groups, funding for the Women's Centre, and a woman's right to choose on abortion."

When Ghomeshi finished his Tetris session he stopped to chat with the young receptionist, who often complained to friends and her boyfriend that Ghomeshi was always "hitting on" her. Then he disappeared into his office, closing the door but always opening it to his visitors, mostly female. Hounslow and others recall a steady stream of young women dropped by every day. In Central Square, outside the student offices, Ghomeshi would wander around chatting to female students.

"I observed Ghomeshi zeroing in on women in the Central Square," Hounslow recalled. "This was when I realized he was predatory. He would see them, go straight to them, and engage."

Hounslow's antenna was up when it came to Ghomeshi partly because he had seen him "zeroing in" on women on campus, and partly because he had his own unusual encounter with him. Following a student meeting, he said, he and Ghomeshi were waiting for an elevator when Ghomeshi made a grab for him.

"With no warning, he just reached over and grabbed my genitals [through his jeans] and started fondling them," recalled Hounslow. Fit and stronger than Ghomeshi, Hounslow says he grabbed Ghomeshi's arm, pulled it behind his back, and then pushed Ghomeshi hard against the elevator doors. "Never do that again," Hounslow said.

Friends standing nearby thought Hounslow was the aggressor. The next day Ghomeshi said he was just "playing around" and accused his subordinate of being "macho, violent, and homophobic." To Hounslow, the student president was a young man who knew no boundaries.

Hounslow noticed that Ghomeshi associated with three types of women. Women he considered above or at his level — those were the ones he went on dates with in public. Women he strung along but never dated — those ones he would tell, while gazing deeply into their eyes, that one day they would marry and start a family. "The third type, the women he really went after, those young women were less confident, not as mature, not as strong, and a bit flighty," Hounslow said.

Along with the rebirth of student activism at York was a strong pro-sex message with warnings about AIDS. In 1991 the World Health Organization estimated that between eight and ten million people world-wide were infected with the human immunodeficiency virus. Two pages in the *Up York* student handbook provided explicit directions on how to use a condom and identified which behaviours were risky and which were not. The handbook also spent some pages on an area of particular interest to Ghomeshi — the women's studies program. Ghomeshi, majoring in political science, was taking a minor in women's studies, and as one of the few men in the course he was very popular. He was also a regular visitor to the Sexual Harassment Education and Complaint Centre across the hall from his offices, dropping in to chat with people from time to time. The student handbook's section on women's studies ends, "Unrelenting pressure is the only way to get what women are entitled to, and we can't let up until we get it."

York University was home to forty-one thousand students in 1991. The campus was seen as bleak, a far cry visually from the ivy and stone of Queen's in Kingston, the University of Western Ontario in London, or the University of Toronto downtown. Not far from York's campus was a rough area, and former students interviewed for this book remember, and newspaper reports of the day confirm, gang shootings and drug busts. That local, urban "war" and its causes — poverty, racial tensions — was of less interest to Ghomeshi and his student government than the coming war in the Middle East. When Prime Minister Brian Mulroney came to campus to speak to business students, some of the student leaders heckled him and pelted the country's leader with hastily cooked macaroni from a Kraft Dinner box.

Saddam Hussein's Iraqi armies had swept into and occupied Kuwait in August 1990, just as students in Canada were heading back to school. Ghomeshi attended most of the protest rallies against the war but insisted he was doing so not as student leader, but as an individual. He was there for the macaroni attack on Mulroney but did not throw any himself, preferring to stand back and watch. Letter writers in the campus paper attacked him for making the student government too political. He responded in the *Excalibur* with a stern letter shortly after the Mulroney incident:

"If my pro-choice, bilingualism, anti-administration, anti-war, anti-Mulroney government stances offend some students on campus, I understand, but I will not apologize. I'm initiating the types of changes and actions that voters democratically — and in record numbers — elected me to pursue during last year's elections."

Ghomeshi was not just a student leader. Until 1989 he and musician Murray Foster were partners in Tall New Buildings, a band that grew out of their jam sessions in high school and a musical friendship that started in seventh grade. "We've been playing with each other for years," Ghomeshi said of Foster during a 1989 CBC interview on a Sunday morning entertainment show. He and Foster were a delight for the young audience, and Ghomeshi's joking sexual reference to his music partner brought squeals from the mostly female fans at the studio.

Tall New Buildings folded; the Chia Pets briefly replaced it, and then, while Ghomeshi was president of the York Federation of Students, he and Foster created Moxy Früvous, a satirical music band they would play in for the next decade. In those early days of Früvous they busked on Bloor Street in Toronto to make pocket money. That's where talent agent Jack Ross discovered them. Ross would be a fixture in Ghomeshi's life and a stalwart supporter for the next quarter century.

Around the time Moxy Früvous was establishing itself, a rumour emerged that Ghomeshi was more than just flirtatious on campus. Stories circulated that the popular and aspiring musician and student-politician was a bad date and more. Like so many other rumours and stories over the next two and a half decades, nothing would be acted upon by anyone official. In 1989, in Ghomeshi's student years before he became president, he liked to set up his bongo drums in the stairwell of a campus residence and play. The residence advisers from the cluster of rooming units got together and held a meeting in 1989. A York student at the time, Kerry Eady, attended with two dozen other female students.

"The [residence advisers] told us they'd had reports from a couple of young women who had 'bad dates' with Jean Ghomeshi. That he had hit them. There was no accusation of date rape but that he'd hit them and one of them had been choked in a stairwell," Eady recalled in a Facebook posting in 2014, twenty-five years later. "They wanted us to have a warning and that if we saw him at parties to get them and they'd make sure he was escorted out of the building."

Eady, who told her story to my colleague Alyshah Hasham, said that as far she knew none of the women felt comfortable coming forward and reporting this to campus authorities or the police. Those comments would be echoed years later by many of the women who would go on to allege to the media and police that they had been assaulted by Ghomeshi.

In their 2003 study, "The Role of 'Real Rape' and 'Real Victim' Stereotypes in the Police Reporting Practices of Sexually Assaulted Women," Janice Du Mont and her colleagues Karen-Lee Miller and Terry Myhr noted that a Statistics Canada report on violence against women found that only six per cent of sexual assaults are reported to police. Du Mont, an applied psychologist and researcher who is now with the violence and health research program at Women's College Research Institute, reviewed available literature with her team and found a host of reasons to explain this desperately low reporting rate: self-blame, guilt, shame, embarrassment, wanting to keep the rape a private matter, humiliation, fear and helplessness, and denial. Their report notes that a woman may fear the blame for the event will be attributed to her, or that she simply will not be believed. The study also found that some women think police have a bias against them and that, coupled with their perception of the police as ineffective and unwilling to get involved in this type of investigation, leads to low reporting.

Du Mont's study focused on an issue that would come up in the Jian Ghomeshi case over and over: stereotypes surrounding what is considered "real rape" and a "real victim." Looking back at previous studies, the researchers found "rape myths" that described a stereotypical rape. Rape mythology, Du Mont's research concluded, "characterizes rape as an act of violent, forceful penetration committed by a stranger during a blitz attack in a public, deserted place. The victim is portrayed as a morally upright white woman who is physically injured while resisting. This classic rape scenario involves highly codified and mutually reinforcing notions of what may be deemed a 'legitimate' or 'real' victim." The researchers' point? When human relationships go off the rails and violence is alleged, it is rarely as cut-and-dry as depicted in rape mythology. Relationships, the use of alcohol and drugs, and various types of behaviour that after the fact can be seen as "risky" muddy the waters. Add to that victims' concerns about reporting — fear, embarrassment, and self-blame — and few sexual assaults are reported.

One day during the latter part of Ghomeshi's time at York, a young woman named Miranda, a student, sat on a bench in York's Central Square, listening to a story she was unprepared to hear. She had gotten to know Ghomeshi that year, and though she had heard rumours about him, she found it difficult to believe that the self-professed supporter of women's rights would do anything to hurt a woman — that is, until another young woman, a friend, asked for a meeting. The friend had been out with Ghomeshi, and she alleged that she was the victim of an incident of sexual assault. Miranda recounted this story to me in an interview for this book, recalling to the best of her ability the story told to her in 1991; the woman who complained to Miranda would not agree to speak to me, and Ghomeshi did not respond to my questions about this incident.

"The young woman who told me this was very upset," Miranda said. "She wanted me to confront him. She did not want to go public, and she did not want a complaint. Yet she wanted him to be outed as the character he was. She was insistent that I do something. So I did."

After her friend spoke to her, Miranda made an appointment by telephone to see Ghomeshi. When the time arrived, her heart pounding, Miranda gathered up her nerve and a notepad and marched across the square to the York Federation of Students offices.

Miranda said hello to Jim Hounslow; he remembers her disclosing her information about Ghomeshi to him back in 1991. Notepad and pen clutched in her hand, Miranda knocked on Ghomeshi's door. The student president opened it.

"Jean, I want to talk about something," Miranda said.

"Sure," Ghomeshi said, smiling. He let her in and closed the door.

Miranda opened her notepad, wanting to make a record of the conversation. This type of confrontation did not come easily to her.

"I told him what this person had said to me, and he just listened for a minute. Then [Ghomeshi] said, 'You know I wouldn't hurt a woman; this girl is just upset because we just broke up.'"

They continued the conversation, but Ghomeshi was adamant. "I don't hurt women. You know me. I don't do that."

Leaving his office, Miranda was "shook up" but not sure what to do. She passed the campus's sexual complaint centre as she left but did not go in because she did not have permission to name her friend. Posters on the wall featured the "No Means No" campaign that was just getting started that year.

"All I felt I could do is warn others by word of mouth," said Miranda, recalling she felt defeated by the incident. If she took anything from that encounter with Jian Ghomeshi, it was this: "If you have a problem with him, you're the problem."

The *Star* reported the York allegations, and university officials checked and found no record of complaints related to Ghomeshi. A spokesperson told us that, given the age of the alleged complaints and York's record retention schedule, it is unlikely "any record exists."

When I heard the stories of Miranda, Jim Hounslow, and other people who knew Ghomeshi during his years at York, it occurred to me that his behaviour apparently started at the same time that women like Carly, Paula, and several others were born, the same women who would come forward a quarter of a century later and tell the stories that would be Ghomeshi's downfall.

10
My Dinner with Jian

Michael Douglas, movie star and son of Kirk, made his way through a crowd of adoring fans. The 2014 Toronto International Film Festival was underway in early September, and he was the main attraction at a private dinner in Toronto's Four Seasons Hotel ballroom. *Wall Street*'s shark Gordon Gekko, *Romancing the Stone*'s swashbuckling Jack T. Colton, and *Basic Instinct*'s Detective Nick Curran — Douglas has had his share of big roles over the years. The opportunity to rub shoulders with a screen legend had brought a hundred and fifty special guests to enjoy dinner and a conversation between Douglas and British-born journalist Tina Brown, a former editor of *Vanity Fair* and the *New Yorker*.

My wife, Kelly, and I rode the elevator up to the sixth-floor ballroom. In the breast pocket of my suit was an invitation for two to the gala, a special occasion for us not at all part of our normal routine. I had been to soirées like this before but usually as a working journalist covering an event when I was a young reporter. When the invitation landed in my in-box — an intimate dinner with actor Michael Douglas that fell on a weekend when both our children would be out of town — I smiled. This was an opportunity Kelly and I could not pass up. Twenty-five years earlier, while attending a friend's wedding in Bermuda, we had been invited to small party at the home of Douglas's mother. Her actor son was there, but I hadn't managed to speak with him. In the elevator at the Four Seasons, I joked that at some point during the evening I would sidle up to him to say hello. Then I imagined referencing *The Streets of San Francisco*, the gritty cop drama he co-starred in that I watched with my father as a kid. I was thrilled to have a second chance to talk to Michael Douglas.

The elevator doors opened onto a festive cocktail scene. I noticed my nails were dirty. I had been building a fence in my backyard in Etobicoke that afternoon. Still, I had managed to find a clean shirt, a decent suit, and even cufflinks. Adrienne Clarkson was over to one side, chatting with someone whose name I could not recall. Kelly and I looked around the sea of ties and tuxedos. Michael Douglas was nowhere to be seen. Toronto television personality Jeanne Beker was moving through the crowd. Also present were Canadian hockey star Wayne Gretzky, his movie actress wife Janet, and leading business couple Gerry Schwartz and Heather Reisman. The financial backer of the event, Credit Suisse, was represented by Ron Lloyd, co-host with Tina Brown. He was the international bank's top man in Canada. It was the kind of event where new arrivals to the cocktail portion were encouraged to make their way to an area where a paid photographer snaps a photo in front of a tall backdrop adorned with the sponsor's name. We were unable to avoid the obligatory photo, and someone handed us drinks. Seeing nobody familiar, we stood and chatted quite happily on our own, looking out over the who's who of Toronto and just taking it all in. I wasn't sure why I had been invited, but I was happy to be there. Kelly took a sip of her drink and paused. She nodded toward a man.

"Isn't that Jian Ghomeshi?"

The *Q* host was standing alone in a corner alcove, checking his phone. His wardrobe — the dark clothes, chest hair exposed — seemed to be a bit of a uniform for him, judging by the many photos I had viewed of him over the summer. His head was down, and he was working his phone quickly. I wondered who he was texting — and what texts were on the phone that would help me. Looking around I expected to see a woman walking toward him, maybe coming back with two drinks, slender, very young. Nobody. As far as I could tell, he was on his own. That was unusual, given what I knew about his dating habits. Perhaps he was being cautious.

It had been five months since the @bigearsteddy Twitter feed had appeared and two months since my last contact with Ghomeshi and his lawyers. Carly and Paula were still in the picture, though during the summer the anxiety levels of both women had been running high. When we failed to find other women to come forward, Paula, in particular, became worried. She withdrew from participating in the story, then came back, then withdrew again, then came back. Their main concern was that they would be outed as sources in some way. I had been honest with them during the process, explaining that while the *Toronto Star* would never identify them, others could. Ghomeshi knew their names, of course, and quite a few of their friends knew they had dated Ghomeshi. All this contributed to a general level of worry and fear. At one point in the summer, Carly told me, "The longer we're in limbo with this story, the more anxious and stressed Paula and I get." She said this was causing her to lose perspective and make her think, well, Jian and I had some good times, do I really want to be part of potentially ruining someone's career and reputation? I did my best to keep her on track. I knew Jesse Brown did, too, even though he was no longer working for the *Star* as a freelancer.

Brown and the *Star* had formally and amicably parted company the week before the film festival dinner. I had told him that we could not publish a story based on the information we had, because, I wrote, it is "not a story that can be proven to the level we demand." I told him I had feelers out, as did he, and that new information could come in at any time "without warning." Brown had written an email to me saying that he might take the story elsewhere. "I believe our sources are credible and that this story is of urgent public interest. I feel a responsibility to report it." I wished him the best of luck. Now, seeing Ghomeshi fiddling with his phone I realized that, at the very least, I would get another shot at putting the allegations to the CBC host.

Kelly suggested we check our table assignment.

"I can pretty much guarantee we will not be sitting near him," I said. My hastily crafted plan was to make my way to the head table area, where Ghomeshi would surely be, and approach him during a lull in the evening. Perhaps the dessert course? Still, we had been given our table number—as far from the head table as guests could be—so we made our way into the ballroom to check.

To Kelly's right was Jörn Weisbrodt, the German-born artistic director of Luminato, the wildly successful annual arts festival in the city of Toronto. To my left was Julie Bristow, a former CBC television executive known for developing *Dragons' Den* and *Battle of the Blades*. And, in what was either luck or the intervention of an unknown party, the small beige place cards with italic writing put Kelly on Jian Ghomeshi's right and me on his left. My mind was racing. On the subway ride to the event, I had been hoping I might meet Michael Douglas. It looked as if this was to be the night I would finally meet Jian Ghomeshi.

I immediately wondered if someone had planned this. Much later, I learned that our table was composed of people whom *Toronto Life* had named one of the city's fifty most influential. The magazine ranked Ghomeshi thirty-seventh. Michael Cooke and I shared the thirty-eighth spot; Cooke declined to attend. Presumably the higher-ranked people were seated closer to the front of the room.

Kelly and I stood as other guests made their way to the table. People milled around us, moving from the cocktail-gossiping portion of the event to the actual dinner. No sign of Ghomeshi. At the head table, quite some distance from us, I spotted Michael Douglas. He was really starting to look like his old man, an actor who was one of my late father's favourites. Tina Brown, was beside him.

Just as I was accepting the fact that it looked like I was again going to miss my chance to meet Douglas, I saw Ghomeshi, phone in hand, walking over. I studied him. He was obviously unaware of his table assignment. Kelly wished me good luck. I remarked that I was definitely going to need her help.

"Nice to finally meet you, Mr. Ghomeshi," I said, stretching out my hand. "This is quite interesting."

Ghomeshi looked at me, then down at my name card on the table, then at his, and then back at me and my hand. His eyes widened. "I'd say. This will be awkward." He looked toward the exit.

"It doesn't have to be," I told him, "though this may be an opportunity to tell me your side of things."

Ghomeshi shook my hand. His was moist and limp. Around us in the ballroom, the final few guests moved to their tables.

The radio host looked toward the exit again but appeared to think better of it and sat down. He unrolled his napkin from his knife and fork and rested his phone beside his plate.

"How is your book doing?" he asked me.

Now that was an interesting question. With it, I saw Ghomeshi relax. He is a polished interviewer and had done his research. I had very recently self-published a mystery book, *The Dead Times*, the story of a homicide detective turned reporter who must unravel a series of murders beginning with the killing of his girlfriend. I told Ghomeshi the book was doing okay, though not exactly a bestseller. I immediately had a fantasy that he would ask me to come on his show to flog my book in return for dropping the investigation. That would have been quite telling. Instead, Ghomeshi congratulated me on the achievement.

Wine was served. Ghomeshi asked for some but did not drink. I had already heard from alleged victims that Ghomeshi was not much of a drinker. For the record, I only had a couple of sips, realizing that I was, out of necessity and unexpectedly, on the job.

Others at the table were talking about the night, the film festival, the weather. Nobody was paying attention to us. Nobody knew what lay ahead for Ghomeshi or that a newspaper investigation was underway. Kelly and Jörn Weisbrodt, the fellow from Luminato, were having a good discussion, and I could tell Weisbrodt was a bit of a raconteur as well as a stylish dresser. He and musician Rufus Wainwright are married and, knowing that Ghomeshi was friends with the musician, I was surprised that Ghomeshi was not looking across the table and trying to engage Weisbrodt or anyone else rather than me, having already denied my request to speak numerous times. I pulled out my phone and told Ghomeshi I had to check on our kids, but what I really needed to do was make some quick electronic notes.

My goal at this point was to come out of the night with something new. At the very least, I wanted to present the CBC host, in person, with the allegations we were pursuing. But to start, I turned to Ghomeshi and began talking about soccer. This was not mindless chatter. The women I had spoken to had told me that Ghomeshi frequently talked about his body image and his age, and his fear that by the time he had children and they began playing sports, he would be an "old, fat, soccer dad."

The salad course arrived, and I kept up my banter. I told him that for many years I had coached soccer, starting with my son's and now my daughter's team. It's something I am genuinely passionate about—youth sports are very important and particularly so for young women. I told him that the character-building aspect of soccer or any other team sport is key. Ghomeshi took the bait.

"I'm getting too old," he smiled.

"No," I said, taking a drink from my water glass. "I have a friend who did not have children until his late forties, and he is very involved with his children and sports." Ghomeshi was forty-seven.

"I am fat," he told me. "I want kids, but I am so afraid that I will be too old to take them to things and be involved. I am still looking for the right person."

I told Ghomeshi he was not fat.

"Really?" Ghomeshi said, smiling at me for the first time.

"You are fine, really. You look like you work out."

Ghomeshi smiled again. "A bit, sure." I knew that Ghomeshi had a personal trainer he visited three times a week.

Kelly then joined the conversation. After a mouthful of salad, Ghomeshi told us that he was still looking for a person to settle down with. The women complaining about his conduct had told me that Ghomeshi would often tell them "You are the one" and that he wanted to marry them. He asked Kelly how we met. We gave him a brief overview of how we were introduced by a close mutual friend. Ghomeshi picked at his food and then put down his fork. I told him how important it was to find a soulmate, and he looked off to one side. I told him we had a son studying math and a daughter in high school, both pretty decent athletes. I was surprised by Ghomeshi's inability to maintain and encourage the conversation.

On the stage, Tina Brown had begun to interview Michael Douglas, the evening's main attraction. I tried another tactic with Ghomeshi, hoping that he had not exhausted his ability to discuss the Billy Bob Thornton interview that had rocketed him to fame. By design, I was not talking about the elephant in the room — the *Star*'s investigation.

"I have to ask you, that Billy Bob Thornton interview, I listened to it this summer because I have been, well, studying you a bit. It was pretty impressive the way you handled him." I paused. He looked uncomfortable until I complimented him. A pattern was emerging. "Is that normal, for an interview subject to request that you not talk about something? That does not happen in print journalism, at least not the stuff I do."

"Kevin, it happens more than you think. It's not like your job where I guess you get to ask any question you want." Ghomeshi paused. I took it as a reference to my questions about his abusive behaviour.

The fall *Q* season was going to launch later in the week, and Ghomeshi told me that in his recent pre-taped interview with Barbra Streisand in a New York hotel room, he had a similar difficulty to overcome. At the interview, which did not air until after the TIFF dinner, he was told by the famous singer's handlers to focus on her music, not her acting career. He said he snuck in questions about acting with a reference to the movie *Yentl*, because it featured "beautiful singing."

"When doing an interview," Ghomeshi explained, "you need to be creative. You need to get an angle on someone."

When he sat down to interview Streisand, Ghomeshi told her that while in his twenties he was coached by an opera singer who had a photo of Streisand in his music room. Ghomeshi told her that the coach complained that Ghomeshi was not the singer Streisand was, which Ghomeshi said he agreed with. He repeated the story in the actual interview. I listened to it when it aired. Streisand, who gives few interviews, obviously liked Ghomeshi. She opened up about her "vulnerability" and "self-doubt." The *QTV* episode shows Ghomeshi looking rumpled and exhausted but thoroughly engaged. He did ask her follow-up questions about her vulnerability.

Streisand: "I get hurt easily. I don't like anyone saying things about me that are not true."

Ghomeshi nodded then shot back. "It comes with the territory." At the end of the interview, Streisand reached forward and clasped Ghomeshi's hands.

I complimented Ghomeshi. "I expect it's not that easy to make some-one as famous as Barbra Streisand comfortable." The main course arrived, and our tablemates looked to their cutlery. Ghomeshi did not touch his food. He started laughing. It was a maniacal laugh, edgy and out of place. His whole body was shaking, and he hunched over his salad plate. I asked him what was wrong.

"This is too surreal, being here with you. You are accusing me of things. I can't be here." The CBC host stood and headed for the exit.

As my tablemates tucked into plates of halibut and vegetables, a few wondered aloud why Ghomeshi had left. Nobody seemed overly con-cerned. Ghomeshi was a busy man, much in demand, and one guest suggested he had gone to make a phone call. Another asked if I had said something to make "Jian get all pissy." I later learned that he had gone to make a call to one of his advisers.

I had a feeling Ghomeshi would return. Tina Brown and Michael Douglas were settling into comfortable chairs on the raised stage. They began an easy back and forth conversation. Douglas told a story about how his father, who was ninety-seven, loved to watch old movies. Kirk called Michael up one day and said, "Michael, I'm watching one of my old movies, and it's pretty good." Kirk called back a few hours later to tell his son that he had realized the movie he was watching actually fea-tured Michael. The crowd loved it.

Ghomeshi returned as dessert was being served.

"Better?" I asked him.

"Yes," he said, checking his phone. He looked stronger, more alert.

Ghomeshi looked away. On the stage, Brown and Douglas were laugh-ing over a bawdy comment that Douglas made about the nine days it took to film the sex scene in *Basic Instinct* and how enjoyable it was spending those days with actress Sharon Stone.

It was time to make a move. I reminded Ghomeshi of the accusations the women were making and the letters we at the *Star* had sent asking questions. I did my best to explain to him how serious the allegations were. Leaning close to him so that our exchange would not become part of the table's conversation, I mentioned the two letters we had sent seeking comment on allegations that he had struck women "with a closed fist or open hand," choked them with his hands "around their neck to the point that they almost pass out," and on occasion covered a woman's "nose and mouth so that they have difficulty breathing." A photographer taking someone else's picture inadvertently captured us talking, and the photo was eventually published in the *Star* online. It looks like a couple of buddies having a serious dinner chat. After giving him a moment to digest these accusations, I urged Ghomeshi to respond and to give specific information to address what these women were saying. His lawyers had only provided a blanket statement saying everything he did was consensual.

Ghomeshi passed a hand over his trim beard and kept his voice low.

"I don't understand why you are still asking questions when our lawyers have told you that I am innocent and there is no story."

"The women who say you attacked them would differ," I told him. "They have made some very strong allegations against you. Are you still carrying on like this with women?"

He dodged the question. "I'm a good person," he said.

I waited. Ghomeshi continued.

"Look, there's no story. Why do you continue asking about this and talking to people? I know who you have talked to and some of them are my friends and they talk to me," Ghomeshi said.

I was surprised that he did not understand how it works, given the nature of his job, which has over the years entailed asking tough questions.

"I am not a journalist," he said, explaining that he was a musician turned host and knew nothing about the way an investigation is carried out. I did my best to explain that when we receive information for a potential story we conduct interviews and try to get to the bottom of the allegations. I told him that was why I had sought comment from him, and then his lawyers, in the summer. I told him the responsible communication defence requires us to be extremely diligent in getting the other side of the story.

Ghomeshi stared straight ahead. The *Q* host had not touched his plate. He toyed with his cutlery, checking his phone frequently. I noticed that he was still not making eye contact with others at the table. "You need to watch yourself," he said. "People in this city need to understand that I have a long memory. You need to understand that and be very, very careful."

"With respect," I said, "it may be the memories of some of these women that you need to be careful about."

On the stage, Brown and Douglas were wrapping up. I had missed the bulk of their conversation.

Ghomeshi stood up to go. I stood up with him and explained that we would continue looking into allegations and that, as part of our policy, I would bring any new allegations to him so that he had a chance to comment.

"I think it is time for you to confront this and tell the truth," I said.

"There's nothing to say. You have the truth." Ghomeshi left the ballroom.

Sandwich Board

Jesse Brown's *Canadaland* studio sits on the third floor of a rental building on Richmond Street near Spadina Avenue in Toronto's fashion district. On Monday, October 20, at the tail end of his weekly podcast (the episode was called "Why I Hate Talking about Israel"), Brown gave his devoted audience a teaser on a news item he promised he was about to break, a "monster" story that he said would be upsetting to its targets. Brown's rich, deep voice was a little higher than normal, the pace of his speech a bit quicker. The self-described media critic told the listeners who fund his show that he was finding stories that the mainstream media couldn't or wouldn't tell, and he was concerned about potential backlash, particularly because his funding structure sought money directly from his audience.

"I am once again getting contacted by people who want to share with me some incredible news stories that have been hidden so far, and I am working on one right now that, I think is a monster, it's a huge revelation," Brown told his audience. "It will appear soon as a post at Canadalandshow.com, and this is a story that is worse than embarrassing for certain parties. I want to flag that now because I think that what is very likely to happen is I will be targeted, that my credibility will be called into question, that my journalism will be challenged, who knows. Now I expect that when you are saying things about people who have a lot to lose, but there is a new element to this now that I am being paid directly by listeners of this show."

Metaphorical alarm bells started ringing at the CBC, at Navigator crisis management, and at Jian Ghomeshi's home office. Once again his employers and advisers reconnected, convinced the story on Ghomeshi's rough sex life was about to break. It had been six weeks since the film festival dinner and, with each week that passed, with no story on the front page of the *Toronto Star*, Ghomeshi and his advisers relaxed. The CBC host had earlier reported to both his advisory team and to senior executives at the CBC that John Cruickshank, publisher of the *Toronto Star*, had told him the newspaper was not interested in the story because it dealt with his private sex life. That was not true — Cruickshank had explained to Ghomeshi that the *Star* was looking into the allegations but did not feel it had a story yet — but that was what Ghomeshi told his team.

Immediately after the film festival dinner, Ghomeshi had telephoned Cruickshank, asking him why I was still investigating. "I thought you guys believed me," Ghomeshi complained. Cruickshank explained again that this was all "part of a process."

Cruickshank was becoming increasingly uncomfortable with these calls. He liked Ghomeshi as the host of the *Q* media panel he appeared on, but he was starting to think the man was lying to him. He had also made it clear to Ghomeshi that *Star* editor-in-chief Michael Cooke would handle any newsroom decisions on the file, since Cruickshank had a conflict of interest because he knew Ghomeshi from the media panel.

"You are just clearing me, right?" Ghomeshi asked the *Star* publisher at one point.

Cruickshank, in his recollection of this period, recalls that Ghomeshi said he would never hurt a woman; he was "very convincing and talked like a feminist," Cruickshank said. At no time did Ghomeshi mention to the *Star*'s publisher his penchant for rough sex.

I heard news of Brown's podcast teaser while on a week's vacation, cycling in Italy with my wife. When I heard that Brown was referring to a "monster" story, I wasn't worried that he was referring to the Ghomeshi investigation. Though we had parted company, I was certain that I would have heard of a planned publication by Brown from the mutual sources we had talked to. Kelly and I kept cycling over the sunny rolling hills of Tuscany, a million miles away from the business of rooting out the secrets of people and government.

Ghomeshi, who already suffered from anxiety, was in a progressively more fragile state as the week wore on. He was also exhausted, having just returned to the *Q* studio in Toronto after a whirlwind trip to Los Angeles where he and his CBC team did a series of *Q Live in LA* episodes featuring such stars as Martin Short and Zach Galifianakis. Less than three weeks prior, Ghomeshi's father, Farhang "Frank" Ghomeshi, had passed away, and Ghomeshi was wracked with grief. In a Facebook post after the death, Ghomeshi referred to his dad as "the greatest man I've ever known." Ghomeshi had a tattoo of his father's name on his right arm, and he shared with his fans that he could not stop crying, thinking about the man who taught him what "love really is."

Ghomeshi often spoke about his father on *Q*, imitating his Iranian accent giving one piece of advice or another, the most frequent being "Please work harder." His father recommended real estate as an investment: when the first Moxy Früvous album went platinum, Farhang advised his son to buy a house. That first purchase tripled in value, and Ghomeshi repeated the pattern three times. Farhang was an engineer for Ontario Hydro after a hard upbringing in Iran, where his own father died when Farhang was only fifteen. Ghomeshi's Facebook eulogy said his father was "terribly loving" and the "finest role model in the world." That he died before the eventual scandal broke was, friends of Ghomeshi later remarked, a "blessing."

At the *Canadaland* studio, Brown continued to develop the story he had foreshadowed. The piece had nothing to do with Jian Ghomeshi and sex. Instead, it involved allegations that Toronto's *Globe and Mail* and the CBC had sat for too long on a story brought to them by Pulitzer Prize–winning journalist Glenn Greenwald about government Internet spying in Canada. Named in the eventual piece were prominent journalists at both organizations.

Back in Toronto that same week, Ghomeshi's busy schedule kicked off with a two-part "exclusive" with Canadian rocker Neil Young. Toward the middle of the week, *Q* had booked an interview with Clint Malarchuk, a former National Hockey League goaltender who nearly died on the job.

Ghomeshi was also in the midst of writing his second book — about how stars deal with anxiety and pressure — and the joke around the *Q* studio was that Ghomeshi was always looking for new material. Producers wondered if he raised the issue with certain stars with an eye toward gathering information for the chapters he was writing.

Ghomeshi had no idea that Thursday, October 23 would be his last day in his beloved, cave-like *Q* studio. Perhaps his greatest adviser in the maelstrom he was living, Navigator's Jaime Watt, wasn't in Toronto as the Ghomeshi crisis deepened. Watt had spent the day before locked down on Parliament Hill, where he had been attending some meetings, unable to leave because a gunman armed with an old Winchester hunting rifle and a long knife shot and killed unarmed corporal Nathan Cirillo at the National War Memorial before rushing into the Centre Block on Parliament Hill, where Sergeant-at-Arms Kevin Vickers shot him dead. Ghomeshi, on the job the next morning in Toronto at CBC headquarters, addressed his listeners, his voice coloured with sadness as he spoke about the events in Ottawa, revealing no hint of what he personally was going through.

"A day later it still seems shocking, it still seems absurd. It still stings. We Canadians spent the day glued to our TV screens, listening to the radio, or online. All following the steady stream of news...out of Ottawa," Ghomeshi began, his Thursday essay riding over somber music, his voice pausing perfectly for maximum yet subtle impact. "And collectively we couldn't believe what was happening. Is this our country? Our Parliament? This is not what we do. This is not who...we are. The images of a fallen soldier being given CPR. Of a caucus room barricaded by furniture. Video of the main hallway of the Parliament Centre Block echoing with gunfire. By afternoon we knew the outcome."

The essay ran four minutes and four seconds. Social media loved it. The words spoke to peaceful people reeling from the attack, but Ghomeshi also noted that Canada was not immune to violence. He mentioned several incidents, including the 1989 attack that killed fourteen women at Montreal's École Polytechnique, which he had referenced twenty-five years previously in the student handbook at York University. He mused that from this day forward that "great stretch of lawn" at Parliament

Hill might be kept locked down, inaccessible, as a result of the violence. Ghomeshi ended by saying that despite the tragedy, good might come, and he talked about how the country came together in the face of adversity. His baritone deepened and quickened as he rushed into the conclusion.

> Canadians from coast to coast reaching out to each other yesterday. Checking in on each other, making sure everyone was okay. We were united in a common feeling as a nation sickened by the news, scared at what might be to come. And by day's end a new resolve. This would not change us. This would not alter our common cause. Our country is bigger than this tragic incident, one lone gunman looking to make a point. We are stronger than this. We believe too profoundly in this country, this culture, this collective. In the coming days, or weeks or even hours, that unity may start to dissipate, fingers may be pointed, at security protocols, access to firearms, religion, political points will be attempted to be scored, and yet let us not forget the feeling of October 22, a day of tragedy and a day when this whole country was united in one voice.

Ghomeshi ended his last essay as he always insisted he should when he gave instructions to his ghostwriters: with a rhyme.

"As for the still-shaken citizens of Ottawa, our oft-maligned parliamentarians, and the civil servants who work with them, the police who protect the Hill, the young soldiers who stand guard at the National War Memorial, a nation is grateful. A nation is thinking of you. This...is Q."

The Thursday show featured a dramatic interview with Malarchuk, the "Cowboy Goalie." His book, *The Crazy Game*, written with *Sportsnet* magazine reporter Dan Robson, told the story of his troubled life, a life affected by depression and other demons, including a diagnosis of obsessive-compulsive disorder. A skate blade sliced open Malarchuk's jugular vein in a hockey game in 1989. The native of Grande Prairie, Alberta, was stitched up and back on the ice in ten days. Years later, his depression worsening and coupled with alcoholism, he fired a .22-calibre rifle bullet into his chin in a suicide attempt, and survived. That began his road to recovery. When he arrived at the *Q* studio and began talking with Ghomeshi, he instantly recognized that they shared similar characteristics. "I saw him as a fellow struggler," Malarchuk recalled later, first in an interview with journalist Rebecca Eckler on SXM Canada's *The New Mid Life* and more recently in an interview with me for this book.

Malarchuk, over the years, has become very passionate about the issue of mental illness. Even before his book was published he spoke openly about confronting his problems. Now a lecturer and writer, he lives on a Nevada ranch with his wife. When he was booked on *Q* he did not know who Jian Ghomeshi was. Friends told him, "You are going to be on with Ghomeshi; he's awesome." He was also told that Ghomeshi struggled with anxiety and would be sympathetic to the ex-goalie's story. The interview was pre-recorded on the Wednesday afternoon, while the Ottawa shooting story was still developing. Before the interview, Ghomeshi was on the phone to his lawyers, hatching a plan that would see his lawyers provide what he believed was exculpatory video evidence to his managers at the CBC in advance of what could be a leak in the alleged sexual assault story. Malarchuk, of course, was unaware of all this. During a quick pre-interview chat with Ghomeshi, Malarchuk felt an instant connection.

"I felt very comforted right from the start," Malarchuk recalled. "His mannerisms, the way he moved from one question to another." Malarchuk was always the funny guy in the dressing room, and before the cameras rolled, the two men chatted about comedian Robin Williams, who had taken his life two months before, and how humour is often used to mask a deep sadness.

The interview was powerful. Sitting in the guest chair, Malarchuk could tell that Ghomeshi had read his book. Many interviewers, he had found on the tour, are so busy they can only skim a few chapters.

"Thank you for being here, man," Ghomeshi began. He noted that it must have been very emotional for Malarchuk to release a book detailing his inner feelings. And he very quickly became personal, with a reference to his own struggles, not something Ghomeshi normally did with a guest.

It happened as soon as Malarchuk told listeners that though he has come to grips with his mental illness, and talks about it openly, the problems have not gone away. Ghomeshi responded, "One of the funny things around mental illness is, when people, I find it almost comical, although they may be well-meaning, when people say to me, well, you know, this can cure you. It's kind of like, it's not that simple! There's no cure. It's always in play. It's about coping."

Ghomeshi commented, in what quickly became a discussion rather than an interview, that when a person is at home and not busy, that is "when it all comes crashing down." People listening to the interview who knew Ghomeshi believed he was not talking about Malarchuk; he was talking about himself.

"Does something trigger the depression, Clint?" Ghomeshi asked. "Is this stressful, doing interviews with the media?"

Malarchuk said no, it was helpful. Ghomeshi spoke glowingly about Joanie, Malarchuk's wife, watching on the other side of the glass in the studio control room. Ghomeshi said she was the hero of the story for toughing it out with Malarchuk, who shot himself in front of her. Malarchuk said that was the worst thing he had ever done, because he blamed her, asking, "You see what you made me do?"

During the interview, Ghomeshi never cut off Malarchuk. He listened raptly to each word that came out of the former goalie's mouth.

"Be true to yourself," Malarchuk said when Ghomeshi asked what advice he would give. "If you need help, be true to yourself. It's not a weakness; it's an affliction. And if you struggle, get help."

At the end of the interview, when the cameras and microphones were turned off, the two men sat there, staring at one another. There were tears in their eyes as they stood and embraced.

"We were spent," Malarchuk recalls. "I left the studio in tears. He was the same, really choked up. There was nothing more for us to say. I think he developed a real connection with me as a fellow struggler...because we both shared a mental illness." Malarchuk and his wife left the studio. Many more interviews followed on the circuit, but this one remains the most memorable.

. . .

Finished for the day, late afternoon on Wednesday after the pre-taping, Ghomeshi brushed past some of the *Q* staff. People stood in clusters, talking about the Ottawa shooting. One stopped him and remarked how emotional he seemed to be about the interview with Malarchuk. It was quite clear to staff that both men had been crying at the end of the segment.

"That interview?" Ghomeshi said as he went out. "Oh, it had nothing to do with that."

Malarchuk had affected Ghomeshi, but he was also grappling with his fear of the "monster" story that Jesse Brown was apparently about to break. Talks with his advisers went on throughout the night before he came in to work Thursday to host *Q*, deliver his essay on the Ottawa shootings, and introduce the pre-taped portions, including the Malarchuk interview. Then he left the CBC building.

At roughly the time Ghomeshi was wrapping up his morning at *Q*, his lawyer Tiffany Soucy was sitting in front of a computer in a boardroom at the Dentons offices on King Street West for a most unusual meeting. Her assistant ushered in two senior CBC employees: chief of public affairs Chuck Thompson and Chris Boyce, executive director of radio programming. Throughout the summer Ghomeshi had kept both executives apprised of the allegations against him, and both men had taken his protestations of innocence at face value. They trusted Ghomeshi. In fact, the entire CBC executive team trusted him. But now, with Brown's forthcoming "monster" story apparently bringing the allegations front and centre again, Ghomeshi and his legal team had a new strategy. They were going to reveal evidence of consent.

Soucy had decided that Ghomeshi would not be present at the meeting. In her brief preamble to the two CBC executives, Soucy explained that she had loaded more than a hundred videos and hundreds of text messages onto the computer in front of her, all from Jian Ghomeshi's cellphone. She said this information would put the matter of Ghomeshi's alleged sexual abuse to rest.

"The plan was to show this as an example of how during consensual sexual relations there could be bruising," a source close to Ghomeshi during that time explained to me.

The videos had all been sent to Ghomeshi from one of the many women he dated over the past decade. The woman recorded them as video "selfies" and sent them to Ghomeshi either at his request or of her own volition. (I interviewed this woman, who wishes to remain anonymous.) Soucy warned that the material the two men were about to see was sexually explicit, ranging from provocative images to text chats about a television show that Ghomeshi and the woman in the videos enjoyed. Boyce and Thompson sat down and began viewing.

The woman was sometimes clothed, sometimes naked. Boyce and Thompson were also shown text messages between Ghomeshi and the woman that seemed to indicate, the CBC executives felt, a completely consensual relationship. One video was very different from the others. Soucy showed it, she said, as an example of how bruising could occur as the result of a consensual sexual relationship. The woman revealed bruising to the side of her body apparently caused by cracked ribs during sex play. Soucy showed the CBC executives a series of accompanying texts that, according to a source, featured the woman telling Ghomeshi that he caused the injury. The video and accompanying messages did not indicate to Boyce and Thompson that the woman was angry or upset with Ghomeshi. No other videos showed any injuries, but Soucy showed provocative videos and text messages the woman had sent Ghomeshi after the bruising video, which the lawyer said was proof the relationship was ongoing, consensual, and friendly.

The videos, particularly the one showing the bruise, stunned Boyce and Thompson. This was not the anticipated reaction. The assignment was suddenly out of the CBC executives' comfort zone. They stood up, gathered the notes they had been allowed to make, and left the law firm offices quickly, hustling into the elevator and then out onto King Street West.

The distance from Dentons to the CBC Front Street offices is nine hundred metres, and both men covered the distance at a half sprint. They were not allowed to take any of the electronic information with them.

Much later, Boyce mused in an on-camera interview that perhaps the CBC should have made a report to the police about the video that showed bruising. Back at headquarters, the two men briefed Heather Conway, the CBC's executive vice-president of English services. Conway was as far from being a CBC "lifer" as possible. She had only joined the year before, coming from a post as chief business officer for the Art Gallery of Ontario. Prior to that she had been executive vice-president at Alliance Atlantis Communications. Boyce and Thompson told their boss that they had been shown information suggesting that this particular relationship seemed to be consensual. It appeared, however, that the sex play had broken a woman's ribs. Conway made up her mind then and there to fire Ghomeshi.

Ghomeshi, who was not in the building, was summoned to the Front Street offices and told he was entitled to have a union representative sit in on the meeting. One could not be found, and Ghomeshi agreed to come to the meeting unrepresented. "There is evidence of abuse against a woman," Ghomeshi was told. "We are going to fire you in twenty-four hours."

Ghomeshi was given an option: resign before that time was up. As one CBC staffer involved in the situation explained, "We cannot have someone who is violent to women on staff." Ghomeshi told those at the meeting that they were wrong and that a "spurned lover" had targeted him. The CBC executives repeated that the conduct they were now aware of from the video showing was not something the national broadcaster could tolerate. He was told to leave the CBC building; a replacement would be found for tomorrow's show. In a closed-door meeting that followed, Chuck Thompson, the public relations chief, was instructed to say, should anyone in the media call to ask about Ghomeshi's absence, that the CBC does not comment on the "private lives" of its employees.

The CBC believed the publication of a story was imminent. Timing was critical. A meeting was scheduled for the next day, Friday morning. With the Friday *Q* host chair suddenly empty, producers called in veteran CBC host Piya Chattopadhyay. *Q* producer Arif Noorani phoned Chattopadhyay, who was in Halifax, asking if she could take over. No explanation was given. Chattopadhyay speculated that either Ghomeshi had landed a last-minute, gold-list interview out of town, or he was taking time off due to his father's passing. She told Noorani she would do it but then was flying to Windsor to host an event. Being parachuted into *Q*, particularly the busy Friday show, was not easy. The Friday episode included several interviews, plus the popular media panel, featuring rabble.ca's Judy Rebick, the *National Post*'s Jonathan Kay and, interestingly, John Cruickshank. The control room also dug up an earlier interview by the suddenly pressed-into-duty guest host so the show would appear seamless and there would be no hint of Jian Ghomeshi. *Q* production staff had an inkling that Ghomeshi's absence was due to the rumoured *Toronto Star* story. They watched the *Star* publisher for clues but saw none.

Meanwhile, a call was made to CBC's maintenance team, who were told to stand by. Something needed to be removed from the CBC lobby.

The Friday morning meeting was held at the Dentons law offices. Ghomeshi was there, joined by lawyers Tiffany Soucy and Neil Rabinovitch. Also present was the Navigator crisis communication team, led by Jaime Watt, who had returned from Ottawa. Representing the CBC were radio chief Heather Conway, Chris Boyce, and Chuck Thompson. CBC's top outside employment lawyer was away on a work retreat in Chicago and so a senior outside counsel named Roy Filion attended as a stand-in. Filion was visibly embarrassed by any mention of the rough sex allegations. Navigator's staff had a request for the CBC at the boardroom table: "Give us the weekend." CBC agreed, and a meeting was set for eleven a.m. Sunday.

At *Canadaland*, Jesse Brown's antenna was up. The media was his beat, and he was always on the lookout for news. A source told him that Ghomeshi had been put on an "indefinite" leave. Brown, whose canvas is very much social media, tweeted that information around four p.m. Immediately, he and CBC public relations chief Chuck Thompson got into a small Twitter skirmish. Thompson tweeted "Jian Ghomeshi is not on indefinite leave from the CBC."

Brown shot back on Twitter. "My info on @jianghomeshi is unverified but from a highly credible source. @CBC should deny now if inaccurate and I will retract immediately." CBC then countered with a brief statement from Thompson saying that Ghomeshi was taking an "undetermined" period of time away from the CBC to "deal with some personal issues." Jesse Brown had publicly forced the CBC into partial transparency. The fact was that the CBC had already determined that Ghomeshi was going to be fired. The only question was whether he would choose to resign first.

The buzz online was that the leave was related to the death of Ghomeshi's father. That was referenced in stories and comments Friday evening in the Toronto media. The response from fans was warm. Of course their beloved *Q* host needed time to deal with this family tragedy. "Thanks for all the well wishes, guys, I'm okay," Ghomeshi tweeted to his followers that Friday afternoon, telling them he was taking some much-needed personal time away from the CBC.

I was still in Italy when Michael Cooke shared the social media announcements with me. "Is this what I think it is?" he asked. It was well past midnight in Rome. Cooke and I talked on the phone, planning a strategy. It seemed a good guess that Ghomeshi's leave was not connected to his father. Cooke quickly put Jesse Brown back on contract. Brown was also away, so the three of us agreed to reconvene in Toronto as soon as possible. My flight back home was scheduled for early Saturday morning.

While I was in the air, high-level meetings were being held at CBC's offices to prepare for the rescheduled meeting at Dentons. The CBC board of directors was notified of the situation. At eleven a.m. Sunday, two groups faced off across a large boardroom table. Present for the CBC were Chris Boyce, Heather Conway, and human resources chief Todd Spencer. Lawyer Filion was also in attendance. Ghomeshi was joined by Jaime Watt and other Navigator consultants, as well as the Dentons lawyers.

Todd Spencer read a short, formal statement informing Ghomeshi that he was being terminated for cause. Spencer cited information that "we have learned in recent days" as the reason for the firing. "Do you have anything to say?" Spencer asked Ghomeshi.

Ghomeshi summed up what he saw as the CBC's position. He said he was being fired for optics: the danger that revelations about his personal life would damage the CBC brand. From his point of view, as he would later write on Facebook, he had kept the CBC informed as a true partner during the past six months. Now, he felt, for the first time in thirteen years, like an outsider.

Spencer, a former journalist thrust into a human resources role, was nervous. Speaking woodenly, he read another document informing Ghomeshi that the representative of an "outplacement" counselling firm, available to help an employee transition to another career, was on hand downstairs should he wish to avail himself of its services. Ghomeshi said no, he was fine. As he told his advisers later that afternoon, he was delighted and "bullish" about his future. He had his second book in the works, was seriously contemplating sinking the CBC with a major wrongful dismissal lawsuit, and he was certain he could be hired by a network in the US. He told his advisers that his plan was to leave Toronto later that day and fly to Los Angeles, where he had friends he would stay with. His only concern was how to leave Toronto without being spotted by the press which, when the announcement of his departure was made, would be looking for a photo and a quote.

Those at the Sunday meeting agreed that the CBC statement announcing Ghomeshi's departure should be brief and avoid referencing any untoward behaviour. After a few drafts, Heather Conway and CBC's chief legal counsel Maryse Bertrand signed off on the statement.

I had been back in Toronto for a day when the CBC issued its statement shortly after one p.m. Sunday afternoon. Jesse Brown and I had already spent many hours talking to sources. The statement that came out, sent by Chuck Thompson, was simple and clean. It came under the header "Statement by CBC regarding Jian Ghomeshi" and read, "The CBC is saddened to announce its relationship with Jian Ghomeshi has come to an end. The decision was not made without serious deliberation and careful consideration. Jian has made an immense contribution to the CBC and we wish him well." There was no hint of the reason he had been fired.

I took the statement and quickly wrote a story, which our online desk put on our website immediately. Then I emailed CBC spokesman Chuck Thompson. "I am trying to find out if this has anything to do with allegations I have been probing since the summer related to Mr. Ghomeshi.

The allegations come from women who allege bad conduct on his part. During the summer I reached out to Mr. Ghomeshi and received some communication back from him and a lawyer he had retained."

Thompson called me, and we discussed the matter. I emailed him my two letters of allegation to him. In an on-the-record interview, Thompson went far beyond the bland statement the CBC had released. I was surprised, and pleased. I had a strong suspicion that these were not words said off the cuff. Someone higher up the CBC food chain must have given Thompson permission. "Information came to [CBC's] attention recently that in CBC's judgment precludes us from continuing our relationship with Jian Ghomeshi," he said. I asked him a lot of questions. When did this happen? Why did it happen? Will there be a financial payout to Ghomeshi? Thompson said he was not at liberty to say anything more. "When an employer parts ways with an employee then for privacy reasons the terms of separation are not disclosed," Thompson said during the interview.

Taking those brief but important quotes, I recast the piece online, foreshadowing that there was more to this story than a simple parting of ways. As to what the "information" was that caused Ghomeshi's departure, we gave no indication.

Ghomeshi, over at the Dentons law firm, saw the quotation from Thompson on the *Star*'s website and, according to a source close to the day's events, went "ballistic." This was not part of Ghomeshi's deal to go quietly into the night. At no time was there a plan to indicate that "information" had been brought forward that led the *Q* host to leave the CBC. His advisers, along with Ghomeshi, were furious. Still firmly in his camp were Navigator, rock-it promotions, agent Jack Ross, and lawyer Chris Taylor. There was general agreement that the next move was to launch a lawsuit against CBC claiming massive damages—$50 million. Rock-it's Goldblatt-Sadowsky wrote a quick press release, and it was sent out around three p.m.

"The action will claim general and punitive damages for, among other things, breach of confidence and bad faith in the amount of $50 million," the statement read, adding that Ghomeshi would also "commence a grievance for reinstatement under his collective agreement." Though the public generally assumed that a big star like Ghomeshi had an employment agreement outside the unionized atmosphere of the national broadcaster, Ghomeshi was, like thousands of other CBC employees, a union member.

With the news release sending the media into a new direction — in the parlance of newsrooms, this was clearly a story "with legs" — Ghomeshi informed his team that he was going to tell his loyal followers what this was really all about. He planned to do so by writing a Facebook post he would release later in the day. Unlike the opening essays on *Q*, Ghomeshi wrote this on his own. He showed it to very few people before he posted it, but one person he did read it to was Debra Goldblatt-Sadowsky. I later asked her if she helped him craft the piece. "No," she replied. "Jian genuinely wrote it, as far as I know. He did read it to me before he posted it live, but he had others advising him at this point."

At the *Toronto Star* newsroom, it was all hands on deck. Bert Bruser, Michael Cooke, Jane Davenport, and I gathered in the newsroom that Sunday to assess how much of our investigation from the summer we could include in the story we were developing. It was one of those spectacularly busy days when there was no time to grab a coffee or do anything other than keep up with a breaking story. Before the Internet burst into our lives, there was no need to update our work until the next day's paper. But with that day's Ghomeshi story, we were filing updates constantly. The firing, Thompson's hint at the reasons behind it, Ghomeshi's lawsuit, and CBC's announcement that it would defend the lawsuit "vigorously" all required updating the online story. It was common practice now for a reporter to include a telephone number and email address at the end of a piece. Already, the public, a very angry public, was calling and emailing. It was a trickle at first, but it grew steadily and the message was unified: how dare the CBC fire our favourite son?

I gave Jesse Brown a desk beside mine, and we got to work assembling information and working the phones. Others in the newsroom were on the story, too. Vinay Menon, our excellent arts and culture columnist, was working his contacts and preparing a column on how Ghomeshi's departure would affect the CBC. The front-page editors were trying rough designs — no matter what we ended up writing, the fact that one of Canada's top stars was out of a job and had launched a lawsuit against the national broadcaster would be front-page news. Our photo department pulled potential photos of the star to run. Dale Brazao, our investigative stakeout king, went looking for Ghomeshi. Just before we convened to discuss how far we could go in the Monday paper, Ghomeshi's Facebook post went up and made our decision much easier.

Dear everyone,

I am writing today because I want you to be the first to know some news. This has been the hardest time of my life. I am reeling from the loss of my father. I am in deep personal pain and worried about my mom. And now my world has been rocked by so much more. Today, I was fired from the CBC. For almost 8 years I have been the host of a show I co-created on CBC called *Q*. It has been my pride and joy. My fantastic team on *Q* are super-talented and have helped build something beautiful. I have always operated on the principle of doing my best to maintain a dignity and a commitment to openness and truth, both on and off the air. I have conducted major interviews, supported Canadian talent, and spoken out loudly in my audio essays about ideas, issues and my love for this country. All of that is available for anyone to hear or watch. I have known, of course, that not everyone always agrees with my opinions or my style, but I've never been anything but honest. I have doggedly defended the CBC and embraced public broadcasting. This is a brand I've been honoured to help grow.

All this has now changed.

Today I was fired from the company where I've been working for almost 14 years — stripped from my show, barred from the building and separated from my colleagues. I was given the choice to walk away quietly and to publicly suggest that this was my decision. But I am not going to do that. Because that would be untrue. Because I've been fired. And because I've done nothing wrong.

I've been fired from the CBC because of the risk of my private sex life being made public as a result of a campaign of false allegations pursued by a jilted ex-girlfriend and a freelance writer.

As friends and family of mine, you are owed the truth.

I have commenced legal proceedings against the CBC, what's important to me is that you know what happened and why.

Forgive me if what follows may be shocking to some.

I have always been interested in a variety of activities in the bedroom but I only participate in sexual practices that are mutually agreed upon, consensual, and exciting for both partners.

About two years ago I started seeing a woman in her late 20s. Our relationship was affectionate, casual and passionate. We saw each other on and off over the period of a year and began engaging in adventurous forms of sex that included roleplay, dominance and submission. We discussed our interests at length before engaging in rough sex (forms of BDSM). We talked about using safe words and regularly checked in with each other about our comfort levels. She encouraged our roleplay and often was the initiator. We joked about our relations being like a mild form of *Fifty Shades of Grey* or a story from Lynn Coady's Giller Prize–winning book last year. I don't wish to get into any more detail because it is truly not anyone's business what two consenting adults do. I have never discussed my private life before. Sexual preferences are a human right.

Despite a strong connection between us it became clear to me that our on-and-off dating was unlikely to grow into a larger relationship and I ended things in the beginning of this year. She was upset by this and sent me messages indicating her disappointment that I would not commit to more, and her anger that I was seeing others.

After this, in the early spring there began a campaign of harassment, vengeance and demonization against me that would lead to months of anxiety.

It came to light that a woman had begun anonymously reaching out to people that I had dated (via Facebook) to tell them she had been a victim of abusive relations with me. In other words, someone was reframing what had been an ongoing consensual relationship as something nefarious. I learned — through one of my friends who got in contact with this person — that someone had rifled through my phone on one occasion and taken down the names of any woman I had seemed to have been dating in recent years. This person had begun methodically contacting them to try to build a story against me. Increasingly, female friends and ex-girlfriends of mine told me about these attempts to smear me.

Someone also began colluding with a freelance writer who was known not to be a fan of mine and, together, they set out to try to find corroborators to build a case to defame me. She found some sympathetic ears by painting herself as a victim and turned this into a campaign. The writer boldly started contacting my friends, acquaintances and even work colleagues — all of whom came to me to tell me this was happening and all of whom recognized it as a trumped-up way to attack me and undermine my reputation. Everyone contacted would ask the same question, if I had engaged in non-consensual behaviour why was the place to address this the media?

The writer tried to peddle the story and, at one point, a major Canadian media publication did due diligence but never printed a story. One assumes they recognized these attempts to recast my sexual behaviour were fabrications. Still, the spectre of mud being flung onto the internet where online outrage can demonize someone before facts can refute false allegations has been what I've had to live with.

And this leads us to today and this moment. I've lived with the threat that this stuff would be thrown out there to defame me. And I would sue. But it would do the reputational damage to me it was intended to do (the ex has even tried to contact me to say that she now wishes to refute any of these categorically untrue allegations). But with me bringing it to light, in the coming days you will prospectively hear about how I engage in all kinds of unsavoury aggressive acts in the bedroom. And the implication may be made that this happens non-consensually. And that will be a lie. But it will be salacious gossip in a world driven by a hunger for "scandal". And there will be those who choose to believe it and to hate me or to laugh at me. And there will be an attempt to pile on. And there will be the claim that there are a few women involved (those who colluded with my ex) in an attempt to show a "pattern of behaviour". And it will be based in lies but damage will be done. But I am telling you this story in the hopes that the truth will, finally, conquer all.

I have been open with the CBC about this since these categorically untrue allegations ramped up. I have never believed it was anyone's business what I do in my private affairs but I wanted my bosses to be aware that this attempt to smear me was out there. CBC has been part of the team of friends and lawyers assembled to deal with this for months. On Thursday I voluntarily showed evidence that everything I have done has been consensual. I did this in good faith and because I know, as I have always known, that I have nothing to hide. This [is] when the CBC decided to fire me.

CBC execs confirmed that the information provided showed that there was consent. In fact, they later said to me and my team that there is no question in their minds that there has always been consent. They said they're not concerned about the legal side. But then they said that this type of sexual behaviour was unbecoming of a prominent host on the CBC. They said that I was being dismissed for "the risk of the perception that may come from a story that could come out." To recap, I am being fired in my prime from the show I love and built and threw myself into for years because of what I do in my private life.

Let me be the first to say that my tastes in the bedroom may not be palatable to some folks. They may be strange, enticing, weird, normal, or outright offensive to others. We all have our secret life. But that is my private life. That is my personal life. And no one, and certainly no employer, should have dominion over what people do consensually in their private life.

And so, with no formal allegations, no formal complaints, no complaints, not one, to the HR department at the CBC (they told us they'd done a thorough check and were satisfied), and no charges, I have lost my job based on a campaign of vengeance. Two weeks after the death of my beautiful father I have been fired from the CBC because of what I do in my private life.

I have loved the CBC. The Q team are the best group of people in the land. My colleagues and producers and on-air talent at the CBC are unparalleled in being some of the best in the business. I have always tried to be a good soldier and do a good job for my country. I am still in shock. But I am telling this story to you so the truth is heard. And to bring an end to the nightmare.

Ghomeshi almost immediately had one hundred and ten thousand people liking his Facebook posting, and he was soon trending on Twitter.

In the *Star*'s newsroom and newsrooms across the country and, more importantly, in the homes of individual CBC listeners, the effect of this

Facebook posting was the journalistic equivalent of a nuclear bomb. Ghomeshi's carefully prepared statement was shocking to those who read it but for different reasons depending on their point of view. The responses would change by the hour as each new piece of information provoked a different type of comment. The majority of phone calls and messages we received from the public were from women, of all ages.

Before news of the lawsuit broke and the Facebook update was posted, I received dozens of emails like this one:

> I am an avid CBC (radio especially) fan, who believes that Jian Ghomeshi is one of CBC's greatest hosts. I would be so very interested in knowing the reason for his leaving. Perhaps we will never know. My husband and I were shocked and extremely saddened by the news. Such a loss for our special public broadcaster, which is currently being systematically degraded terribly. In our opinion, Jian is an exceptional interviewer, of many interesting guests. He appears to be an honourable, sincere individual, admired by many, including my family. I sincerely hope that our judgment is accurate. We shall miss his enjoyable, thought-provoking contributions on CBC. I trust we shall hear soon that Jian will be back, to continue his good work. I hope there are plenty of supporters for Jian Ghomeshi.

Upon publication of the news that Ghomeshi was suing for $50 million, a reader from Kelowna, British Columbia, contacted me with this comment about the Ghomeshi situation.

"Wow! Smells like Stephen Harper conservatives to me! The CBC is still in Canada isn't it or did it move to the US? Jian speaks out with the highest values and integrity. The CBC has made a big mistake, $50 mil is a lot. Jian will do a lot of good with it. LOL! You can't keep a good man down. He will rise above this even stronger! Thank you for your coverage."

And: "Love the *Star*. Thanks for your reporting re Ford, et al. Now, this Ghomeshi thing. Hope you stay on it. I smell financial irregularity."

With Ghomeshi's Facebook post released at the supper hour on Sunday, the conversation online and my contacts from readers changed. There was targeted anger toward the CBC and people demonstrated, at least for now, how tolerant a society Canada truly is.

"I am horrified at what CBC has done. Do they remember what Pierre Trudeau had to say? CBC is no longer welcome in my house. I am a monthly cash contributor to the CBC and that will end tomorrow. Shame, shame on them. And shame on this woman who is obviously a jilted lover. I hope he sues the ass off CBC and wins."

The most remarkable call I had that afternoon and evening was from a person who knew Lights, the young singer Ghomeshi managed. The caller, who requested anonymity, told me several things. First, he indicated that Ghomeshi was known for hurting women during sex, information we had not yet published. He also said that Ghomeshi was known to tell women he wanted to "hate fuck" them, which was the comment that CBC producer Kathryn Borel had heard. Again, we had not reported that. Finally, and most intriguingly, he said that Ghomeshi had skipped an important meeting that afternoon with Lights. He told me that the next day, Monday, Lights would come out with a statement throwing her full support behind Ghomeshi, her beloved manager. But on Friday, at the end of the week, the man told me, Lights was going to turn her back on Ghomeshi and issue a statement showing she did not support him. I made notes of our conversation, but at least for now, this was just "nice to know" information.

One very important part of the Jian Ghomeshi story puzzle was still missing for the public: at seven p.m. Sunday none of the coverage across the country hinted that Ghomeshi was alleged to have hurt anyone. As evidenced by the fellow who called me, there were whispers, but nothing had been said or written publicly. Instead, the story that was building online was of a human resources travesty, a valued employee fired because he had unusual taste in sex. Only the *Toronto Star* was in a position to alter that narrative. Ghomeshi's Facebook post pulled open the curtain on his enjoyment of rough sex and suggested that his behaviour may be "offensive" to some. He also gave his side of the story, alleging that an ex-girlfriend was spreading lies about him. He said there was no truth in the allegations and no complaints against him. All of these comments by Ghomeshi opened a door for us. It was time to move ahead.

Ten p.m. was the newsroom deadline for tomorrow's print edition, which would give a short window to lawyer and edit the piece, then set it for the presses and an online publication before midnight. Online stories can be posted at any time, but there are times when we release a story on the web at six a.m., when the print edition is delivered. This would not be one of those times. We wanted the story out online as soon as possible, and there was a great deal of work to do to get there. Despite the Facebook post and the lawsuit, the story was still a legal minefield. A tremendous amount of information had to be distilled and formed into a relatively short story very quickly, and that task fell to me. Jesse Brown got to work writing what we call "z copy" — short synopses of information, pulled from we had gleaned over the summer from interviews.

We had to get the story as it had been investigated into the paper, fairly, correctly, and quickly. It had to be written as soon as possible, but it still needed to pass all the tests of the responsible communication defence. The story could not make it seem like Ghomeshi was guilty. Rather, we had to present the information as allegations and be honest about the information we could not prove or did not know. We had to show how diligent we had been in trying to obtain Ghomeshi's side of the story. As soon as the news of his firing broke in the early afternoon, I reached out again to Ghomeshi, his civil lawyers and his public relations company, and the CBC, asking all of them to respond to allegations of violence involving the women we had interviewed. Due to our agreements with the sources, we still could not provide the identities of those making the allegations. Still, we provided all parties with enough information to show them that the claims related to violence — hitting and choking. From Ghomeshi, we already had his summer responses, what he said to me at the TIFF dinner, and most importantly, his Facebook defence. We also reached out to Carly, asking her if there was any truth to the comment in Ghomeshi's Facebook posting that Ghomeshi's "ex" had tried to contact him "to say that she now wishes to refute any of these categorically untrue allegations." Carly denied Ghomeshi's claim.

With input from Jesse Brown, I wrote the front-page story quickly.

Bert Bruser hovered near my desk, providing advice when asked but also making sure I had the time to do the job. The news was out that Ghomeshi was fired, so our story focused on *why* he was fired. Our sources at the CBC, bolstered by the CBC sources of colleagues in the newsroom, told us that the firing decision related to sex allegations and that "consent" was the central theme. Ghomeshi said everything was consensual, and the women alleged it was not. Michael Cooke, Bert Bruser, Jane Davenport, Jesse Brown, and I met for a lawyering session. Tensions that would increase dramatically over the next three days began to emerge. Brown was nervous about the way we were crafting the story and becoming more agitated the closer we came to publication. By ten p.m. the story was being edited, and just after eleven it was off to the presses and posted online. The first line of the story — the "lede" — read:

> CBC star Jian Ghomeshi has been fired over "information" the public broadcaster recently received that it says "precludes" it from continuing to employ the 47-year-old host of the popular *Q* radio show.

That was not news for some, but for our loyal print readers who do not always follow breaking stories online, it would be. The next few paragraphs were news for all readers, particularly these sections, which appeared on the front page before the story turned inside:

"Over the past few months the *Star* has approached Ghomeshi with allegations from three young women, all about 20 years his junior, who say he was physically violent to them without their consent during sexual encounters or in the lead-up to sexual encounters."

We also reported:

"They allege he struck them with a closed fist or open hand; bit them; choked them until they almost passed out; covered their nose and mouth so that they had difficulty breathing; and that they were verbally abused during and after sex."

Michael Cooke wrote a column that ran as a companion piece, in which he tackled the issue of why we had not published the story in the summer, and why we were publishing it now.

The reason the *Star* did not publish a story at that time was because there was no proof the women's allegations of non-consensual abusive sex were true or false. They were so explosive that to print them would have been irresponsible, and would have fallen far short of the *Star*'s standards of accuracy and fairness.

In view of Mr. Ghomeshi's extraordinary statement on Facebook on Sunday evening, and his high public profile in Canada, we now believe it is in the public interest to detail those allegations, which appear to have led directly to his sudden firing from the CBC.

The effect of the story and Cooke's column late on Sunday evening was dramatic. First, the tone of the emails and calls changed dramatically. In a turn that suggested a herd mentality, the general public seemed to go from strongly supportive of Ghomeshi to aggressively angry at him. This email from a woman arrived at 11:45 pm, the beginning of what would become known as a "national conversation" on this important social issue. "Thank you for bringing the matter of Jian Ghomeshi to the attention of the CBC and to *Star* readers," she wrote. "I believe you have done women across this country a great service. I stopped listening to *Q* years ago when it became noticeable to me that this host appeared inappropriately preoccupied with sexual content in unrelated stories. Canadian women deserve a higher standard in a major CBC radio host and I now hope that CBC will stick to its decision." Julie Macfarlane, a law professor from the University of Windsor, emailed a note that further substantiated the importance of the story and the issue: "Thank you for this story, from hundreds and hundreds of frightened women who do not want to come forward for the very same reasons."

Publishing the reason for Ghomeshi's termination had a second result: it signalled to the world that the *Toronto Star* would be interested in learning more. The long-awaited sandwich board was officially on the street.

12

CBC God

Jian Ghomeshi stuffed a suitcase in the back of his car. With a female friend, a long-time confidant, in the passenger seat, he headed down the Queen Elizabeth Expressway towards Buffalo.

As the world he knew was collapsing, the former *Q* host's eyes were fixed south, on Los Angeles. Soon his lawyers would file his suit in Toronto court, and he had said his piece, at least for now, via Facebook. Los Angeles was a favourite destination. He visited often to get away from the grind of his busy job at the CBC, and he had some friends there. As he told his advisers when he was fired, he felt this was a door opening for him, at the same time that another door had closed.

Flying to California would put some much-needed distance between Ghomeshi and the story. The question remained, though: how would he get there without being spotted? His advisers, including the Navigator crisis team, tried to spirit him away on an Air Canada flight as the *Toronto Star* was preparing its story detailing the reasons behind his firing. The hope was to get him on a plane without having to go through the regular security and US customs lines. Now that news of his firing had hit television and radio, it was a certain bet that everyone with an iPhone would document his journey at Toronto's Pearson International Airport. Worse, once news spread across social media that he was on a plane bound for LAX, media from Los Angeles and the paparazzi corps would be waiting at the other end in full force. Social media and its ability to convey information broadly and instantaneously has transformed the news landscape, making it much harder to hide out than in the old days. Though Ghomeshi was no Rob Ford, he was news in America; his show was syndicated there. Air Canada representatives told Ghomeshi's advisers that rules put in place after 9/11 prohibited circumventing regular security. Someone suggested he drive to Buffalo and take a flight from there.

Monday, as the media scoured the city for Ghomeshi, the *Star*'s team in Toronto came up empty-handed. He was not at his house or his mother's house, nor was he at the CBC or the Dentons law offices. A source told us Ghomeshi was in or on his way to Los Angeles, and we were given the name of a hotel, the Sunset Marquis in West Hollywood, where it was believed Ghomeshi had registered; in his high school memoir, Ghomeshi had thanked the Sunset Marquis for putting him up in a rock-and-roll setting while he was writing. *Toronto Star* reporter Tim Alamenciak was on the next flight.

The newsroom pooled its tips and resources so that its man in LA would have the best possible chance of finding the now former *Q* host. For example, Ghomeshi was known to be friends with Ryan Adams, an American singer-songwriter who had been a guest on *Q* over the years. Alamenciak had, with *Star* investigative team member Jesse McLean, located the infamous crack house where Rob Ford partied, and he was perfect for this hound-dog assignment. Alamenciak was armed with telephone numbers for people, all women, whom Ghomeshi was supposed to know in the city.

Why look for him? In the news business, that is akin to asking why people breathe. Realistically, finding Ghomeshi at this stage would only result in a photograph and a terse "no comment." The story developing in Toronto was, in the long term, more important. Yet the need to locate and photograph someone who is at the centre of a news maelstrom remains an imperative part of news coverage. To track Jian Ghomeshi down would be a scoop; plus, whom he was with could prove important to the investigative arc of the story. And yes, we would try and interview Ghomeshi again, though his lawyers were insisting there would be no comment. Judging from the calls and emails rolling in, we would soon have more questions.

Jesse Brown and I were being deluged with tips regarding Jian Ghomeshi's conduct. Many of the allegations we had heard over the summer, and many of the new allegations appeared criminal in nature.

In his Sunday Facebook posting Ghomeshi asked: "If I had engaged in non-consensual behaviour why was the place to address this the media?"

For Carly and Paula, the first two women making allegations, the answer was simple. They had absolutely no intention of coming forward to the authorities. They did not want to have to testify in court and be the target of a sharp, well-paid criminal defence attorney. They did not want to be linked publicly to embarrassing details regarding their conduct with Ghomeshi, perhaps becoming the target of an Internet shaming campaign. Both expressed fear that Ghomeshi would sue them for defamation of character. They wanted the story out with the help of the media, not law enforcement.

The reality is that reporting allegations to the media first is not unusual. Talk to the police, and there is no guarantee that you will not end up on a witness stand. Talk to a reporter, and if the journalist is trustworthy, you can remain a confidential source. As I've said, a newspaper investigation can kick-start a police probe. Ghomeshi's point in his Facebook posting was a relevant one, however, and it certainly resonated with me, the newsroom, and the public. The public typically places a higher value on a law enforcement file than it does on a newspaper story. On Sunday, immediately after Ghomeshi was fired, I contacted Mark Pugash, the well-known and steady spokesman for the Toronto Police. I asked him if the police had any ongoing investigations relating to Ghomeshi. He checked and told me there was no Ghomeshi investigation. I suspected that one would begin shortly.

Over the days that followed, my notebook filled with new allegations. Some of these new cases differed in significant ways from Carly's, involving women who, in many instances, had much briefer relationships with Ghomeshi. I also realized, as the timeline grew, that Carly was just one in a long line of allegations stretching back as far as Ghomeshi's early days at the CBC and even to his time at university. The allegations against him spanned a period of more than fifteen years.

Linda Redgrave was the first to get in touch, sending a brief email to me just after midnight on Sunday. Our story had been online just over an hour.

"Hello, my name is Linda Christina Redgrave and I too was subjected to Jian's abuse. It was winter 2003 and I had met Jian at a CBC Christmas party. I have friends who have known him for many years. He and I went out a couple of times after I went to his show taping of >*play*. I did go to his house the last time I saw him which is where he got extremely violent and there was no forewarning or safe words." She closed with contact information where I could reach her.

I met and interviewed Redgrave the next day at a Starbucks in Toronto's underground. She shared the two incidents, one in December 2002, the other in January 2003, that still haunted her. As soon as she learned of the *Star*'s story, she decided it was time to tell hers. She mused about talking to the police. I said that was up to her. I asked about follow-up contacts she had with Ghomeshi, and she said there were none. The incidents were so upsetting to her that she stayed away from the CBC host. Lucy DeCoutere was the next contact we had. Jesse Brown spoke to her first. Her story was very similar to Redgrave's: she had gone on a date in 2003 and been assaulted. She was the first source who was willing to tell her story with her name attached, a bold step. I questioned both DeCoutere and Redgrave closely about their motivation for coming forward, and I asked why they had not done so at the time of the assault, either to the media or to the police. Redgrave, as noted, was very clear on this point. "At the time I thought, Jian Ghomeshi hit me. I am going to go to the police? What are they going to say? It seemed so easy for me to be made to seem the bad guy."

Redgrave said she moved past her fear because she found strength in the stories, though anonymous, of Carly and others in the first piece we published. She wanted to add her voice. At first, she spoke to the *Star* and other media on condition of anonymity. Later, following the criminal trial, she successfully asked the court to lift the publication ban on her name. When Lucy DeCoutere made her very public statements, she said she had decided to "own" the situation and have full control over it.

Both women would tell their stories first to the *Star*, and then to the CBC. It was apparent to me by the start of that week that CBC was having a tough time reporting on a story that involved one of its own and the organization itself. I received a flurry of calls from producers of *As It*

Happens and other CBC programs who wanted to cover the Ghomeshi story and needed help. I told them I could not provide them with a way to contact alleged victims, but that if they began reporting on the story they would likely hear from some. The producers indicated to me that they were receiving pressure from above to be extraordinarily careful with this legally sensitive story, which involved their own organization. Unless they could get accounts from two alleged victims, they had been told they could not cover the story. All week long, I was repeatedly booked as a guest on CBC shows and then cancelled as CBC journalists worked to track down victims. The CBC did take one significant action that Monday. Two maintenance workers scraped off the twenty-foot-high poster of Ghomeshi adorning the Front Street lobby of the CBC headquarters. People walking through the lobby tweeted photos of the removal.

In the *Star* newsroom, we were working toward a new story, to be published on Thursday. The news was out that four women had made allegations against Ghomeshi — Carly, Paula, Molly, and the still-anonymous Kathryn Borel — but there was still a great deal of pushback from the public. In the same way that the *Toronto Star* had been attacked for using "anonymous" — confidential — sources in the Rob Ford investigation, we were criticized in this case as well. Of course, the women were only anonymous to the public — to the *Star* they were confidential sources, and with good reason, as they were alleging sexual assault. Some members of the public simply did not believe that the allegations could possibly be true. Mississauga lawyer Jia Junaid later wrote in our sister paper, the *Hamilton Spectator*, that at first she did not believe the women who came forward, particularly Carly.

"When I read Ghomeshi's Facebook post, I sided with him, believing that this twenty-something-year-old woman was in fact, as he described, 'a jilted ex-girlfriend,'" Junaid, who describes herself as an "ardent supporter of human rights" and is a survivor of sexual assault herself, explained. She "imagined a scorned ex-lover with an agenda to destroy his reputation." Junaid "pictured [Carly] as a beautiful model or a socialite, maybe someone who didn't get her way and was now spewing defamatory material to get back at him. Maybe she wanted a relationship. Maybe she wanted money. When other women anonymously reported similar sexual attacks by Ghomeshi, I dismissed their claims, largely because they were anonymous and their anonymity somehow made their statements less real and less credible, at least in my mind." Junaid would come to regret her original position, and she told me that it was "personally important" for her to publicly apologize for doubting the original allegations. She did not want to add her voice to those who might blame the victims of Ghomeshi's alleged attacks.

At the *National Post*, columnist Christie Blatchford weighed in, criticizing the *Star* for listening to "anonymous" women and writing a story about their claims. She noted that the *Star* had a "crack team of reporters" on the file but pointed out that we are not "properly trained sex assault investigators." Blatchford, who has equally condemned other investigative work we have done, concluded her missive with these words: "What we have here is another sordid modern tale of bullying; another low water mark in journalism, and another man vilified by anonymous accusers. McCarthyism, anyone?"

Faced with this storm of pushback, the *Star* determined it needed to develop the story further and interview more alleged victims. If they would not go on the record, then we should do our best to provide as much detail as possible so that the public would understand these people were real. For many Ghomeshi supporters and some of his key advisors, two details — a teddy bear and a panini — would eventually cause them to question their loyalty. But as the week got underway, Navigator, rock-it promotions, Chris Taylor, Lights, and Jack Ross were still firmly in the former CBC host's camp. So were Dentons and lawyers Tiffany Soucy and Neil Rabinovitch, who that Monday filed against the CBC a $55 million lawsuit alleging defamation and breach of trust. Judging from the claim, Ghomeshi was particularly angered by the CBC's use of information — the video and texts — he said he provided in good faith to fire him. CBC responded that the suit had no merit and it would seek to have it tossed out of court. Eventually, Ghomeshi dropped the lawsuit, paying the CBC $18,000 in legal costs.

New allegations came to us from across the country. We did our very best to interview the complainants thoroughly, to obtain text and email information to bolster the claims, and to verify and corroborate certain details in each case, such as the time and place of an event. Was Ghomeshi in the city at the time of the allegation? Did he provide any information to the woman that would prove the two had an interaction? The *Star* did all of this with the understanding that in cases of he said/she said it could never present these allegations as anything other than that — allegations. Some allegations came in as telephone calls, others as email contacts. In some cases, I received tips suggesting I contact a person who had a story to tell. That's how the tip came in regarding Jim Hounslow, the former York University Federation of Students official who said Ghomeshi fondled him. A second man also called in with a startlingly similar story from the same time period.

We interviewed a female graduate of the journalism program at the University of Western Ontario, who alleged inappropriate conduct by Ghomeshi when she attended a *Q* taping in 2012. The woman first met Ghomeshi in early 2012, just as she was finishing her studies, when he visited Western to speak. She later saw him again during his fall 2012 book tour. A recent graduate, she told Ghomeshi she was interested in working at *Q*, and he suggested she get in touch with the show's executive producer. That led to her being invited to a taping.

She said in her interview with the *Star* that Ghomeshi, seeing a familiar face in the control room, invited her into his studio after the show. Alone in the room, they chatted about the show, and she recalls Ghomeshi telling her how good she looked. When she was leaving, she said, he asked her, "Aren't you going to give me a hug?" She said Ghomeshi lifted her off the floor in a bear hug. She turned to leave a second time, and she said Ghomeshi came up behind her, placed his hands on her waist, and pressed his body against her backside.

"As I'm walking towards the door, he was behind me, kind of hugging me from behind and walking with me. That's when I thought, whoa, this is kind of a bit much," she said when I interviewed her for a story by *Star* reporters Katrina Clarke, Alyshah Hasham, and me, who were following the university angle. The woman also said that, an hour later, she received a text from Ghomeshi, who asked her if she would meet him for a "non work-related drink" and added a winky face —;)— to the message. She said she would if it would be a "friendly meet up" and that she hoped he could help her get a job. Ghomeshi responded, she said, that he did not want to be a "conduit to a job" and was not interested in a personal friendship. The text messages stopped shortly after that. The woman eventually told Jeremy Copeland, her former journalism professor, what had happened, and Copeland later brought it up with other faculty, in the fall of 2014, when another student listed Q as one of her top three internship choices. Copeland, one of the faculty members who supervises internships, said it was agreed that the student not be placed at Q.

"For her to go down there and have that happen, have someone abuse his authority and position to hit on her in a very strong way, crossing her boundaries, is unacceptable and unprofessional behaviour," Copeland told the *Star*.

One new tip led me to an interview with Janine, a woman with a story from 2003. Like DeCoutere and Redgrave, Janine later testified at Ghomeshi's criminal trial. She wrote an account of the incident, and the story I eventually wrote about her experience was based on her writings and my interview with her. Janine was in her early thirties at the time of the incident, and she knew Ghomeshi from Toronto's arts scene. They dated a few times in the past but had never been intimate. In 2003, Janine ran into Ghomeshi at a music and dance festival in Toronto's Withrow Park, and he asked her to take a walk with him. They stopped to sit on a bench and chat. Ghomeshi suddenly grabbed her shoulders and began kissing her forcefully. Then, she recalled, "he put his hands around my neck and choked me." This was in broad daylight, and Janine was shocked. "He smothered me," she said, and pushed her down on the park bench and "groped" her. "I pushed him away. It really scared me. He was so aggressive," Janine recalled.

"He smothered me. He grabbed my arms, very hard. He bit me. He pushed me down on a park bench and forcefully kissed and groped me. Not once, I should point out, was there ever a conversation about consent," she wrote in a Facebook account.

That week I had spoken to researchers and practitioners of BDSM keen to corroborate and uphold the need for consent in any BDSM play. The people I spoke to said they were upset that something they practised was being maligned by people who had no understanding of the rules.

They put Ghomeshi in that category, since he had raised BDSM in his Facebook posting, though he said he practised it consensually. One man who described himself as a "kinky fellow that is active in the BDSM community," told me that consent is vital to a healthy BDSM relationship. "The way that I do this sort of stuff is looking for enthusiastic consent. If I'm talking to a new partner, I'll ask them what they like. If they like choking I'll explain where it can be dangerous (which becomes informed consent) and the rules I have around it. Usually, I'm looking for a response of 'OMG, I love the feeling of being choked.'" Bottom line: the man, along with other BDSM practitioners and researchers, said that a person agreeing to "being aggressive" does not mean consent. "Forcing anything on someone is straight-up sexual assault," the man told me. Later, when I approached Lord Morpheus for this book, he provided his own thoughts as a sex educator.

"As anyone in the wide, diverse BDSM community can tell you, the very cornerstone of BDSM play is consent. We don't indulge in kinky play without the consent of another. There can be no coercion or begging involved; it must be a consensual exchange of sexual and physical energy. One of the most delicious feelings we can experience in kinky sex is the feeling of surrender, of opening up physically, emotionally, and mentally. With this feeling of exposure comes the responsibility of making sure your partner is experiencing it in a positive way. We can reassure our partners in many ways. Physically, we can offer reassurance during playtime and cool-down, and [we] never underestimate the power of cuddling and holding either before, during or after a scene."

I asked Janine to think over her time with Ghomeshi in the park and recall if there had been any request for consent, or any discussion of what he was going to do. She said no. In a comment that seemed indicative of a pattern with the Q host, Ghomeshi contacted her by text the next day as if nothing had happened. She told me that while she saw Ghomeshi at public entertainment events after the incident, they were never intimate again.

The profile of Ghomeshi I had built in my mind over the summer was changing. It seemed to me that Ghomeshi's behaviour was much more serial in nature than I had originally thought. With just how many women, I wondered, had the former Q host tried his approach? It seemed he had a voracious appetite for meeting new women. Perhaps he was trying his moves on multiple occasions with many partners, looking for ones who would enjoy it his behaviour, or at least tolerate it. With Carly, he maintained a lengthy relationship after selecting her from a crowd. They had become intimate relatively quickly. Paula was different. He chased her for some time before the one incident and then became angered and not tried again. The woman in the stairwell, Molly, whose relationship overlapped with Carly and Paula, had an incident similar to Janine's on the park bench. And judging by the growing number of women with allegations related to the year 2012, it seemed that his book tour, and perhaps his rising celebrity and a feeling that he was untouchable, created a golden opportunity. He seemed to be seeing more women than ever before and increasing his aggressive behaviour toward women. Was the CBC star never worried that someone would make a complaint?

Not all of the women who contacted us alleged violence, but each one added a piece to the puzzle.

Penny was in her late twenties in 2012 when she decided to go hear Jian Ghomeshi speak. This was a big night out for her, a new beginning after a decade of rocky times. As she later told me, she had been raped in her early twenties, battled depression, and seriously contemplated suicide. I was struck by how open she was. Penny said it had taken many years to come to grips with her past.

Penny grabbed the last book and stood in line at the tail end of a queue that was a hundred fans long. "That night I remember I felt a really positive energy," she told me. "I was working again, a good job, and when I got to the front of the line I felt this look on me, his eyes, and I could instantly tell he was attracted to me. I could tell he felt my positive energy."

Penny and her sister, who was with her that night, posed for photos with Ghomeshi, who insisted on putting his head very close to hers in the picture. Penny's sister remarked she felt like a "third wheel." The *Q* host asked for Penny's name and inquired where she worked. Penny said those questions seemed natural. She left at eleven p.m. and headed home. Talking to a famous radio host was exciting. A good night all around, and she was glad she got out of the house. The next day her job was taking her to New York on a very early flight. An hour after she arrived home, as she was getting ready for bed, her cellphone rang.

"Hi, it's Jian. What are you doing?"

Penny almost dropped the phone. Ghomeshi explained that he had Googled her name and company and found her cell number online. "He told me he felt I had good energy and he wanted to meet me somewhere." That a celebrity had telephoned Penny was a significant event in her life and made her feel even better about herself. She explained she could not see him that night, so he suggested a rendezvous in November when he had another book event in a city several hours' drive from her home.

"We can hang out," Ghomeshi suggested. Penny agreed. Over the next month they exchanged "flirty" text messages. She was nervous, anxious, and excited to see him at the arranged event and made plans to stay with a cousin. Ghomeshi was staying at a hotel.

"You look great," Ghomeshi said, greeting her in the lobby. Ghomeshi explained he had spent hours finding the perfect restaurant. They walked to it, a short distance from the hotel. They sat at a table and ordered a bottle of red wine. The chef asked Ghomeshi to come to the kitchen for a tour and he left Penny, waiting, wondering what the night would bring. When he returned she began telling him about her life and some of her struggles. As a fan of Q, she imagined he was a good person to share her thoughts with.

"He had no empathy, though, for me. He was supposed to be so worldly, but I found him closed-minded when discussing my issues. We talked about anxiety, but when I told him I do not take meds, he completely tuned out." She said Ghomeshi became quite angry during their dinner.

"What's your deal? Are you cold and jaded?" he asked her, referencing her flirty texts over the past month and how standoffish he felt she was at dinner. He insisted she must be twenty-six, though she was in her late twenties. He criticized her hair, which was up that night, not long and flowing as it had been the first time they had met. But when the appetizers arrived, Ghomeshi pulled his chair to her side of the table and started kissing her. She resisted, reminding him that they were in public and barely knew each other. After dinner, she walked back to the hotel with him. Against her better judgment, she went up to his room. It was a regular-sized room, and Ghomeshi remarked that he normally "gets a suite."

Ghomeshi fiddled with his iPod and put on one of his favourite bands, Spoons. She said his mood improved immediately. I made a note. Carly and other women had mentioned his love of that band.

"I am so excited to share this music with you," he told Penny, sitting close to her in a chair and asking her again if she was twenty-six. He tried to take down her hair and began kissing her. Penny said she pushed him away, laughing.

"Someone who laughs when you try to kiss them is just being malicious," Ghomeshi said. "You know, I almost cancelled on you. I know a lot of people in [this city]. I could have been with anyone tonight. What would you do if I had cancelled?"

Penny became extremely uncomfortable and left. Outside the hotel she stopped, took out her phone, and sent out a tweet: "I went on a date with @jianghomeshi and I don't think he likes me."

Ghomeshi texted her within a few minutes. "I don't like my personal life being discussed."

Penny apologized and deleted the tweet. Over the next few days they exchanged texts. Penny told him she was sorry about how the evening deteriorated. "Good luck on your book tour, you deserve it!" she wrote.

Ghomeshi's last text to her put the blame on Penny.

"Well I'm not sure what was going on but it made me feel really shit. At one point I just felt ridiculous. Why was I, a grown man, taking someone to a nice dinner who was showing very little indication of wanting to know me or even be friends? It was pretty lousy. If you are more forthcoming and sweet to others all power to you (and them!). I'm sure you can be very charming and you're super cute. But sadly — since you're continuing to discuss this — i'd think it better for my self-esteem to avoid you. :) all the best."

Penny's story was not one of abuse, but it was instructive. It did not form part of the main stories we were producing, but it helped me understand Ghomeshi's character. The man was struggling with issues of depression and anxiety, and despite his fame, he desperately wanted to be liked. The women who spent time with him described him as a master manipulator and a narcissist.

One of the young women I interviewed that week, Beth, told me that when she met Ghomeshi she "felt like Jian was CBC God." I underlined her comments in my notepad. Beth's description would become a prominent part of a story we published that week, and it went to the heart of the problems that Janice Rubin's scathing report on the broadcaster identified as the "host culture" that allowed Ghomeshi to get away with his bad behaviour for so long. (The CBC commissioned the Rubin report shortly after the Ghomeshi story broke. Rubin, an employment lawyer and expert in workplace harassment, was assigned the task of investigating allegations of harassment, discrimination, violence, or other inappropriate workplace conduct at *>play* and *Q* during Ghomeshi's time on those shows. "Host culture" describes an environment where the host is boss and those around him feel they have no choice but to be obedient.)

Beth was another twenty-something woman whom Ghomeshi met on his 2012 book tour. She was a CBC producer in a Canadian city but was, as she put it, "a real fan [who] really, really wanted to work on *Q*." CBC featured Ghomeshi on a local show, and Beth heard he was doing a book signing. At the local venue, she found a long line of fans. She toughed it out, just as Carly, Penny, and Molly had in other parts of the country.

When Beth presented her book for signing, she leaned in and told Ghomeshi that she worked at the CBC and wanted to work at *Q*. "He was so nice," she remembered. They exchanged telephone numbers, and Ghomeshi invited Beth to join him and some friends for drinks later that evening. He said it would be an opportunity for her to meet some others from the CBC. Beth went to the lobby of the hotel where he was staying and waited. Ghomeshi showed up alone, telling her he had "lost" his friends. He hugged her, holding the embrace longer and more firmly than she felt was appropriate.

"This isn't a professional meeting," Ghomeshi told her. It was dark out, about nine o'clock. They walked to a local pub and sat in a booth. Ghomeshi asked her a lot of questions about her job. He sat close to her and began rubbing her legs with both of his hands, explaining, "I have anxiety. Touching helps."

Looking into her eyes, Ghomeshi said, "There's something about you. You are coming to Toronto to spend the weekend with me."

Beth was both flattered and taken aback. Her mind was racing. "I want to work for you, not date you."

Ghomeshi replied, "The two worlds can co-exist. I've done it before."

During their conversation that night, she said Ghomeshi revealed that he had previously dated CBC producers and at least one of them enjoyed having rough sex. In an even more unusual comment, Beth said Ghomeshi described how one woman told him she felt like she was being raped every time they had sex. (I was unable to verify either of these allegations.) Leaving the pub, they walked to a Tim Hortons and shared a panini. They walked back to his hotel at about one a.m. Beth said Ghomeshi explained he had dry contact lenses and had to go up to his room to take them out.

"I felt like a big moron," she said. "I should have seen it coming." Ghomeshi used the bathroom, saying he had to at least splash water on his contacts. She used the bathroom after him and came out to find that he had dimmed the lights. She said Ghomeshi then roughly threw her against the wall and kissed and fondled her forcefully. She told him, "I don't want to do this. I want to work for you." To herself she said, "Don't insult him; don't ruin your chance of getting a job at his show."

She said Ghomeshi got her on to the bed, pinned her there with his weight, and told her, "Don't worry, we don't have to have sex." Beth said she performed fellatio on the Q host "just to get out of there." He never struck her, never choked her.

After the oral sex, Beth, who had remained clothed, began to cry and said she was leaving. As she left, she heard Ghomeshi call out, "I'll talk with my executive producer [Arif Noorani] about you."

Beth said she went home, feeling "gross" and "used." The next morning, she received a text from Ghomeshi.

"Happy Thursday!" read the text. Ghomeshi told her that he had spoken to Noorani on her behalf. Noorani contacted her and invited her for an interview. Beth did some checking and booked her interview for a day when she was certain Ghomeshi would not be at the studio. When she walked into the Q offices, however, Ghomeshi was there.

The interview took place between Noorani and Beth. The executive producer told her that he could give her some "casual" production work on *Q*, but she would have to live in Toronto. Beth left the CBC building. Ghomeshi texted her as soon as she was out the door. "You look sexier than ever," he wrote and invited her for drinks that night. She declined.

Beth said a friend suggested she make a complaint to the CBC, their mutual employer. She did not, deciding that she had gone willingly to his room and that "it didn't feel like rape." In retrospect, she understands that this was a clear case of sexual harassment, given that Ghomeshi had indicated he might be able to improve her career with a job at *Q*. Going up against the "CBC God" was not something she wanted to do. Beth left the CBC soon after the incident.

As this part of our investigation deepened, I was dealing with a controversy of my own creation. I had used the descriptor "educated and employed" to describe the four women who initially told their story of alleged abuse. This was my doing, not Jesse Brown's, and I took and take full responsibility for that phrase. My intention, since we had promised not to identify the women, was to explain to the reader a bit about who they are. Each source had different concerns—some said we could mention their city but not their line of work. Others said we could not give their exact age. Generally, our source agreement did not allow me to be specific about where they worked or had recently attended university. They all had jobs, and they all had significant education credentials, which is why I wrote that line. That's not how literally hundreds of angry readers took it. The emails and calls rolled in within a few minutes of the story being published:

"Your line makes it seem as though claims made by educated, employed women should be taken more seriously than those made by unemployed, uneducated women," wrote one woman. Another: "I query why it would matter that these women were employed or educated. Would that make them more likely to be lying or telling the truth? Or perhaps the violence harder to justify? This rides the edge of victim blaming."

Flare magazine responded that afternoon with a critical online story, focusing more on those few words than on the *Star*'s investigation and what it had revealed. I understand how the line could be interpreted. However, I have done investigations in the past that revealed the abuse of people who were unemployed and, due to a wide range of circumstances, had very little education. In both cases, I described the victims as they were, which is to me appropriate and fair. My goal was to be descriptive, not to pass judgment.

With each new allegation in those first few days came a duty to try to get Ghomeshi's side. I provided written questions to Ghomeshi's lawyers and contacted executive producer Arif Noorani, but they did not respond. On the overall issue of the CBC's response, the *Star*'s Jacques Gallant was the go-to reporter, pushing CBC brass every day for interviews, trying to find out what management knew about Ghomeshi and when. The CBC had already acknowledged to me that it had been aware of the severity of what we were exploring as soon as I sent the original allegations to Ghomeshi in late June; it just had not believed the allegations.

In covering the developing story, Gallant found CBC public affairs chief Chuck Thompson "generally quick and helpful" in his responses. But Gallant was critical of the CBC executive team above Thompson. "The CBC never granted the *Star*'s multiple requests for interviews with ex-head of radio Chris Boyce and executive vice-president of English services Heather Conway," he noted. Both spoke to other media, but not the *Star*.

As the story continued to develop, a question I was often asked in the newsroom, by both male and female reporters, was why women whom Ghomeshi accosted did not simply tell him to, as one woman said, "screw off the moment he tried something."

Some did. Jim Hounslow had, back at York. One of the women who would not stand for Ghomeshi's rough moves was Darlene. In 2006, she was in her early twenties and working at the CBC. She met Ghomeshi, who was about to begin working on the new *Q* show, at a CBC Christmas party. He zeroed in on her and struck up a conversation. He suggested she meet him for a drink one evening downtown. Darlene did not like this suggestion. She told Ghomeshi that she lived with her parents in the north part of Toronto. If he wanted a drink, he could come up to her area. He did, and they went to a pub near her parents' home.

Leaving the pub, they walked back to Ghomeshi's black and red Mini. Darlene said that with no warning, Ghomeshi "put his hands around my throat and pushed me against the car. He was choking me."

Darlene pushed him back roughly. "What the fuck? I have three brothers."

"Your loss," Ghomeshi said as he pulled out his keys, slid into his car, and sped off.

Darlene, stunned, started walking. Her cellphone rang. It was Ghomeshi.

"I am driving really fast on the highway and I am under a lot of stress right now and if I crash it will be your fault."

"I told him to calm down," Darlene recalled. Ghomeshi hung up. "I closed the book on him." She thought Ghomeshi "acted like that because he was in the public eye and well known and felt he could do no wrong."

Jesse Brown was in and out of the newsroom working on the story and also dealing with *Canadaland* business, which was booming, thanks to the Ghomeshi stories in the *Star*. His Twitter profile jumped from ten thousand followers pre-Ghomeshi to thirty-one thousand in the months right after the Ghomeshi story. In timing that was pure coincidence, just before the Ghomeshi exposé was published in the *Star*, Brown announced that he was starting a campaign to crowd-fund, encouraging his listeners to donate money with the promise of being named on the show for donating as little as four dollars a month. He went from eight hundred donors prior to the Ghomeshi story to over two thousand. Listeners who donated ten dollars a month were rewarded with a T-shirt and a book. In the months that followed, *Canadaland*'s audience continued to grow, a sign of an increasing appetite for independent media criticism.

Late that Wednesday afternoon, we finished the story for the Thursday paper that included information from DeCoutere, Redgrave, some of the other new cases, and also delved more deeply into the original cases. We convened around five p.m. to lawyer the story with Jesse Brown, Bert

Bruser, Michael Cooke, Jane Davenport, and city editor Irene Gentle, who was very much involved in the story from that point. We sat down with printouts of the story draft.

Although this was the second time we had lawyered a story with him, Jesse Brown was still struggling with the hierarchy at the *Star*. While we had collaborated on the draft, I had again taken the lead on the writing, given the time pressure we were under. As the meeting opened, Brown loudly raised questions about the story as written, identifying problems big and small that he didn't want in a draft he was involved in creating. The meeting quickly grew uncomfortable.

"Jesse," I said when I felt enough time had passed, "this is their meeting." I pointed to Bert, Michael, Jane, and Irene. "We are the reporters. They ask us the questions."

Brown was clearly angry, but he got the message. We went through the story, which was a long piece with plenty of detail. It was a time-consuming process. Bruser asked how many of these new allegations had been presented to Ghomeshi. I told him that as they had come in this week, I had gone back to Ghomeshi's lawyers and provided written questions relating to as much of the allegations as we were allowed to reveal, given the source issues. As for DeCoutere, we had her permission to name her in the story and in our requests for comment. At the time, Redgrave had not given permission to use her name, nor had others we had spoken to.

When I first learned about Big Ears Teddy and how Ghomeshi would allegedly face the stuffed animal toward some women and away from others during his aggressive sex play, I wanted that to form part of the story. After all, the fake Twitter account used to pressure Ghomeshi bore his teddy bear's name. Brown, as we went through the copy, was concerned about the inclusion and placement of descriptions of the bear watching or not watching sex acts. He believed that doing so would trivialize the serious allegations. I argued, with backup of the *Star* team at the table, that this misuse of a "comfort bear" was a key detail that revealed a great deal about Ghomeshi's personality. The detail stayed in, up high, though I removed a second reference to the bear later in the story at Brown's request. The bear's existence would spark much online discussion in coming days as readers speculated it contained a hidden camera. That speculation was never resolved. The bear itself, Ghomeshi told people at *Q* and some of his female friends, was lost in early 2014 with some luggage on an Air Canada flight.

The partnership between the *Star* and Brown was uneasy at best, and growing volatile. Throughout this session, Brown argued aggressively on behalf of Carly and Paula, particularly Carly. He considered them to be his sources, not our sources or the *Star*'s sources, and from his point of view, he was in a partnership with them. He had never been comfortable with asking them tough questions, a sore point between us. We also differed about encouraging sources to come forward publicly, resulting in conflict when I said in a *Star* video explaining our investigation that, despite "our best attempts," the original women we interviewed declined public identification; Brown issued a tweet to make it clear that he never encouraged any source to use her real name. He also did things that I did not think belonged in an investigation where all moves and comments might one day be dissected in a courtroom. One evening, for example, for reasons I never understood, he tweeted a photograph of the back of my office chair—which, like all *Star* chairs, has the reporter's name on it—with the suggestion he was "working late with Kevin Donovan." On another occasion while he was still working for the *Star* and on a day I thought was going well, he gave an interview to *Toronto Life* in which he said his relationship with me was "unspooling." Managing editor Jane Davenport acknowledged the difficult working relationship with Brown but told me later she recognized that at times when we were playing devil's advocate on the allegations and the story, Brown had a different approach.

"On a human level, I also felt that he fundamentally believed his sources and treated their stories as if he had been entrusted with them. I think this put him in a difficult position on a team operating with different objectives and with sometimes different journalistic values."

The second investigative story went live online just before ten p.m. Wednesday night. It began: "Eight women from across Canada now accuse former CBC host Jian Ghomeshi of abusive behaviour ranging from allegations of beating and choking without consent, to workplace sexual harassment." The story introduced Lucy DeCoutere and quoted both her and other women speaking out about their experience.

When the story went live, I was sitting in the middle of the newsroom with Bert Bruser, discussing where to go next on the investigation. I heard a shout from the end of the newsroom where the investigative team sits, and where I had left Jesse Brown a few minutes before. Looking up, I saw Brown barrelling towards us.

Brown passed us all in a dead run and strode inside Michael Cooke's office. He stormed around Cooke's desk, and there was an altercation of some sort. Cooke said he stood up and there was some sort of "chest bump," which he immediately regretted.

At the same time, our web desk discovered a problem: Brown's byline was not on the story. The problem was a system glitch that happened when a staff reporter (in this case me) had his byline blended with a freelance byline (Brown). The latter has to be separately coded, and this hadn't been done. We had a similar problem with the first story I did with Brown, but only on the mobile version of the story. This time it was the online story. The print edition, produced separately, was not affected.

Even as the alert web desk was on the case, Brown left Cooke's office, Cooke in hot pursuit, to complain to the editors who were fixing the problem. I sent out a tweet, and so did Cooke, alerting the world that Jesse Brown was the co-author of the story. We fixed the byline issue quickly, and over the next thirty minutes Brown and Cooke argued via email. Later, in an email interview for this book, Brown said he understood the byline issue was a "glitch" that was sorted out quickly.

The next morning, Brown returned to work full time on his podcast. "Please know that this decision has little to do with the friction we experienced with each other on a personal level," he wrote in an email. "I have great esteem for each of you. I learned an incredible amount and I consider it a privilege and a career highlight to have worked with you. Sincerely, Jesse."

Brown would do his own soul-searching in weeks to come. After all, he had heard of issues with Ghomeshi as far back as 2007 and had done nothing. In an interview with the radio host known as Ed the Sock, he said that after the story broke, he felt remorse and wondered if he should have done something when his friend Kathryn Borel first told him her story. "When she was sexually harassed by Ghomeshi, I knew about it," Brown said on the show. "There's all this talk about people who looked the other way, who knew what was going on and did nothing. I was one of those people. I knew this was happening to my friend." Brown, who was at CBC at the time, said he could not have gone to management: "I would have been fired."

Though Brown did not work for Ghomeshi, he had through his friend Borel encountered the host culture. Would Brown have been fired? Likely not. Should he have done something more for his friend? Possibly, though it is not clear that his speaking up would have altered the situation. As the Rubin report found, "there was a belief that as a host, Mr. Ghomeshi was somehow exempt from the behavioural standard" of the national broadcaster. This had the effect of making people at the CBC "less assertive in terms of pursuing formal complaints." Further, Rubin found that "management knew or ought to have known" of Ghomeshi's conduct and failed to take steps to ensure "that the workplace was free from disrespectful and abusive conduct." In its most damning statement, the Rubin report stated: "It is our conclusion that the CBC management condoned this behaviour."

Thursday morning, our story was on the street. The *Q* guest host parachuted in for the day opened the show's segment, a slight tremor in her normally steady voice.

"Hi, I'm Piya Chattopadhyay. It is Thursday, October 30, 2014. We're reading what you're reading. We're hearing what you're hearing. It is tough. And we want to thank you for being here. We are *Q*." The upbeat theme music tried, unsuccessfully, to shudder away the emotion.

In Los Angeles, *Star* reporter Tim Alamenciak had come up empty-handed, through no fault of his own. Ghomeshi had made a two-day booking at the Sunset Marquis for Monday, October 27, but then cancelled. After a day or two with friends, he flew back to Toronto and drove out to Minden, Ontario, to a cottage owned by Toronto entertainment mogul Jeffrey Latimer, whose clients had appeared on *Q* over the years. Ghomeshi had called him the previous Sunday asking if he could stay at the Minden retreat as a favour. As the *Star*'s Mary Ormsby and Dale Brazao determined, Ghomeshi stayed on his own in the secluded cottage for several days before returning to Toronto.

Joining Lucy DeCoutere as the only named woman making an allegation against Ghomeshi, Toronto lawyer Reva Seth wrote an account, with her name attached, of her attack. It was published in the *Huffington Post* under the heading, "Why I Can't Remain Silent About What Jian Did to Me." In a follow-up interview that Thursday with the *Huffington Post*, Seth, a mother of three, explained she was motivated to write her piece after DeCoutere came forward and asked women not to be afraid to tell their own stories. "After much thought, I decided to answer her call."

The combined effect of the *Star's* new story providing the intimate and specific allegations of eight women, Reva Seth's account, and the barrage of online discussion had an instant effect on Ghomeshi's stalwart advisers. In the twenty-four hours that followed, one after another, the people who had stood by Ghomeshi for months dropped him.

Debra Goldblatt-Sadowsky, who had been with Ghomeshi since he started his run at CBC, had been inundated all week with questions from the media. On Friday, she and rock-it promotions announced they had cut ties with Ghomeshi. "Going forward, rock-it promotions will no longer be representing Jian Ghomeshi. We won't be responding to or receiving media requests." Navigator issued a similarly terse statement: "The circumstances of our engagement have changed and we are no longer able to continue."

Jack Ross, the agent who discovered Ghomeshi busking for coins back in his university days, was also out. A source called to tell me that Ross quietly, with no news release, dropped Ghomeshi's name from his website's client list.

Lawyer Chris Taylor dropped his public association with Ghomeshi.

Lights released a second statement, as I had been told she would. "I posted comments about Jian Ghomeshi the day after he was dismissed by CBC where I rushed to defend my manager of twelve years," the singer wrote. "I am now aware that my comments appear insensitive to those impacted and for that I am deeply sorry. This is to confirm that as of now

I will be parting ways with Jian Ghomeshi as my manager. I hope everyone can heal from this. Lights."

One of Ghomeshi's advisers later explained what happened as the week developed. "Everyone bought his story that there was a crazy girlfriend trying to destroy him. But as more and more stories came out, with details like the panini and the weird stuff with the teddy bear, things changed. Ultimately, Jian Ghomeshi was a guy we all believed in, and it didn't turn out that way. So we all left."

Ghomeshi, having returned from the cottage retreat, went to see Eddie Greenspan, arguably the most famous trial lawyer in Canada. Ghomeshi visited Greenspan not to hire him but to ask whom he should hire if he needed a criminal lawyer. Greenspan, who died later in the year, told Ghomeshi his best bet was to hire his former law partner, Marie Henein.

Just before the dinner hour on Friday, eight days after Ghomeshi's civil lawyer showed the video to startled CBC executives, Toronto Police announced it had begun an investigation into sexual assault allegations involving the former *Q* host. Detectives put out the word that they were interested in speaking to anyone who had information. At an impromptu news conference, Chief Bill Blair said that until a complainant came forward, there could be no active probe.

"When these crimes are committed, we need a complainant, we need someone to come forward and say, 'this is what's happened to me,' and we will investigate that and we will do that as quickly and compassionately as we possibly can." In comments that would foreshadow the difficult road ahead for police and complainants, Blair told reporters he understands there are "many circumstances" in which a complainant would be reluctant to speak to police. He renewed this call the following week, saying that if complainants "come forward to police, they will be treated with respect, they will be treated professionally, and they will be treated with care." The sex crimes unit of Toronto Police was handling the case, Blair told reporters. Two women came forward overnight: Lucy DeCoutere and Linda Redgrave.

Watching these events unfold, I could not help but wonder how many of the others I had spoken to would come forward, either to the police or to other media, and how many other complainants were out there. Those who did come forward to police would be asked all sorts of questions, or at least I assumed they would be. Why did you return to Ghomeshi after an incident? Did you flirt with him before? After? Is there an electronic record of your relationship? The rules of disclosure in Canadian criminal law are such that if charges are laid, Crown counsel has to turn over all information it obtains to the defence team. The women I spoke to had deleted much of their electronic communication. But I knew there was one person who did not delete: Jian Ghomeshi.

13

"One More Young Woman"

Sue Montgomery was in an enviable position. In an industry starved for jobs, teetering on what doomsayers warned was annihilation, she was a newspaper reporter, and an accomplished one, for Quebec's leading English-language newspaper, the *Montreal Gazette*. She had been front and centre at many big stories over the years, reporting from South Africa, Botswana, Angola, Rwanda, Thailand, Cuba, and Haiti, where she covered the 2004 coup and the 2010 earthquake. Her stories chronicling sexual abuse at schools and other institutions run by the Brothers of the Holy Cross had won her the 2009 Beyond Borders award from an organization dedicated to stopping child exploitation. I had known Montgomery when she worked as a summer intern at the *Star* in the late 1980s. Now age fifty-four, in the fall of 2014 she was covering the sensational trial of Luka Magnotta, accused of murdering and dismembering Lin Jun, a Chinese national studying engineering at Concordia University, but she was also following the Ghomeshi story. After a conversation with Antonia Zerbisias, a friend and columnist at the *Toronto Star*, Montgomery sent out a powerful tweet using the hashtag #BeenRapedNeverReported.

Montgomery and her husband had two teenaged children and a busy life. She insisted on teaching their kids certain lessons, lessons informed by a difficult personal past. She taught them that their bodies were their own. Should anything untoward happen, they must speak out. "If anyone touches you or threatens you in any way you have to tell us, you have to tell someone," Montgomery would tell her children.

As a young adult, Montgomery found the courage to tell her family and the police about the sexual abuse she and her sister had suffered between the ages of four and nine at the hands of their grandfather — and to confront their abuser. On one unforgettable day she stopped the car, full of her siblings and parents on their way home from the family cottage on the shores of southern Lake Huron, to march up the driveway to her grandfather's house and confront him. She and her sister had already reported their grandfather to the police in the sleepy town of St. Mary's, where he was a well-known and well-liked citizen involved the local church community. A senior local police official, who knew her grandfather well, was incredulous: "What, Arch?" The case went nowhere. Her family was supportive but powerless.

Arch Montgomery was sitting when she came in the door that late summer day. She recalls the conversation was brief and forceful.

"Granddad, I have stuff to say to you," she started. He immediately cut her off.

"You are a goddamn liar!" Arch hollered.

His wife, Montgomery's grandmother, looked at her, red-faced but resolute. "Well, you'll never be a virgin when you get married," she said.

The grandmother's remark was so bizarre that it stopped Montgomery cold. Turning to leave, she had one parting shot. "God knows what you did, I know what you did, you will rot in hell." The next time she and her sister saw Arch, he was in a casket at his funeral.

Montgomery experienced a second assault, when she worked as a flight attendant before she became a reporter. After an overnight from Toronto to Frankfurt, Germany, she was in her hotel room, changing out of her uniform to go out for a beer with a male colleague, when he knocked at the door. She let him in, and he was immediately aggressive. She was twenty-one; he was in his mid-thirties.

"He attacked me. It was so sudden. I figured I must have given him the wrong signals. The next thing I knew he was holding me down. I was so embarrassed. I was confused. I had let him into my room."

Her recollection of the events is honest and open. Thirty years later there is still a cloud of pain. She said the flight attendant undressed her. "I am going to fuck you!" he yelled.

"Look, I did not fight back. I remember his eyes, like a wolf's eyes. There was penetration, and he said horrible things to me." Her experiences with her grandfather "allowed me to go other places in my mind," she said. "At a certain point in that room I decided, 'let's just get this over with.'"

He left. Montgomery tried to sleep, but she could not. She was a wreck. The next morning at the hotel breakfast, her attacker ignored her "as if I did not exist." Montgomery did not report the attack. She needed the job to pay her university bills and was "seriously afraid I would lose my job if I told this story about him."

The stories of the women who had spoken up about Ghomeshi's behaviour inspired Montgomery to take action. It offended her how people, men and women both, did not understand the many factors that conspire to prevent victims of sexual assault from going to the police or telling their stories publicly. When she thought of people she had met who struggled with disclosure, Montgomery wondered when the tide would turn and what it would take to make a difference.

"It's like piles of brush were gathered all over the world just waiting for someone to light a match," Montgomery said in an interview months later.

Montgomery lit the match with a text message to Antonia Zerbisias the Thursday afternoon that the *Star* published the story detailing the eight women who were alleging abuse. The story raised issues that struck a chord with both journalists, and Montgomery told Zerbisias it was time to remove the stigma and encourage people to speak up. "Enough already!" She proposed starting a list — "I was raped and didn't report it" — and seeing how many names they got. "I'll start with my name," Montgomery offered.

Zerbisias joined Montgomery, saying she had been raped in 1969 and again in 1970. Before posting, both women took a deep breath. "My heart is pounding," Montgomery texted.

#BeenRapedNeverReported was a global Internet phenomenon, which a Twitter expert estimated reached, through tweets and retweets and views of the hashtag, nearly eight million people in the first two days. People all over the world, in many languages, began to share their stories. It was painful, but as Montgomery had hoped, it was positive. While reporting on the Ghomeshi story, I watched the social media response to

Montgomery's tweet snowball, as one after another person tweeted an explanation for silence. "Because even my 'friends' told me I shouldn't cause I would ruin HIS life," read one. Another: "because when you're young and no one really believes you anyway."

It was heartening to see that such a distasteful story as the Ghomeshi allegations could be a touchstone — so many people who had kept secret a difficult part of their lives were now empowered to come forward. Two women had an idea, and social media gave that idea a platform: a safe space for people to tell the world what had happened to them. Twitter, it seemed, was making it harder for people to ignore the very real issues of sexual assault and rape.

On March 4, 2015, Women's College Hospital, which runs the Sexual Assault and Domestic Violence Care Centre, the first hospital-based program in Ontario to provide emergency care and counselling to survivors of sexual and domestic violence, hosted a panel discussion called Beyond the Headlines: How High-profile Cases are Drawing Attention to the Complex Issues Surrounding Violence Against Women. The moderator for the dinner-hour event was Valerie Taylor, the psychiatrist-in-chief in the Department of Medicine at the hospital. The panel, Taylor announced, was an effort to "move the conversation forward." The event was put on in conjunction with International Women's Day.

The elephant in the room that night was the looming Jian Ghomeshi criminal trial, eventually set for February 2016. In November 2014, after Toronto Police Chief Bill Blair called for complainants to come forward, police laid a series of charges involving six women; charges related to two women were dropped before trial. The allegations in the four remaining cases were not the most severe of the cases I was aware of, but they seemed clear-cut. These complainants did not have long-term relationships, or appear to have had much or any follow-up contact with Ghomeshi, that would muddy the waters of a criminal trial. At least, that was what they told me and other media when first interviewed.

Of approximately one hundred people in the room that night, I was one of only four men. I shared the panel with Nneka MacGregor, a survivor of sexual assault and the executive director of the Women's Centre for Social Justice, and Catherine Classen, a psychologist who leads the trauma therapy program at Women's College. We each gave ten minutes of opening remarks; Nneka MacGregor spoke about the power structures that often prevent women from telling their stories. Then, for the next two hours, one woman after another rose to tell her story of abuse at the hands of a man. Grief counsellors were present, prepared to provide comfort to anyone who needed a reprieve, though MacGregor was always first on her feet to offer a hug and consolation. It was a very emotional evening, and it ran longer than anticipated because so many people wanted to be heard.

There was a great deal of anger in the room: anger at the abusers for what they had done, anger at "the system" for allowing the abuse to happen—and anger at the media, too. I was the only journalist present. Vocal audience members told me that reporters were wrong to use the word "alleged" to speak of assaults against women and should instead use the word "said." The word "alleged," Catherine Classen argued, "conveys that the reporter may question the truth of the event, whereas using 'said' is neutral." MacGregor took issue with the word "choked" to describe the allegations in the Ghomeshi stories. She said she would prefer "strangled."

"In the Jian Ghomeshi case, they call it 'choking.' Choking means something radically different from strangling. And how when you talk about it as choking it tends to minimize. Strangulation is what he was doing. Choking is very different. When you call one the other . . . you're not actually explaining the high-risk nature of the act. For us, language is important and language matters."

I tried to explain the importance of due process and the concept of innocent until proven guilty, the role of responsible journalism in this type of story, and to clarify that I used the words the women used—choked, not strangled—but more than anything, the women present wanted to be heard. They wanted the audience to understand what they had been subjected to, because they believed that it would help the greater cause of reducing sexual violence committed by men against women. As one after another speaker took the microphone, I thought of two women who reached out to the *Star* after the initial week of Ghomeshi stories. Both had terrible tales to tell. The first, Kim, was thoughtful and poised as she explained the circumstances that led to the incidents with Ghomeshi, and she seemed to have a coping mechanism that had allowed her to process the situation and begin to heal. The second woman, Cindy, was the complete opposite.

Kim contacted me after a great deal of soul-searching and prior to Ghomeshi's arrest.

> After contemplating, obsessing, and not sleeping for a week straight, I'd like to share my experience with Jian Ghomeshi, whom I dated for a month shortly after moving to Toronto from my home turf [removed]. It was in 2011 — I was [mid-twenties]. There was assault, there was bad behaviour, there was a lack of respect for myself as a woman and a human. My account would have to remain anonymous.
>
> As a news story, this reveal has been consuming me — so many of the accounts shared by the women who've come forward read like my own. Some are worse than mine. As more and more comes out, I feel the need to add my own "piece to the puzzle." Not sure why exactly or what more it can bring. I've been carrying this stuff around for 4 years now and a lot of it got suppressed. I can't tell you the emotional stir I've felt through all the news and updates, though. I had no idea of the extent and serial aspect of Jian. It is very unnerving. It makes sense. I don't want one more young woman to be preyed on by him. What yourself, Jesse, and the *Star* team are doing is incredible work. I can't even tell you...

Kim would not come forward as a named person, but she wanted her story known so that, as she said in her first note, not "one more young woman" would fall under the former CBC host's spell.

One more young woman: that comment really resonated. I had just interviewed a recent journalism school graduate who believed she could have been "next." She told me Ghomeshi had picked this woman up in his usual flattering you-may-be-the-one way at a holiday party two years before, and a photographer had taken their picture. Ghomeshi suggested "you could be my secret Christmas girlfriend," but they never got together. Then in October, just before the story broke, Ghomeshi emailed her. "We should get together and take more pictures," he suggested. In the end, Ghomeshi cancelled the date because his father was ill. "When the story came out I was shaking, just shaking," the woman told me. "I keep wondering: was I the next one?"

When I interviewed Kim she told me she moved to Toronto in 2011. She longed to be a writer and had hopes of starting a career in Canada's biggest city. She was in her mid-twenties. So many of the women Ghomeshi was with—no matter his age at the time—were that age, and he wanted Penny, who was in her late twenties, to say she was twenty-six. In another case, I was told he promised a twenty-six-year-old woman he was dating that as soon as she turned twenty-seven, he would propose. Something about the age twenty-six appealed to Ghomeshi—was this his "type"?

Kim arrived in Toronto with one suitcase. A friend told her that Q host Jian Ghomeshi was looking for a junior assistant. He had a senior assistant, and a good one, Ashley Poitevin, but had posted a job looking for someone to make him cold smoothies and crisp salads at his home while he was preparing for his Q shows. Kim applied and was invited to an interview with Ghomeshi and Poitevin at Ghomeshi's Cabbagetown house. The interview lasted fifteen minutes. Ghomeshi was stern and very serious. That night, he left a message asking her to meet for coffee and a second interview in the morning.

Ghomeshi was a different person at the coffee meeting. "I am a pretty anxious person and I was taken aback," Kim said. "He asked a lot of personal questions. Did I have a roommate? Where was I last night when he called? Did I know people here?"

She said he criticized her for mispronouncing his name and calling his show The Q instead of Q. He accused her of wearing clothes that were "too granola." He listed what he saw as her shortcomings, asking, "How could you run a room of people?"

Kim left the job interview feeling a panic attack coming on.

"He gave the impression I had sincerely offended him, and I genuinely felt so bad about it at the time. I look back on this now as the tactic of a manipulator with a mandate," she told me.

She wrote him and took herself out of the running for the job. He thanked her for her "candour" and invited her to a live broadcast of *Q*. After the broadcast, he began sending texts, including one many other women reported receiving: "Happy Monday!"

They began dating. She wondered if the job she had applied for was just a ploy to meet new women. On their dates she noticed that he persistently tried to improve her appearance. "You should dress like that," he said once, pointing to another woman. Or, "Let's get you a jean jacket," he'd say. On another occasion: "That's the first time you have worn something to highlight your breasts." He criticized her posture, saying that he knew a woman in her forties who clenched her shoulders in the same way, then took his hands and firmly pushed her shoulders into what he considered the proper position. One time he warned her that her meal choice of french toast contained "a lot of carbs."

"I don't know if I want to make love to you or hate fuck you," he told her that day.

On a visit to his house one evening, she said, they were standing in his kitchen, looking at his laptop, "when out of nowhere he pushed me into the fridge and made a snarling sound." Kim recalled. "I want to ravage your little body," Ghomeshi told her.

During one of several intimate encounters they had, she said, he took her into the washroom at her home, telling her, "I have something exciting planned for us." He slapped her hard across the face. He asked if she liked choking. She said she had never done that. He tried to convince her. Kim told me she let him try it but did not like it. The acronym BDSM was never mentioned, nor the concept of a safe word.

Kim did recall that the first time they were intimate, Ghomeshi said, "Tell me if I am too rough." At times she did. She'd ask him if "we can just chill, nothing too crazy," she remembered. "There were so many times when I was uncomfortable with him. I could have cut it off, and I should have."

The behaviour continued. She felt degraded and disturbed by the whole experience. "One time he hit me really hard, on my head and face, with an open hand. I pushed him back once and he grabbed my wrists and said he did not like that," she recalls.

Kim broke the relationship off after, she said, Ghomeshi pushed his finger between her legs as they walked into the Sony Centre to see an Adele concert. "Then he put on his Jian Ghomeshi face to everyone and I felt like a piece of arm candy."

"I was not with him very long. This is not a story of strength or one I am very proud of," said Kim, who is still seeing a therapist. "I still struggle with self-blame on this since I still . . . went back. I still wanted him to think something of me."

Kim pushed back, literally, on just one occasion. She said Ghomeshi grabbed her wrists and told her in no uncertain terms that "he was the one who would dominate."

The Ghomeshi story that I found the most troubling came from a woman, Cindy, who seemed shattered by the experience and angry at everyone, on and off, including other victims, Ghomeshi's legal counsel, and me. By the time I interviewed her, the stories of Carly, Paula, Lucy DeCoutere, Linda Redgrave, Reva Seth, and others were out. Cindy believed that her case revealed the strongest allegations, and in my conversations with her, she was demeaning and dismissive of the other women. She wanted to make sure I understood that she had endured abuse for longer than most of the others. There was a time in the fall of 2014 when Cindy considered coming forward publicly, though she eventually rejected that notion because, she said, she was fearful of a lawsuit by Ghomeshi, and particularly of being summoned to a criminal witness stand by Ghomeshi's lawyer Marie Henein, a woman she did not know but whom she said she placed in a category slightly below the devil incarnate. Cindy was also concerned about the effect of coming forward on her own career.

When I interviewed her, Cindy had many questions for me. Did the *Star* pay the other victims? (No, we do not pay for interviews.) Why was the *Star* not interested in doing a specific story on her case? (I explained that we believed it was better to group the stories together to show a pattern.) Should she consult a lawyer? (I did not answer that, as it is not my place to advise people.)

Cindy's time with Ghomeshi spanned about six months in 2012, that key year when Ghomeshi's book was published and his *Q* show featured one after powerful guest after another, including feminist Gloria Steinem and actor Kim Cattrall. According to my timeline of Ghomeshi allegations, at least five of the women who made allegations against Ghomeshi to the media experienced incidents with the former CBC host during a relatively short period of time in 2012. In some instances, it appears that one woman ended a visit with him on a weekend and the next woman arrived on the Monday.

In Cindy's case, she was interested in a career in the media, and she met Ghomeshi purely by chance when she was visiting a friend at the CBC building. They struck up a relationship. She was in her early twenties; he was forty-five. She told me his work ethic impressed her; Ghomeshi toiled eighteen hours a day and wrote a "new essay every day," Cindy told me, not knowing about his team of ghostwriters. Still, Ghomeshi often bragged about how difficult his job was and of his goal to be the most famous person in Canada. "He was like the Canadian Jesus. Everyone adored him, and he had shone his light on me."

During their time together, she said, he was often violent, and he became progressively more violent with each sexual encounter. Afterward, Ghomeshi would become nice and charming and would ask her to "cuddle" in bed. Barely out of university, in an unbalanced power situation, Cindy went along with the CBC host. "I was in awe of him and wanted so much for him to like me." She found him moody a great deal of the time.

On what was to be their last evening together, he led her to the bedroom of his Cabbagetown home. She said he pushed her down to a seating position on the hardwood floor. "He put his hands around my neck and started to press, increasing pressure, choking me. He had done this before. This time was worse. He was looking into my eyes. I couldn't breathe and I started to panic." Ghomeshi had placed Big Ears Teddy in a small wooden child's chair, and the bear was facing her.

Cindy said she tried to stop the choking, and he did stop momentarily, but then he put his hands over her nose and mouth. She felt herself starting to lose consciousness and recalled thinking, "I could die here tonight and no one would know where I was or what had happened." She tried to move his hands but could not. She said he then struck her four times, in rapid succession, "pounding the heels of his hands into my temples." Her eyes watered.

Her gut reaction told her to leave, but she stayed, and they went to the bed. She felt Ghomeshi was "disappointed in me," she said, and she wondered if this was something she "needed to learn." During sex, she said, he pinned her down. She struggled and managed to get on top of him. He promptly lost his erection, saying he was tired. Cindy went to the bathroom and texted a friend, who told her to leave immediately. Ghomeshi convinced her to stay a while and watch television. When he fell asleep, she left. She never saw him again.

Kim's and Cindy's stories became part of a piece I did for the *Star* in November. The story revealed that of fifteen women we had interviewed by that time who alleged abuse, not a single one said she consented to the choking, beating, or other mistreatment she allegedly experienced at the hands of Jian Ghomeshi, contrary to what Ghomeshi claimed. What disturbed me most about Cindy's story was not just that the allegations were so severe, among the worst I had heard so far. It troubled me that beyond her telling the story to the *Star*, there was no follow-up, no therapy as far as I could tell, and no way for her to come to grips with what had happened.

According to Janice Du Mont, who has studied the prevalence and consequences of intimate partner violence in a variety of communities, disclosure is a key step in the healing process.

"If a person reports a sexual victimization, some of the person's well-being psychologically is restored," Du Mont told me in an interview for this book. "If the person is believed and supported then that can be a powerful healing experience."

I expressed my concern that there were women in the Ghomeshi case, many of them quite young, who were not seeking or had no access to support. Du Mont could not speak about the Ghomeshi case specifically, but she told me that women often feel guilt, shame, and embarrassment in these situations and blame themselves. "Some women believe the best in people," she said. "They might ask, 'did I bring this on?'"

I described the different reactions I had encountered with women I had interviewed. In my impression, Kim appeared to have begun to heal; others had not.

"Women are not a homogenous group," Du Mont said. "Some are more resilient than others. For some, the healing process will be lifelong."

Du Mont observed some women find it hard to even come to the conclusion that they have been sexually assaulted. Society still considers sexual assault to be the knife-wielding stranger in the bush. Academic studies show that ninety per cent of the women who are sexually assaulted are attacked by men they know.

The Beyond the Headlines panel was a continuation of a conversation started not by Jian Ghomeshi but by Carly and Paula. Aiding the conversation was the work of the *Star*'s Emily Mathieu and Jayme Poisson, whose investigation of campus sex assault and the lack of protocols for addressing them was published within weeks of the Ghomeshi stories. Their reports prompted the Ontario government, and universities and colleges across Canada, to vow to do better. Kathleen Wynne, the premier of Ontario, committed $41 million to a three-year initiative she called Taking Action Against Sexual Violence and Harassment. "Many women in the province do not feel safe," Wynne said when she announced the plan. "I have a problem with that." The government's slogan was "It's never okay," and Wynne promised to beef up workplace safety legislation to require employers to investigate all forms of harassment. She also vowed to bolster and speed up the prosecution of sexual assault cases in the courts.

At Beyond the Headlines, Nneka MacGregor gave a rousing call to arms. "I'm a woman who is filled with hope, and I'm a woman who is filled with fire and a little bit of anger," she told the audience. "As a survivor, the courage that lives in me and all of the other women who have experienced one form of violence or another, the courage it takes for us to stand up and talk about our experience is incredible. The reason why

I continue to do the work is because I find myself daily surrounded by incredibly courageous women."

Victims of abuse have to learn how to speak up against the "sense of oppression" that makes women "go into your room, get into your bed, get under the covers, and not come out," MacGregor argued. Women get out for one reason. "That is really about a sense of justice. If I don't speak, if I don't use what has happened to me, if I don't use it to bring about change, nothing will be different in the world that my children go into." She said she continues to campaign for social justice for women, for her children and other youngsters.

"I do this work so my daughters will never, never end up in a situation where some man feels that he has the right to violate and torture and abuse, and they will have no recourse. I do this so my son will grow in a world and have the voice and the courage himself as a man to speak up and to speak out in support of his sisters and other women."

14

The Trial

"Kevin Donovan got it wrong," Linda Redgrave told the court. "Kevin Donovan gets a lot wrong."

She was sitting to the left of the judge and facing defence lawyer Marie Henein, who circled in front of the first complainant in the Jian Ghomeshi criminal case like a prizefighter with an opponent hard against the ropes.

"Kevin Donovan got it wrong?" Henein asked, looking at Redgrave over the top of her glasses.

"What I have been led to believe is he gets a lot of that wrong," Redgrave replied.

My heart knocked hard in my chest. I was sitting with sixty other reporters in the gallery of the courtroom on day one of the Ghomeshi trial. In the row in front of me, Jian Ghomeshi's mother, sister, and other family members stared hard at Redgrave, whose long blonde hair cascaded from her head. Ghomeshi sat quietly to the left of his lawyer. I looked around. Christie Blatchford, the *National Post* veteran of many court and media battles, seemed unconcerned. Younger reporters who did not know me very well were suddenly busy on their phones and computers. I checked Twitter and saw quite a few were spreading this minor bombshell, making me, unfortunately, the story. I had a sense I was about to disappear under the wheels of a bus.

Redgrave was telling the court, presided over by Mr. Justice William Horkins, that I did not properly tell her story when she gave me her first interview back in 2014. The issue at hand: kissing. Redgrave told the court that when Ghomeshi assaulted her on two occasions it was during kissing, sensual kissing. Our stories did not mention kissing. Redgrave shared with the court another detail: she said that when she was sitting in the passenger seat of Ghomeshi's car, facing him, he asked her to undo some of the buttons on her blouse, but she said no. They began to kiss, and Redgrave told the court that it was at this point that Ghomeshi roughly yanked her hair.

As Redgrave took a sip of water, I reached into my briefcase and dug around until I found the notes from my interviews with her back in the fall of 2014. Redgrave was the first woman to reach out to the *Star* after our initial story on the Ghomeshi allegations was published. The story had been online for just over an hour when she emailed me, giving her real name and writing: "I too was subjected to Jian's abuse." Her email briefly detailed an allegation when she visited the CBC star's home, and I interviewed her the next day in person. During that interview she had told me the first incident took place in Ghomeshi's car after a taping of *>play*. She said that, as my notes confirmed, he suddenly yanked her hair back sharply, asking her if she liked it "rough." On another occasion, at his home, she alleged that Ghomeshi again yanked her hair roughly, pulled her to the floor, and delivered three sharp punches to the side of her head. In her account to me, there was no kissing. In fact, and I had a clear recollection of this, Redgrave had told me the assaults were sudden and unprovoked. When she told me this I was not surprised. It was similar to what other women had said, and Ghomeshi, as I had learned from many interviews, was not particularly into kissing. On my phone I pulled up my stories that dealt with Redgrave. No mention of kissing.

Marie Henein had cautioned Redgrave about fabricating evidence and obstructing justice. Pressed by Henein on the kissing/no kissing question, Redgrave dug in, focusing her attack on me. "He twists it," she told the court. Henein smirked incredulously. She was no fan of mine, of that I was sure, but she was using my reputation to sink the Crown's first witness.

I didn't like this. It occurred to me that if my interviews became more of the story, I might not be able to cover the trial.

I recalled Redgrave sending me regular emails after the story ran, and I pulled them up on my phone while Henein pondered her next question. Redgrave's emails to me were extremely positive. Surely if she thought I got the story wrong she would have told me at the time. I leaned forward on the wooden bench to catch every word of Redgrave's testimony. Her eyes moved around the room, but they did not rest on me. Something had made her change her story, but what? After Redgrave again told the court that I had not "characterized" her story properly, Henein introduced Redgrave's CBC interviews, including one on the evening radio show *As It Happens*. No mention of kissing. Then Henein played Redgrave's first police interview. No kissing. Asked about this by Henein, Redgrave relented.

"I had the memory [of kissing]," she told the court. "I just didn't put it out." When interviewed initially she was, she said, "high on nerves" and omitted her recollection of kissing, a "sensual kiss" she told court. Later, in a subsequent police interview and now to the court, Redgrave said there was kissing, both in the car and on the later occasion at Ghomeshi's home. It seemed pretty obvious to me what had happened. A charge of sexual assault could only be justified if an assault occurred in a sexual context. Kissing had been added later, as she retold her story to the police, and it made me wonder if someone along the way had aided her recollection. Without the kissing, or some other sexual act, only a charge of assault could have been laid.

Walking back and forth in front of Redgrave, Henein reminded me of the late Eddie Greenspan, her mentor and someone I had watched in various court cases over the years and even gotten to know once when he was a source on an investigation. There is a lot of the theatrical about Henein and her former boss. Glasses on and off, prowling the small space in front of the judge and the witness, both had the ability to radiate indignation like a white-hot fire. To her right, Crown attorney Michael Callaghan's face showed the first hint of concern. Though he did not know it, Callaghan was watching the beginning of the end of his case.

Henein had laid her trap, and it was a trap she would set for the other witnesses over the next two weeks. She began by asking questions to establish the story the witness wanted to tell, often by going over details that the witness had testified in chief, when Michael Callaghan first introduced their account. In quick succession, she then brought up inconsistencies. Redgrave said one of the features of Ghomeshi that made her feel safe was that he drove a yellow Love Bug, a Volkswagen Beetle. An alarm bell went off when I heard her say that, because she never told me she knew what kind of car it was. Henein, having established Redgrave's firm memory of a yellow Beetle, then suggested to her in cross-examination that Ghomeshi did not own a yellow Beetle until months later. This was later part of an agreed statement of facts entered into the court. That jived with what I knew. Other women who saw Ghomeshi later in the year certainly recalled that car — but not Redgrave. Ghomeshi had driven a Volkswagen before the Beetle, but it was a GTI, not a Bug.

Henein then went over Redgrave's purported anger at Ghomeshi after the two incidents of assault. "I left, and I didn't go back, and I didn't have any more dealings with him," Redgrave testified. Henein, glasses perched on her nose, consulted her notes. Six times you told police you had nothing more to do with him, she put to Redgrave. Redgrave agreed. You didn't want to watch him; you didn't want to listen to him? Redgrave agreed. She never has; she never will. In fact, she told the court, she will not even listen to Shad, the new host of *Q*. Henein moved in for the legal equivalent of a kill. Sixty reporters leaned forward, and if you could hear social media draw a deep breath, it did at that moment, waiting. With more drama than was required, Henein revealed that not only had Redgrave reached out to Ghomeshi subsequent to the assaults, but she had first done so with an email — subject line "Hello Playboy" — that said "good to see you again." Six months later, she sent another email, this one with a photo attachment, showing herself on a Toronto beach, wearing a red string bikini. Redgrave, flustered, told the court she sent the photo as bait to get Ghomeshi to respond, so she could confront him. He never responded, the court heard.

Henein had scored her points. She had no more questions for the witness.

Redgrave's explanation that she did not mention the kissing because, the way her mind works, she has to sit with a memory before she is sure of it, prompted Christie Blatchford to write, in one of a series of devastating columns: "This witness sat with memory for 13 years and it's wreaking havoc with her credibility." It was not that many veteran reporters on hand did not believe the witnesses' central accounts of assault, but they knew that too many troubling inconsistencies would finish the Crown's case.

. . .

Old City Hall Courthouse is my favourite building in Toronto. It's a grand, Gothic structure dominating the corner of Bay and Queen Streets, and it became, over the days that followed Redgrave's testimony, the site of a media circus. Built in 1899, its stone comes from two places: the Credit River Valley in Ontario, and a quarry in New Brunswick. A series of grotesque stone carvings — suggestive, historians say, of councillors of the day — dominates the impressive entrance and its castle-like doors. Protestors gathered in front of these doors throughout the trial to chant "We believe survivors" and savage Marie Henein who, it seemed to me, was just doing the job she was hired to do: give her client the best possible defence.

To gain admission to the trial, reporters and spectators had to line up at seven a.m. in cold February weather to get what I dubbed the golden ticket that granted access to Courtroom 125. The room reminded me of the set of the 1962 movie *To Kill a Mockingbird*: all oak panelling and polished rails. Reporters of all types were on hand: columnists like Christie Blatchford and the *Star*'s Rosie DiManno, both female legends in the Toronto newspaper world; highly experienced court reporters like the *Star*'s Alyshah Hasham and the *Sun*'s Sam Pazzano; and journalists who normally cover arts and culture, like the *Globe and Mail*'s Simon Houpt and my colleague Vinay Menon. I was the only reporter present who had the advantage of having interviewed many complainants and also people close to Ghomeshi.

From Jian Ghomeshi's perspective, the trial went from good to great following Linda Redgrave's testimony. From the Crown's side, it went from bad to dreadful. While the protesters chanted outside, inside Courtroom 125 witnesses fell before Marie Henein's sword.

When I interviewed Lucy DeCoutere, I had serious concerns that she would be a poor witness at a trial, not because I disbelieved the essence of her story, but because I worried that her irreverent personality would work against her in a courtroom. She told a compelling story when she first took the witness stand. She told the court Ghomeshi choked and slapped her at his home years before, while they were kissing. Her account was identical to the one she told me and other media. DeCoutere said the assault so angered her that she wanted nothing to do with him again. She had told me and the police that while she had seen him from time to time at arts and entertainment events, there had been no flirting after the night she said he choked her until she had trouble breathing.

But Marie Henein's cross-examination revealed a series of post-incident contacts and shredded DeCoutere's credibility. Using emails and handwritten correspondence that Ghomeshi had apparently saved for more than a decade, Henein exposed inconsistencies and mistruths that ultimately proved fatal to the Crown's case regarding DeCoutere's allegations, just as in Redgrave's. Henein produced a photo, a selfie of the two cuddling in a Toronto park soon after the choking incident. Henein also produced an email written the day after the incident, in which DeCoutere wrote "you kicked my ass last night and that makes me want to fuck your brains out. Tonight." A handwritten letter she wrote a few days later read: "Jian you are great. I want to have more fun times with you.... I am sad we didn't spend the night together." Marie Henein, in a flourish that I suspect was planned at her offices days, weeks, or even months before, asked DeCoutere to read from the stand the last line from the letter that Ghomeshi had saved for fourteen years. DeCoutere, who had testified that Ghomeshi choked her with both of his hands, studied the letter on the witness stand, then read the last line: "I love your hands, Lucy."

The third and final complainant to testify was Janine, the woman involved in the Toronto arts and culture scene as a performer. She had alleged in an interview to me that Jian Ghomeshi sexually assaulted her on a bench in Toronto's Withrow Park in 2003. As Janine settled into the witness chair and took the oath, I flipped through a notepad looking for my 2014 interview with her and a written statement she had shared with friends on Facebook hours after the original Ghomeshi stories broke. Janine's story, as originally told to me and documented on Facebook, was simple. Ghomeshi, she said, "pushed me down on a park bench and forcefully kissed and groped me." In court, the Crown attorney took his time with Janine, going over her evidence more carefully than he had done with other witnesses. Responding to Callaghan's questions, Janine laid out a story that seemed identical to what she told me.

When she was a teenager, Janine had seen Ghomeshi perform during his Moxy Früvous days. They saw each other from time to time at arts and cultural events and once had dinner together on the Danforth in Toronto. In 2003, while performing in a music and dance festival at Withrow Park, she saw Ghomeshi, and they went on a stroll through the grounds, ending up at a secluded area and sitting on a park bench. They kissed for a few minutes. She compared what happened next to Jekyll and Hyde.

"All of a sudden I felt his hands on my shoulders and his teeth. And his hands were around my neck and squeezing," Janine told the court. Janine, her voice shaky, said she recalled one of Ghomeshi's hands covering her mouth and "smothering" her. She said it did not feel "safe or sexy." She had struggled to recall what happened after, she testified, and much was a blank. She knows she went home, and she recalls they went out again, a few days later, on a date. The Crown asked why. She said she found Ghomeshi charming. She thought that if she went out again with him, it would be different. She said she is "notoriously" known for giving people second chances. They went back to her home. She gave him a hand job, he fell asleep, and Ghomeshi left later in the evening.

I watched Marie Henein during this interchange. She stared at Janine, impassive. Janine's testimony did not appear to be news to her. It certainly was to me. The story of the assault was the same, although oddly Janine told the court she never used the word "grope," which was untrue; she had written that word herself. More dangerous to her case, though, was that she had apparently only recently divulged the post-incident contact, and it was of a sexual nature. That was not something Janine had told me when I interviewed her.

The Crown continued, pulling more of the story from Janine. After this sexual encounter, she went with Ghomeshi to a party. At the party, Ghomeshi, standing beside her, blurted out to another man, "We are not seeing each other; we are just fucking." I made a note. This *was* something Janine had told me. In fact, she had omitted only the sexual encounter when she spoke to me. It was a big omission, but it did not change her central allegation. I could not help but wonder, though, how we at the *Star* would have treated this if we had known about the hand job at the time of publication. Given that we knew that Carly and others had repeated post-incident contact, I am pretty sure we would still have published the Janine story, but with the added detail. After the comment at the party, Janine said she told Ghomeshi she wanted nothing more to do with him. "You are fucking crazy, lose my number, don't ever call me again."

After a lunchtime break to go over what she termed "late disclosure," Henein stood up to begin her cross-examination of Janine. The late disclosure, Henein told court, was Janine's decision on the eve of her testimony to reveal that, just days after the alleged sexual assault, "you messed around and gave him a hand job."

"I tried to stay in public with him, as best I could," Janine told Henein. "It was an absolute misjudgment and one that a lot of women make."

"I don't care about a lot of women," Henein said, whipping off her glasses and fixing her gaze on Janine. Janine stared back. For several heartbeats the only sound in the court was the tapping of laptop keys. #Ghomeshi was once again trending on Twitter.

Henein took Janine through a new statement she had given police just before testifying, a nine-minute interview in which she disclosed that she had not mentioned the sexual encounter when she first spoke to police because she did not think it important.

Henein said she was baffled that what occurred was not deemed sexual and important enough to be discussed with police at the first interview. "He magically appears in your home, his penis ends up in your hand, he sleeps over?" Henein asked.

Janine said police only asked her if they had ever had sex. "It wasn't sex; intercourse, I mean," Janine responded.

For the first and only time in the two-week trial, Crown attorney Michael Callaghan got to his feet and objected to what he called Henein's "abusive" questioning. The judge waved it off, saying Henein was simply conducting a cross-examination.

"So when the police asked you to tell the truth, the whole truth and nothing but the truth, you lied?" Henein asked.

"I omitted," Janine shot back. Henein sat down. The trial was over, but for closing summations and the judge's verdict. With a veteran journalist's gallows humour, Christie Blatchford turned to me.

"Hey, Kevin, want a hand job?"

For Blatchford and *Star* columnist Rosie DiManno, the women who testified were an embarrassment, in some instances for how they behaved but mainly for the fact that they were not truthful. "It's the lying, stupid," DiManno wrote in a column. "*Falsus in uno, falsus in omnibus.* Latin for 'false in one, false in everything,' the common-law legal principle that a witness who testifies falsely about one matter is not credible to testify about any matter. Just as the judge would rule six weeks later, both columnists said that the withholding or outright lying about their many post-incident contacts was the complainants' undoing. DiManno did note, in her closing to a column: "I believe you, ladies. Multitudes do. If there's to be any solace found in that."

On Thursday, March 24, 2016, Mr. Justice William Horkins acquitted Jian Ghomeshi of four counts of sexual assault and one count of choking to overcome resistance. "At the end of this trial, it is impossible to determine, with any acceptable degree of certainty or comfort, what is true and is false," Horkins told the packed courtroom. "I find Mr. Ghomeshi not guilty on all of these charges and they will be noted as dismissed."

Justice Horkins's ruling noted that he was not saying "these events never happened." Instead, he found the three witnesses' "inconsistencies, questionable behaviour," and "outright deception" of the court tainted their evidence. Horkins also felt that conversations between two of the complainants cast doubt on whether they were telling the truth. Lucy DeCoutere and Janine exchanged *five thousand* electronic messages, many describing how they wanted to destroy Ghomeshi. At one point Janine wrote, "it's time to sink this prick." In the days before instant messaging, text and emails, those discussions would likely have been oral discussions and never be discovered. Marie Henein simply had to ask the court to get the witnesses to turn over their electronic correspondence.

After Linda Redgrave's second day of testimony, Rosie DiManno stopped me on our way down the worn stone steps for a coffee near the cells. "Is that it?" she asked me. "Is that all the cops have? Why did this even go to trial?" This is a complicated question, and it's not one I'm sure I can answer. The Ghomeshi allegations and Jayme Poisson and Emily Mathieu's reports in the *Star* about sexual violence on campus prompted a strong reaction from the Ontario government. With so many women telling stories of mistreatment by Ghomeshi, police and provincial justice officials felt compelled to do something. A small number of women came forward, and they laid charges. The problem, as became evident in court, was that the police apparently stopped their investigation at a simple interview. As far as I could determine, there was no search of Ghomeshi's computer or phone, no attempt to obtain the many videos that Ghomeshi had stored and his lawyers had shown to the CBC, no interviewing of people who worked with Ghomeshi and were aware of some of his behaviours. Nor was there a reference or an attempt to get into evidence at trial Ghomeshi's Facebook posting in which he described his love of rough sex.

The fact that Ghomeshi did not testify hampered the Crown. Had he taken the stand, Callaghan could have put his Facebook and other statements to him and questioned him extensively. Throughout the trial Ghomeshi sat in a chair beside his lawyers, looking a little sad, a little lost, and making notes and doodles on a pad of paper. Still, even without his testimony, many observers in the court believed that the police and Crown dropped the ball on this case, myself included. Of great interest to me, given how the trial developed, was the fact that the Crown had earlier withdrawn two other sets of charges brought by two women. In one case, that of Simone, the woman who alleged she was assaulted at a music festival in Owen Sound in 2002, the charges were dropped after Simone provided police with a short chain of emails that showed she exchanged friendly words after the alleged incident. Simone said she was friendly with Ghomeshi post-incident because she thought his aggressive behaviour in the Owen Sound hotel room had been an aberration. She later told me she was "up front about everything" with the police when they interviewed her and asked for further information. She said the Crown was concerned that in her follow-up emails she seemed "extremely friendly" with Ghomeshi and did not later "confront him about what he did." Simone said the Crown told her: "It is not that we don't believe you; it's that we don't think this is a case we can win."

As soon as the judge left the courtroom, Ghomeshi stood and hugged his mother and sister. Tweets from inside the court reached protesters outside. They reacted, shouting: "Guilty! Guilty!"

Lucy DeCoutere, Linda Redgrave, and Janine had sat together in court for the verdict. They left in tears.

As Michael Callaghan told reporters he would review the judge's ruling to see if he would appeal, a protester standing among a group of journalists tore off her sweater and launched her semi-nude body at the Crown attorney before police wrestled her to the ground. Her chest bore the words "Ghomeshi Guilty."

Marie Henein, in a brief statement in court, said that despite the unprecedented scrutiny and pressure, the case was determined on the "evidence heard in a court of law." She said Ghomeshi would take time with family and close friends "to reflect and move forward from what can only be described as a profoundly difficult period in his life."

Outside Old City Hall, the chants of the protesters grew louder.

15
Déjà vu

"Do you mind if I record this interview?" I asked Grace, the young woman sitting across from me in the *Toronto Star*'s investigative team office. A whiteboard with a list of stories done and to come was behind me. A coffee maker somebody really needed to hook up sat on the floor beside a box of documents.

"No, that is fine."

This meeting with Grace reminded me of the first interview on the story, with Carly, two years earlier on the fourth floor of the *Star*. Grace had come down to the paper at my request. Testimony in the first Ghomeshi trial was done and the judge would not deliver his verdict for several weeks. A second trial involving allegations made by former CBC producer Kathryn Borel was more than two months away, and sources in the court system were predicting the single charge of sexual assault in that case would either be withdrawn or fail at trial. Ghomeshi's legal team was simply too strong, legal observers and fellow journalists told me frequently. Grace had followed the coverage of the first trial in the *Star* and emailed me to ask whom to contact at the Toronto police department about Jian Ghomeshi. I told her I would be happy to provide that information, but I asked if she would be interested in talking to me as well. She agreed. This would be one of three interviews I conducted with her. On the table between us was a two-inch stack of text messages. Grace had earlier provided me with copies of electronic communication she and Jian Ghomeshi exchanged between January 2013 and September 2013, a time that overlapped with many of the women I had already written about. During the interview she let me compare the printed texts to those on her phone. That was one of a number of things that made me trust Grace.

Grace had followed the trial coverage closely. She had read how defence lawyer Marie Henein dug up evidence of post-incident contact between the complainants and Ghomeshi and used that to impeach their testimony. The story she had to tell, she noted, was a different one than those of the women who testified in court against the former CBC host. She was not passing judgment on the women who had post-incident contact after an incident; her story was simply different. "Every single one of those women reached out to him in a way that could be flirtatious. I am not one of those people," Grace told me.

A little bit about Grace: she is in her mid-to late-twenties and works in the music promotion business in Toronto. She likes her job, and from what I was able to determine when I looked into her work history, she is good at it. In 2013, when Jian Ghomeshi was at the top of his game, *Q* on CBC was a coveted slot that would be of interest to bands Grace promoted. Get on *Q*, and your band might make it big.

Grace and I went over the ground rules. If I was to tell her story, I had to be able to ask her any question. She agreed. I would have to be able to put the substance of her allegations to Ghomeshi. She agreed. I would have to be able to call her friends and ask them what, if anything, she had told them about this incident. She agreed. Her main concern was that associating her name with this case would, she feared, jeopardize her future. She did not want to lose her job and her status in the music industry, and we agreed that I would not use her name or her exact age.

Grace was physically similar to many of the women I'd met to whom Ghomeshi had been attracted. At the time of the incident, she was a little younger than most of the women he allegedly assaulted. What stood out about Grace—and I have this from friends of hers I interviewed—is that "she does not take shit from anyone."

Grace first met Ghomeshi at a music industry party in January 2013. After the party, he texted her a lot and wanted to take her for drinks or dinner. In one text message, in February, Ghomeshi asked Grace if she had plans for the night. Grace responded: "Hello sir! Yes I am isolated and working all night, now that I am not so sick." Grace was not interested, but she wanted to make a name for herself in the Toronto music scene. In March, she texted Ghomeshi about two of her firm's budding artists. Ghomeshi responded, "when are we having that much anticipated drink?" He volunteered to, as she put it, "blow off" a friend, joking they could spend the first hour "seeing if you know how to pronounce my brown person name."

"Hahahaha just awful. And no I actually can't tonight ill (sic) probably be working late," Grace responded. The back and forth continued into the summer. Grace provided him with two tickets to a show, to which Ghomeshi said he would take a girlfriend. When Ghomeshi asked Grace if she would have dinner with him the following Monday, she agreed. Ghomeshi was pleased. He said he was an optimist and expressed his delight that she would see him. He began counting down the hours in text messages, something he stopped doing after acknowledging it might be "creepy." For dinner, he offered to cook butter chicken, and she arrived at his home, the former peanut factory in Cabbagetown, early on a July evening. It was pouring rain. Grace arrived feeling apprehensive but with a plan to show Ghomeshi clips of her bands on her laptop.

"In my mind I was so hell bent on keeping this professional. I can keep this totally platonic, I can keep this business, I have the ability to turn this whatever way I want, and I am going to keep this totally business minded, which it was," Grace recalled. Ghomeshi was a perfect gentleman. They had one glass of wine, ate dinner, looked at the bands. Ghomeshi did express shock that she had not listened to his monologue on *Q* that day, a riff on climate change, and played it on his sound system for her. Rain lashed the Sackville Street home, and when a drip developed from the ceiling Grace positioned a bucket. By eleven p.m. she was out the door. She arrived home soon after. Before midnight, Ghomeshi texted, asking her out the following week. She told him she was busy. The next morning, as Toronto work crews cleared storm drains, Ghomshi texted: "Happy Tuesday... when do I get to see you." Grace responded that she was sick and joked it was the butter chicken.

Sitting across from Grace that afternoon at the *Star*, I frequently referred to the stack of text messages. I asked if she really was sick, either at this point or others in the text chain. Grace said no, she was trying to keep her distance from Ghomeshi. She did not want a relationship. "I didn't want to hang out with him," she said. "I wanted to pitch my artists."

Over the next few weeks, Ghomeshi asked on five occasions to see her. Grace continued to make excuses — she was ill, cleaning up after the flood, a relative was in town. The fifth time, he contacted her from Los Angeles in late August, and she agreed to meet him for a drink on a Monday night. She asked where he wanted to go.

"I don't know where. I didn't think it through that far. Just know I wanna see you. By which I mean...Jian wants to see you." When Monday arrived, he suggested she just drop by his house. Grace said she would drive, something she said was her way of telling Ghomeshi she was not going to drink very much. She also told Ghomeshi she had a very early morning meeting.

At nine p.m., she texted she was heading to his house.

"Text when you're here cause I'm on roof and may not hear the door. Also — I hope you like red wine. Also, it's fucking gorgeous up here." Ghomeshi came downstairs when Grace arrived and met her on the main floor, where the kitchen and living room were situated. They chatted for an hour, and then Ghomeshi led her to the rooftop. The top floor of Ghomeshi's house was a deck with a cedar fence surround, a table and chairs, and two chaise lounges, one for a single person, the other for two. Grace was on alert, a young woman in her early twenties who had the inkling she had made a mistake. When she walked in earlier, she noticed the wine was already poured. "There was a different vibe than the first time," she explained. "I thought, oh no, this is a thing."

It was nice on the roof. The stars were shining, and the sky was clear. Ghomeshi began talking about his anxiety. He told her he was writing a second book, a follow up to *1982* that would focus on his anxiety and the anxiety that top performers suffer from. Grace said he told her he was "stressed and anxious" because Air Canada had recently lost a "keepsake" he always kept in his luggage because it helped him with his anxiety when he travelled. She asked Ghomeshi what it was, and he muttered that it was a kind of "stone," but he was not ready to give her the full details. "That's for another time. I am not sure I can talk to you about it yet," she remembered him saying.

Grace sat in an upright chair, choosing her spot carefully. Ghomeshi lay on one of the chaise lounges. He would stand up, walk over to her, and then go back and lie down. Several times he asked her to get off her chair and walk over to the other chaise lounge and lie down. Eventually Grace relented. "I didn't know what to do."

"I was mid-sentence, and the next thing I knew he was on top of me. I had no leverage. He is bigger than me, that's for sure. I remember being in complete shock. Every moment I felt I was mentally prepared to get out of. I was always three steps ahead. I always had an excuse. I always had a reason to leave. I had my car close. I had everything planned out just in case it went creepy. I just never anticipated something like that happening."

In our interview, and two subsequent interviews, I went over, and over, the details of her interactions with Ghomeshi, including what transpired in a short few minutes on the rooftop, asking her the sort of questions that I expected Marie Henein would ask her if she ever chose to go forward. She did not waiver in her account. It remains an incident indelibly marked on her mind. I put the description below to Ghomeshi and Henein, in a written letter exactly as it appears here, to seek comment or clarification for a story I published after the verdict in the trial. Neither responded.

> You encouraged the woman to lie on a one-person chaise lounge looking at the stars. You were sitting in a chair beside her. While she was looking at the stars, without consent, you jumped on her, putting the full weight of your body on the top of the woman. You put both hands around her throat and choked her, while kissing her aggressively and trying to force your tongue down her throat. You removed one of your hands and thrust it between her legs. The woman was wearing tights. You said to the woman, "I'm going to fuck you so hard you won't be able to walk for a week," and "I am going to stick my finger inside of you and fuck you so hard." During this time, according to the woman, you made deep, guttural, 'animal' style' sounds. The woman managed to extricate herself from the situation by pushing you away.

She recalls saying "too fast, too fast." She made an excuse to leave and you insisted on walking her to her car a few blocks away. You gave her a kiss on the cheek.

The animal rage Grace had seen in Ghomeshi was gone as quickly as it appeared. As soon as Ghomeshi was off her, she said she began making a series of excuses, going into "fight or flight mode," and was out the door almost immediately. During the walk to her car he asked her to text when she was home. Grace drove two blocks, pulled her car over, and cried. When she got home, she sent him a single-word text: "home!"

I imagined Marie Henein spending a great deal of time dissecting that message, asking Grace why she would send such a happy-sounding text complete with exclamation mark to a man who she said had just choked and violated her. I went over that with Grace. She told me that she felt "like an idiot" for putting herself in that situation and thought the easiest way to extricate herself was with a simple, short text. Using an exclamation mark is not unusual for her.

"You send a text to him at 12:12 a.m. with a happy exclamation mark. Why?"

Grace leaned forward in her chair and looked at the printout of her texts. "For me reading that now, that, to me, is something wrong. I am not a short texter. I am like a, 'Hi, I'm home, thanks for having me, blah blah blah.' I am that person. But he told me as I left, 'Text me when you are home.' I remember thinking, should I text him? Should I text him? I think I was even home before that, and I thought text him 'home now,' and end it at that." She thought that if she didn't text him, Ghomeshi would "start suspecting that I was going to talk to someone about it."

The next day, at 11:27 a.m. Ghomeshi texted her. "Hi. Happy Tuesday. Thanks for an amazing night."

Grace did not respond. He texted again at 6:36 p.m. "Not even texting me back today? That makes shit awkward."

Grace told Ghomeshi by text that she had left her phone at home.

"I'd like to see you," Ghomeshi texted the following day. Grace made occasional excuses.

"It's like that?" Ghomeshi texted at one point. Grace replied she was having a tough week at work and was now living at a friend's place.

"I'm supposed to be in studio for the next two weeks. Most night/weekends and I have the time booked so I can't bail at this point."

Ghomeshi made a few more attempts, which Grace ignored. Ghomeshi had the last word, before giving up.

"Happy almost September," Ghomeshi wrote, the last text in the pile of communication Grace had shared with the CBC host.

I interviewed Grace two more times and spoke to two of her friends who confirmed key elements of her account. The *Star* published the story in late April 2016, six weeks before the date set for the next Ghomeshi trial. While Grace, unlike many other complainants, had no post-incident contact with Ghomeshi, we used her story as a way to try to understand the issue surrounding such contacts. Why do they happen? What bearing, if any, should they have on a criminal case?

Ottawa law professor Elizabeth Sheehy, one of the experts I spoke to about this issue, said the focus on post-incident contact makes it very difficult to prosecute these kinds of cases. She said it "gives a profound message that unless you govern all of your behaviour from the moment of the assault, say nothing, record nothing—unless you perform absolutely perfectly in the days, weeks and months after the incident, then you run the risk of not being believed."

That was the main reason Grace said she reached out. She had no further contact and thought it was important to tell her story.

University of Windsor law professor Julie Macfarlane said that for many women there is immediate confusion after an incident. "Here you have someone who until a few minutes ago you really liked, and they have done something that you are not comfortable with. It is perfectly normal to later try and reach out and figure out if this was an aberration. The professor said the woman may ask, did I make this happen? Is this my fault?

In the first Ghomeshi trial, the women were faulted for not disclosing their post incident-contact, but the judge also criticized them for behaviour that, in his opinion, was "out of harmony" with what he would suspect of a victim of sexual assault.

Macfarlane said many judges do not seem to understand the dynamics of these situations. She said a person's charm, or perhaps a desire to offer someone a second chance, can draw the woman back.

Grace had no intention of doing that and rebuffed all of Ghomeshi's further attempts to see her. And while she originally contemplated going to the police with her allegation, the judge's comments when he eventually acquitted Ghomeshi soured her on that idea. "I got spooked on it after seeing all of the reactions of people saying how they had 'known all along these women were liars,'" she later told me.

16

Her Day in Court

Kathryn Borel was running on little sleep, almost no food, and her nerves were stretched piano-wire taut. Living in Los Angeles, the former *Q* producer should have felt a long distance from the Jian Ghomeshi case. Instead it was with her morning and afternoon, and she woke up at night wondering if she was doing the right thing. Trial, or no trial? Courtroom drama, or courtroom steps? Was accepting a deal in the public interest? In her interest? And what would Ghomeshi say if and when a deal was done? Ever since Toronto Police laid a single count of sexual assault against Ghomeshi based on her statement, she had been ready to testify. But the words of a friend, an American prosecutor, rang in her head as she imagined being grilled by Ghomeshi's lawyer, Marie Henein: "A courtroom is not your house, Kathryn. It's hers."

Friday, May 6, 2016, was cool in LA, an unseasonal nip in the air. Screenwriting work she should be dealing with lay idle on Borel's desk, because the carefully crafted deal that would stop the second Ghomeshi trial was unravelling. Borel was frequently on the phone to her lawyer in Toronto, Susan Chapman. It did not look good. Two months ago, Borel said, Chapman had told her that she and Marie Henein had talked about the upcoming case, and Henein had asked if Borel would consider a "creative solution" to avoid a trial. Borel said her lawyer told her that Henein, the tough lawyer who had done so well at the first Ghomeshi trial, was "tired" and did not want to do the second trial. At first, Borel thought the solution would involve a plea bargain. Borel, who recalled this story to me and later to Jesse Brown on his *Canadaland* show, said Susan Chapman told her she had the impression that Henein "meant money" and was "talking about cash." That allegation—that the defence was trying to buy its way out of a criminal trial—is something that Henein's office strongly denied when I posed the question in research for the *Toronto Star* and this book. Her law partner, Scott Hutchison, said in an email on behalf of Henein that any such suggestion was false and defamatory. "Offering money to someone in exchange for not proceeding with a criminal charge is highly improper and contrary to the Criminal Code.... At no time did anyone by [*sic*] or on behalf of Mr. Ghomeshi suggest any payment of any kind to Ms. Borel."

It's impossible to know the content of the conversations that took place between Henein and Chapman, as neither will discuss them. For her part, Susan Chapman said she could not comment, and that I would have to rely on Borel's recollection. Henein asked her law partner to respond to the money allegation. I went back to her on the issue of her being "tired" and not wanting a second trial. Henein did respond to this and several other questions, telling me she would consider giving an interview, as "much of the information you have set out...is actually not correct. I expect it is being filtered." Ultimately, Henein wrote back to me that she would not provide an interview. "After much consideration," she wrote, "it is my view that professionally I am unfortunately not in a position to discuss, correct or comment on without prejudice discussions with counsel."

Faced with the suggestion that the Ghomeshi side wanted out of the trial, Borel said she jokingly responded to her lawyer that she would only agree to drop the charges for one billion dollars and chemical castration of her former boss. Those settlement discussions went no further until, a month later, during a trial preparation call between Borel and Crown attorney Michael Callaghan, the Crown said Henein had approached him with the suggestion of resolving the trial with a court-approved peace bond. Callaghan explained that Ghomeshi would agree to be of good behaviour and to stay away from Borel for a period of one year. The trial set for June would never happen. Borel said she was not interested.

"There's something more," Callaghan said. "He will give an apology."

Borel thought about it. It was not ideal, but maybe it was enough. The first trial, from her perspective, had been a disaster: the accused acquitted on all charges; the complainants roasted by the judge for lying and withholding information. If, in her case, Ghomeshi apologized for his inappropriate sexual behaviour in the workplace, that might help move the conversation forward.

In anticipation, the Crown booked a courtroom — the same courtroom, 125, where Ghomeshi's trial took place — for Wednesday, May 12. Nothing was entered into the court file, so curious reporters who heard rumours of a deal could find no proof. But now, the Friday before, the deal was breaking down over the wording of the planned apology. Borel had sent a suggested version that was strong but was told Ghomeshi's team rejected it. In its place, Borel recalls, Henein sent Susan Chapman a proposed statement that prominently described how difficult the whole case, including the media circus, had been on Ghomeshi's mother and sister. There were also some words about Borel's "jocular attitude" in the Q studios, which Borel interpreted as Ghomeshi blaming her for encouraging him to put his hands on her behind and, to use her words, "sport hump" her, something Toronto Police had told her was a sexual assault. She wanted something positive to come out of her decision to press charges. The difference with the Borel case was that she had a trump card — two, actually.

The allegations brought to court by Linda Redgrave, Lucy DeCoutere, and Janine, relied solely on the testimony of the complainants. Borel's case was different. Sitting at her computer at home, Borel pulled up an email that would be part of the case if it went to trial. The day after Ghomeshi had put his hands on her in the Q studio in 2008, a colleague had referred to the host as a "CBC stud." Borel fired back in an email: "Ew. CBC stud? Yesterday he came up behind me, put his hands on my hips, and pretended to fuck me from behind. Grosstown. I yelled 'QUIT IT,' then he slinked off, tail between his legs, among other things. I can't wait until I'm out of here."

Borel also had the corroborating testimony of Roberto Veri, who had worked at Q and had previously publicly acknowledged on Jesse Brown's *Canadaland* that he had seen Ghomeshi come up behind Borel. He "grabbed her by the waist and humped her like four or five times," Veri said. "He drove his pelvis into her buttocks and [had] a big smile on his face."

Borel told her lawyer that she was not going to settle for a weak apology. She would have preferred an apology "to all of the women," but it was made clear that if Ghomeshi was going to apologize to anyone, he would only apologize for his actions to her. The other cases were over. "If we don't get an agreement that he will give a strong apology then the deal is off," Borel told her lawyer. The Crown had arranged for her to fly to Toronto on Tuesday evening, the day before the hearing. Borel said she would only get on the plane if the deal was in place. Saturday, Sunday, and part of Monday passed. None of the news was good for Borel.

In the eighteen months since he was arrested and charged with sexual assault, Jian Ghomeshi had been seeing a counsellor described as both social worker and psychotherapist, something Jaime Watt and Navigator had first advised, unsuccessfully, back in the spring and summer of 2014, before the story broke and charges were laid. Ghomeshi had logged sixty-one therapy sessions. Sometimes he met with the therapist in person, sometimes on the phone or over Skype. To help Ghomeshi achieve a deal that would see the charges dropped, the therapist wrote a letter to Marie Henein in late April.

"In our conversations, Mr. Ghomeshi and I have explored dynamics of power and control, and the intersection between gender and social constructions of status and influence. We've looked closely into the distinctions between intention and impact, especially when there are differences in power between persons. We also examined the effects of discourses related to male dominance and success, strategies for managing stress and anxiety, effective expressions of anger, and paradigms of intimacy."

Kathryn Borel arrived in Toronto on the evening of May 10, having been given assurances that the apology would be sound. Early Wednesday morning, May 11, Toronto police detectives picked her up at her hotel and, as a courtesy, drove her to Old City Hall Court. On the flight, she kept thinking of a line from human rights activist Malcolm X that appealed to her and the situation she was in. "A ballot is like a bullet," Malcolm X had said in 1964. "You don't throw your ballots until you see a target, and if that target is not within your reach, keep your ballot in your pocket." She planned to give a brief statement on the courtroom steps following the courtroom apology, if there was one. In Borel's case, her ballot was her prepared statement. If Ghomeshi did not give an apology, she felt she could not give her speech. "I would have no target," she explained to me later. *The ballot or the bullet*, she kept thinking.

Journalists packed the courtroom, most of whom had covered the previous trial. On the steps outside were protesters. Crown attorney Michael Callaghan joked that he would not be speaking outside this time, a reference to the topless protester who charged him after Ghomeshi's acquittal. Mr. Justice Timothy Lipson, the regional senior judge in Toronto, entered the court and took his seat. Ghomeshi and just one lawyer, Marie Henein, were present. The former CBC host's mother and sister sat in the front row. Callaghan stood and described how the high-profile host, as he was in 2008, thrust his pelvis "repeatedly" into Borel's buttocks as she leaned over a desk to look at some papers. Both were fully clothed. Callaghan said these actions comprised the criminal allegation of sexual assault. Then Ghomeshi stood to make his statement. He faced Justice Lipson. Borel sat in the body of the court with friends and family. She drew a deep breath.

It was the first time Jian Ghomeshi's voice had been heard in public since he went off the air almost two years before.

> I want to apologize to Ms. Borel for my behaviour towards her in the workplace. In the last 18 months, I have spent a great deal of time reflecting on this incident and the difficulties I caused Ms. Borel, and I have had to come to terms with my own deep regret and embarrassment.
>
> I enjoyed a position of privilege in my job at the CBC as host of a program I loved. I was a person in a position of authority and leadership, and I did not show the respect that I should have to Ms. Borel. I did not always lead by example and I failed to understand and truly appreciate the impact of my conduct on Ms. Borel's work environment. That conduct in the workplace was sexually inappropriate. I realize that there is no way for me to know the full impact on her personally and professionally.

I now recognize that I crossed boundaries inappropriately. A workplace should not have any sexualized tone. I failed to understand how my words and actions would put a coworker who was younger than me, and in a junior position to mine, in an uncomfortable place. I did not appreciate the damage I caused, and I recognize that no workplace friendship or creative environment excuses this sort of behaviour, especially where there is a power imbalance as there was with Ms. Borel. This incident was thoughtless and I was insensitive to her perspective and how demeaning my conduct was towards her. I understand this now. This is a challenging business to be in and I did not need to make it more difficult for Ms. Borel. The past 18 months have been an education for me. I have reflected deeply and have been working hard to address the attitudes that led me, at the time, to think that this was acceptable.

I apologize to my family for letting them down and in particular for the impact that all of this has had on my dear mother and my sister. I apologize for the burden my actions have placed on those dear friends who have stood by me throughout this difficult time. I regret my behaviour at work with all my heart and I hope that I can find forgiveness from those for whom my actions took such a toll.

The judge agreed to the peace bond, and Ghomeshi signed it with his lawyer by his side. The forty-eight-year-old unemployed radio host let out a sigh, looked up at the courtroom ceiling, and sat down. Borel stood and left the courtroom. A half hour later, she strode out the front door of Old City Hall Courthouse and walked to waiting microphones, clutching her ballot. Her long black trench coat flapped in the light breeze.

Hi everyone. Thanks for coming out and listening. My name is Kathryn Borel. In December of 2014, I pressed sexual assault charges against Jian Ghomeshi. As you know, Mr. Ghomeshi initially denied all the charges that were brought against him. But today, as you just heard, Jian Ghomeshi admitted wrongdoing and apologized to me.

It's unfortunate, but maybe not surprising, that he chose not to say much about what exactly he was apologizing for. I'm going to provide those details for you now.

Every day, over the course of a three-year period, Mr. Ghomeshi made it clear to me that he could do what he wanted to me and my body. He made it clear that he could humiliate me repeatedly and walk away with impunity. There are at least three documented incidents of physical touching. This includes the one charge he just apologized for, when he came up behind me while I was standing near my desk, put his hands on my hips, and rammed his pelvis against my backside over and over, simulating sexual intercourse. Throughout the time that I worked with him, he framed his actions with near daily verbal assaults and emotional manipulations. These inferences felt like threats, or declarations like I deserved to have happening to me what was happening to me. It became very difficult for me to trust what I was feeling.

Up until recently, I didn't even internalize that what he was doing to my body was sexual assault. Because when I went to the CBC for help, what I received in return was a directive that yes, he could do this, and yes, it was my job to let him. The relentless message to me, from my celebrity boss and the national institution we worked for were that his whims were more important than my humanity or my dignity. So I came to accept this. I came to believe it was his right. But when I spoke to the police at the end of 2014, and detailed my experiences with Mr. Ghomeshi, they confirmed to me what he did to me was, in fact, sexual assault.

And that's what Jian Ghomeshi just apologized for: the crime of sexual assault. This is the story of a man who had immense power over me and my livelihood, admitting that he chronically abused his power and violated me in ways that violate the law. Mr. Ghomeshi's constant workplace abuse of me and my many colleagues and friends has since been corroborated by multiple sources, a CBC *fifth estate* documentary, and a third-party investigation.

In a perfect world, people who commit sexual assault would be convicted for their crimes. Jian Ghomeshi is guilty of having done the things that I've outlined today. So when it was presented to me that the defence would be offering us an apology, I was prepared to forego the trial. It seemed like the clearest path to the truth. A trial would have maintained his lie, the lie that he was not guilty, and it would have further subjected me to the very same pattern of abuse that I am currently trying to stop.

Jian Ghomeshi has apologized, but only to me. There are 20 other women who have come forward to the media and made serious allegations about his violent behavior. Women who have come forward to say that he punched, and choked, and smothered, and silenced them. There is no way that I would have come forward if it weren't for their courage. And yet Mr. Ghomeshi hasn't met any of their allegations head on, as he vowed to do in his Facebook post of 2014. He hasn't taken the stand on any charge. All he has said about his other accusers is that they're all lying and that he's not guilty. And remember: that's what he said about me.

I think we all want this to be over. But it won't be until he admits to everything that he's done. Thank you.

Jian Ghomeshi was celebrated during his eight years on *Q* for starting conversations. In kitchens, offices, doctors' waiting rooms, coffee shops, restaurants, on subways and streetcars — any place where people gathered and talked about ideas. Big issues that challenged the mind; small, fun stories that made people smile. The guests were A-list. As former staffer Joe Mahoney explained, *Q* began in a very un-Canadian way, shooting to be bigger than its roots. "We did not set out to do Canadian content. We were Canadians making it but there was no reason we could not go for big stars from the get-go." And they did. Joni Mitchell. Al Gore. Jon Stewart. Barbra Streisand. Joan Rivers. Julian Assange. Ghomeshi never landed his teenage idol, David Bowie, but not for lack of trying. Inspiring Canadian guests also graced Studio 203: astronaut Chris Hadfield, environmentalist David Suzuki, author Margaret Atwood, and actor Kim Cattrall among them.

Not all of the episodes were excellent. At times the host failed to make a connection with his guest. Producers noticed that he struggled with strong female guests who were close to his age or older. British television journalist and food writer Nigella Lawson was one of these, and Ghomeshi's attempt to control the interview failed miserably. She was simply too strong for him. With younger female guests who were the age of women he dated, Ghomeshi had much more "game," as Carly might have put it. One of his last interviews was with *Pitch Perfect* star Anna Kendrick. The interview's undercurrent of flirtation lasts until the very last question.

Ghomeshi saw himself as a star, and of course he was in many circles. But he was a star because he interviewed celebrities. In one of the last times he would be seen in a gala setting before the story broke, Ghomeshi was standing at the downtown watering hole dbar in Toronto's Four Seasons Hotel. Next to him was movie actor Ryan Reynolds. A crowd of very young and attractive women pressed forward — to talk to Reynolds. Cellphone cameras were out, and one after another woman asked for a picture with the movie star. Ghomeshi, sitting off to one side, had his head down. Nobody asked for a photo with him. The uncomfortable Thornhill teen who chased Wendy, the older girl of his dreams, struggling to be seen, was back. All of a sudden, he was invisible.

Undoubtedly Ghomeshi had his detractors. Jim DeRogatis, the Chicago rock critic who was interviewed about the R. Kelly sexual abuse allegations, found Ghomeshi to be a "shitty, unctuous interviewer" when he brought big names on to his set. From DeRogatis's point of view, Ghomeshi landed big stars because he "fawned over everybody he interviewed."

I asked DeRogatis to cast his mind back to that December 2013 interview with Ghomeshi and the now ironic topic — should the public still listen to the art of a person who has allegedly hurt people? DeRogatis said that he now has trouble with the portion of Ghomeshi's work that focused on "portraying himself as a friend of women and a feminist."

"With what has happened," DeRogatis said, "Jian Ghomeshi's hypocrisy is now legendary." He will not be digging into the Q archives any time soon.

Yet the real legacy of the Q host's time on the airwaves was not the broadcasts at all. Rather, it was the allegations regarding his actions and behaviour toward young women that, once revealed and explored, started a national conversation on the topic of undisclosed sexual assault and harassment in the workplace, on university campuses, and in bedrooms. Ghomeshi's downfall came from the stories told by a group of women he dated—sometimes for one night, sometimes for months—and from people who worked on his show at CBC, like Kathryn Borel. Like soldiers who have fought in Afghanistan, some of the women who made public their allegations have formed a bond, brought together by their shared intimacy with this famous and now tarnished Canadian personality. When they talk, and they do talk, their conversations are often about the eerily similar experiences they endured.

Ghomeshi's fall from grace was staggering. Since the stories first broke, he has been unemployed and undergoing counselling for his behaviour, including issues of male dominance and how his actions impacted others. There was a significant shakeup of CBC brass following the scandal. Arif Noorani, producer of Q, was put on leave and then reassigned to a new post; he is in charge of developing new programs and podcasts. CBC first suspended, and then fired, Chris Boyce and Todd Spencer, two executives involved in looking into the allegations. In late May 2016, Spencer, who had been director of human resources, fired back at his former employer, suing the CBC for wrongful dismissal and seeking a payout of $640,000. CBC has claimed in a statement of defence that Spencer failed to conduct an "appropriate" investigation into Ghomeshi.

For the women involved, for CBC staffers, for the public, and for his friends, the case of Jian Ghomeshi is being viewed with an increasingly widening rear-view mirror as people search for clues from the past. What made Ghomeshi tick? CBC producers involved in Q recall the episode where a California neuroscientist discovered that his own brain scan revealed he was a psychopath. Women the scientist worked with said they could no longer be around him. Producers, who behind Ghomeshi's back had called him a "narcissist," "sociopath," or "psychopath" for years, wonder if that episode or others on related mental disorders had an impact on their famous host. These were the same producers who watched his behaviour worsen over the years and, like others, endured it because they needed Ghomeshi. Women who dated Ghomeshi and endured his "rough lovemaking" are traumatized with embarrassment and guilt; some who stayed liked Ghomeshi or needed him. The public and his friends are also looking for clues as the conversation he inadvertently started continues. Musician Owen Pallett, twice a guest of Ghomeshi's on *Q* and a friend away from the microphone, wrote the following on his Facebook page on October 28, 2014, shortly after the first story broke.

> I too have heard endless rumours that he's been a bad date, and have heard stories of shadiness and strange behaviour. I have heard about his ridiculous pick-up lines and have (to my shame) tittered about them with my friends. But I have never heard, until today, that Jian Ghomeshi beats women. I am skeptical of arts reporting. I am skeptical of Canadian journalism. I am sensitive toward shaming of people who are so-called sexual deviants. But let's be clear. Whether the court decides that predatory men are punished or exonerated does not silence the voices of the victims. It does not make victims liars. Whether our culture continues to celebrate the works of predatory men is another issue. It does not silence the voices of the victims.
>
> Jian Ghomeshi is my friend, and Jian Ghomeshi beats women. How our friendship will continue remains to be seen.

Janice Du Mont argues the Jian Ghomeshi story has provided a "watershed moment" for Canada. She laments that it took a high-profile case to do this, noting that sexual violence against women occurs on a daily basis across the country. Still, Du Mont will take it. "Talking about what happened is the starting point," she says. "It makes the invisible visible."

Kathryn Borel, back in Los Angeles, is pleased that she helped make a difference.

"This is not the end of the conversation. It is the beginning of the conversation."

Acknowledgements

This project was conceived by two extremely talented literary agents, Samantha Haywood and Jesse Finklestein, who saw a book behind the headlines. It was given life by Pieter Swinkels and the Kobo team, but it grew and developed into a published book thanks to the brave people at Goose Lane, notably Susanne Alexander, Karen Pinchin, Martin Ainsley, and my new favourite person in the world, editor Jill Ainsley, who took what was at times a muddled mess and made it so much better.

There would be no book without the support of the *Toronto Star*, which allows so many of us to do great investigations. Editors Michael Cooke, Jane Davenport, and Irene Gentle provided inspired leadership and deft guidance on these stories. During the tough times of the investigation and the book writing, my mentor and long-time lawyer Bert Bruser helped me figure out problems and urged me to keep going. To lawyer Iris Fischer, who provided both able legal advice and keen editing suggestions, thank you! All journalists would be lucky to have a Bert and an Iris on their side.

Thank you to the women and men who spoke up and out. As with all investigations, the investigators are only as good as the information they are provided.

Finally, thank you to my wife, Kelly Smith, who excels as a sounding board and behind-the-scenes editor and collaborator.

Kevin Donovan is an investigative reporter and editor at the *Toronto Star*. A thirty-year veteran of the paper, he has won two Governor General's Awards (Michener) for public service journalism, three National Newspaper Awards, and three Canadian Association of Journalists Awards. He is also the author of *ORNGE: The Star Investigation that Broke the Story*.